American Business
in the Twentieth
Century

American Business in the Twentieth Century

Thomas C. Cochran

Harvard University Press
Cambridge, Massachusetts
1972

Preface

Some fifteen years ago, in a book considerably shorter than this one, I treated both economic and business developments in the United States of the twentieth century. In order to consider the history of business in more detail, I have omitted economic discussion from the present volume except where directly necessary to an understanding of business change. Furthermore, when the earlier book was written there was very little secondary literature devoted to the then-recent history of business, and much of the text had to be based on my own experiences as an observer of, or occasionally a participant in, business processes. By 1971 a multitude of books and articles have recorded aspects of the twentieth-century history of business. Articles in *Explorations in Entrepreneurial History* and the *Business History Review* alone serve as an adequate introduction to the period. Moreover, able scholars have offered challenging interpretations of business in relation to politics and society in general, while others have explored the nature of bureaucratic organizations and personal behavior in business roles. In all, there is now a large and varied literature which permits the synthesis of business history from secondary sources with almost as much factual evidence as is usual in the older fields of study.

The present book is neither a hostile critique nor an apology for the actions involved in modern business, but rather an effort to record well-authenticated parts of the history that should be of importance to both businessmen and scholars. Too frequently, in my own experience, executives have assumed they remembered all the details that led to or surrounded a previous decision or policy, only to find that a reexamination of the evidence revealed the situation in a quite different light. It should be the aim of "objective", academic writers to inform business leaders, not to praise them — since for that function they have their own more adept public-relations departments.

While in many minds business history is most closely associated with economics, in interpreting such history the theoretical association is not necessarily closer than with the other social sciences. Although its purpose is producing and distributing goods and services for profit, business is a *social institution*. For many years of scholarly reinforcement in this point of view, I particularly thank Professor Arthur H. Cole, whose wide-ranging ideas may be read in his *Business Enterprise in Its Social Setting* (Harvard University Press, 1959).

T. C. C.

Radnor, Pennsylvania

Contents

American Business in the Twentieth Century

Part One
The Old Order, 1900–1930

1 Business as an American Institution

From colonial times on, the American environment encouraged a preoccupation with business. Expanding settlement, abundant resources, increasing population, and rising land values made every successful farmer an entrepreneur — and made operations in real estate the universal business. In addition, continued migration made for impersonal, market-oriented economic appraisals, unaffected by sentimental attractions to place or dutiful obligations to old friends or relatives. A lack of well-entrenched customs reinforced the utilitarian or pragmatic attitude and encouraged innovation.

If the term "businessman" is used to designate anyone who participates in decisions for organizing the production and distribution of goods and services for profit, there are many kinds of American businessmen, ranging from commercial farmers and the great army of small- to medium-sized operators to the comparatively few executives of big corporations. Some businesses have been run in much the same way for generations and have altered but little between the nineteenth and twentieth centuries; others have been forced into continuous adjustment to meet changes in markets or technology. The big business executive in a luxurious office is likely to be there because mass-production machinery, efficient transportation, and a broad market necessitate big, highly capitalized business. The small proprietor behind a counter mirrors the fact that no computer has yet eliminated human activity from retailing or service.

As used here, "businessman" includes an indefinite fringe of policy-making executives in large companies together with all partners and proprietors of smaller enterprise. But no matter how broad the definition, most Americans in the twentieth century have not been businessmen. Aside from farming, in 1900 scarcely one American household in six had a member who managed a business or occupied an important managerial position. By 1970 the number had risen to nearly one in five, but even if farm managers and proprietors and all corporate executives were included, less than a quarter of the working population were in positions permitting or requiring decisions concerning business policy. Working in a large company might subtly condition the lower-level administrative employee to business folkways and beliefs, but it did not make him a businessman in either his own or the public's estimation. Although to foreigners America was a land of business, to most Americans business managers were a group apart.

The Business Heritage

Compared with businessmen of other nations, those of America have always enjoyed unusual social prestige. Even in the seventeenth and eighteenth centuries, when the manorial lords of great estates on the rivers and bays formed the traditional elite, merchants in the seaports had been able to attain high social rank. In Charleston, South Carolina, center of a proud plantation aristocracy, planters apprenticed their younger sons and married their daughters to the men of the countinghouses. The status of merchant generally rose still higher as one went north, until on the seacoast of New England the social supremacy of the great merchant was unquestioned.

In spite of the plans of kings or proprietors, the forms of feudalism were never securely fastened on the American colonies and there were no lasting titles based on landed estates. Since Great Britain garrisoned the colonies and appointed the chief civil servants, army and government careers were either closed or less attractive to Americans than would have been the case in an independent nation. The Church of England had no American bishops, and the other churches tolerated in the colonies were nonhierarchical. Only in New England was much prestige attached to the ministry and even there its position was declining by the end of the colonial period. Unhampered, therefore, by strong and repressive competition from titled nobility, army, navy, government, or church, business and the businesslike profession of the law offered the broadest and shortest avenues to financial success and public recognition. Whereas in Great Britain the title of barrister, attorney, or merchant was looked down upon by the aristocracy, in America each of these carried social prestige in itself, the title of merchant generally being reserved for men of large affairs in overseas trade.

By the close of the Civil War, the prestige of the land had waned in the metropolitan circles that dominated American society and no new occupations had arisen to threaten seriously the leadership of business and the law. For some years after the war, the military title of "General" carried weight; but the army shrank to a garrison for strategic seaports and Indian posts, and the hundred days of the Spanish American War produced no great leaders to perpetuate *la gloire militaire*. The ministry and the learned professions grew in numbers but scarcely in social prestige, and practitioners of the arts, other than journalism or literature, were – to say the least – not widely acclaimed.

Although the power of the pen was not to be neglected as a source of social control or political or economic position, this power was wielded increasingly by and for business. Following the lead of Thomas Paine, who write for the Pennsylvania Bank in the 1780s, literary men in the service of trade rationalized in books and articles the needs of corporations or industries. At the top levels of metropolitan journalism the distinctions between the publisher's functions as a big businessman and those of the purveyor of news were by 1900 becoming blurred.

In some of the less developed parts of the nation politicians, particularly those in the upper reaches of federal government, enjoyed high prestige, but in the wealthy industrialized and urbanized areas, business leaders looked upon politics as an inferior occupation. While the exact balance in prestige between business and politics in America as a whole was difficult to determine, perhaps it need not be struck. Of national politicians in the decade 1900 to 1910, selected in a study by William Miller as the most important, over 30 percent had been or were in business or business law as well as in politics.[1] Furthermore, the personal wealth of successful politicians was usually invested in business ventures. Consequently, while individual politicians might seek favor with the voters by supporting acts not favored by most businessmen, political leaders as a social group had no desire to lessen the power or prestige of business.

Competing Values and Ideals

While by 1900 business values and attitudes were developed and accepted by a large part of the upper classes or social elite, the mass of the people gave only a grudging acceptance to the buisness system as represented in the careers of "masters of capital" and "captains of industry." Boys and young men were taught at home and in school to seek success, but were also advised that there were spiritual values superior to money-making. "The supreme vice of commercialism," said Bishop Potter in 1902, "is that it is without an ideal."[2] This statement, made to an assembly of Yale students, illustrates the unwillingness of the bishop and other clergymen to accept the validity of ideals less spiritual than those of the church. He failed to recognize the goal of a higher standard of living as an "ideal" of commerce adhered to implicitly by most Americans. A generation after the bishop's statement, an astute French observer called the American standard of living "a sacred acquisition . . . in which they will allow no reduction, and which they will defend to the uttermost against both competition and surreptitious invasion of other countries."[3] Henry Ford saw the increasing standard of living as leading to new and better ways of life and "contributing something deep and lasting." The authors of *The American Business Creed* aptly term Ford's view the "spiritualization of material progress."[4] "Commercialism" or business was the source and protector of the rising standard of living, and hence shared in its "sanctity."

Yet many persons regarded business as unscrupulous, undemocratic, and materialistic. The paradox resulted in part from the distinction between "commercialism" or capitalism as a way of life, an approved social system, and "business" as a particular institution within the system through which a minority group controlled production and distribution.

No culture can be satisfactorily characterized by a single phrase. Yet businesslike values and respect for them seemed the most pervasive common element in American culture, more so than religion, world mission, the democratic spirit, or similar formulations of American ideals. Of the primary business belief that the American way rested on the chance for any able individual to gain wealth, Ralph H. Gabriel wrote:

This faith and philosophy became the most persuasive siren in American life. It filled the highways with farm boys trekking to the city. It drained the towns and countryside of Europe. It persuaded the educated young man that the greatest rewards in life were to be found in the business world. It taught the ambitious that power lies in wealth rather than in political office. It penetrated the workshop and paralyzed the effort of the labor leader undertaking a crusade for justice to the working man.[5]

Reinforcing the earlier Protestant ethics stemming from Calvinism, now becoming partly secular, the business philosophy emphasized the importance of choosing a proper calling, of doing one's appointed task, and of success as a sign of God's grace. The frontier environment had also emphasized success through business enterprise and planning for a future always expected to surpass the present. The Calvinist and frontier traditions had been absorbed in the business life of thousands of country towns and small cities whose citizens strongly influenced the surrounding countryside. Even in the farming areas Lewis Atherton wrote of "the mingled fear, distrust, and respect with which citizens regarded the small circle of leaders in frontier towns."[6]

The ambiguous position of business as such was reflected in attitudes toward its leaders. People of the upper intellectual levels gloried in the strength that prodigious economic development gave to the nation, extolled the American system of individual initiative, competition, and material success, but refused to acclaim business leaders as the topmost representatives of the culture. A magazine writer in 1902 noted that "when the prince of one of the reigning houses . . . came to explore somewhat in the Strenuous Land, it was . . . the captains of industry he most desired to meet. . . . Yet, for the most part these men's records are to be found in no dictionary of American biography, many are not in 'Who's Who'; they figure but little in the columns of the press; they are not the types that have been chosen to stand for American greatness in the Hall of Fame."[7]

Americans of 1900 who collectively typified business culture to foreigners, and who, if we had means to measure, may in reality have been chiefly conditioned by this omnipresent environment, obviously thought of themselves as primarily representing other qualities. They liked Theodore Roosevelt's emphasis on "the fundamental qualities of courage, honesty and common sense."[8] They dramatized themselves as part of an inevitably conquering Anglo-American civilization, or as the leaders of democracy in the world, or as God's chosen instrument for creating the perfect society. One might say that the business habits and values were so much a part of the American scene that they were taken for granted as part of the natural order.

Yet these habits and values with their emphasis on saving, investment, and efficient work were far from usual in the rest of the world. While every society "saved" part of its income, the ends for which income was saved or spent took many forms, such as the miserably poor Tibetans investing hundreds of thousands of hours of their labor in weaving the largest banner in the world to hang on an outer wall of the Dalai Lama's palace. In general, static class-bound agricultural societies showed little tendency to invest in tools for further production, except for the amounts necessary to keep existing equipment in repair. The rich of many nations of Asia, Africa, and South America preferred to spend their income in London or Paris rather than to save for investment at home. The people of these countries viewed work as a necessary evil and would have found it hard to understand Henry Ford's belief that "thinking men know that work is the salvation of the race, morally, physically, socially. Work does more than get us our living; it gets us our life."[9]

The Importance of Small Business

In his famous Cross of Gold speech at the Democratic Convention of 1896 William Jennings Bryan specifically mentoned the "crossroads merchant" as part of the group oppressed by big business. Yet a count of businessmen would show them to be chiefly crossroads or corner-store merchants, or other small distributors. It has been the position and prestige of this latter group in society that has probably been most important in making America a business culture. These were the men who were active in town affairs, whose buildings gave the towns form and character, and who for their own ends, if no other, improved the streets and formed civic bodies. No manor houses in the surrounding countryside overshadowed their residences, no country gentry dictated the tone and temper of local affairs, in this business "democracy."

It was probably misleading even by 1900 to call back-country Americanism a "grass-roots" culture. "The history of the Middle Border," says Atherton, "has been largely the history of its towns."[10] The middle- or upper-class townspeople were the ones who had the business folkways and mores, and who spoke for society in both praise and criticism of business. William Allen White, the "Sage of Emporia" (Kansas), noted many times in his autobiography that his businessman father belonged, because of his strictly local success, to the ruling class. "I knew definitely and with conscious pride that I belonged to the governing class. . . . We were the people."[11] Of Miller's 334 men systematically chosen to represent the topmost business and political elite of the first decade of the present century, only fifty had fathers who were farmers; only four, moreover, had fathers who could be classed as "workers."[12] Local politics were largely run by the mer-chants, manufacturers, and lawyers, and the same group directed the charities, schools, and clubs. "Every country town," according to Atherton, "had an inner circle whose own personal interests were so tightly woven with those of the community at large that one cannot determine where self-interest ended and public spirit began."[13] The newspaper publisher, large or small, was a member of this local business group, and its opinions were those most often expressed in print, because in the eyes of the publisher they represented "ordinary common sense."

The Opponents of Business

How then did it happen that at the end of a century of massive physical achievement by entrepreneurs, "business" came under a mounting attack from the general public and its political representatives? One answer was that employees did not identify their personal interests with those of the companies for which they worked. Another was that in the nineties farmers were still numerous, depressed socially and economically, but well organized and favored politically by geographic representation. In varying ways farmers thought themselves both exploited and despised by other businessmen. Many of them hoped that government regulation or ownership could curb such exploitation.

Furthermore, when hostile critics used the word "business," they generally meant big corporate business. The political influence of such business was evident in the varied pressures of the big corporations upon state capitals or upon Washington. Representative Mills of Texas had said in 1894 that the emasculation of Cleveland's effort at tariff reduction posed the question whether this was a government of the people, or one of taxation by trusts and monopolies. The Bryan campaign of 1896 abounded with charges that big business controlled the government and had bought the Cleveland administration lock, stock, and barrel.

On most specific political measures business was arrayed against itself: a few entrepreneurs were able to build trusts, a larger group of small enterprises wanted trusts curbed; manufacturers usually lobbied for tariffs, the railroads opposed protective duties; chambers of commerce might favor slum improvement, the local real-estate group fought the necessary regulations. The economic debates of the late nineties in Congress were not so much concerned with the issues of individualism against regulation as with those of conflicting business interests.

Business as a whole seldom came under attack, even from the farmers. Bryan said approvingly: "The man who is employed for wages is as much a businessman as his employer."[14] The Populists, the most radical agrarian party of the late nineteenth century, wanted government ownership of some of the utilities that served the farmer, but only government aid for the free enterprise of commercial farming. Few people attacked what an anthropologist might regard as the central themes of the business culture. Such elements as belief in the virtue of labor, particularly for those lacking in material goods; the importance of material success; the obligation of men to work for a higher general standard of living; the idea that competition was good within "reasonable" limits — all these were accepted by both critics and defenders of specific business or industrial practices.

Such criticisms as there were of the central business values came from a few spiritual or intellectual leaders and a scarcely larger number of extreme radicals. In spite of the protests of Bishop Potter and other clergymen, the age-old challenge to renounce the things of this world and live only for God was muted; it had in fact seldom been emphasized in nineteenth-century Protestantism. Quite generally God was assumed to approve of material progress and the higher standard of living, and therefore God's work and one's own could be regarded as the same. Social welfare rather than metaphysical considerations increasingly provided doctrine for the churches.

Henry and Brooks Adams, as well as William Graham Sumner, thought, for different reasons, that the society was decaying, but the elder Adams and Sumner had no program for reform. The native Marxian labor leaders, such as Debs and de Leon, denounced capitalists and exploitation, but only because they held socialism a better way for achieving the same material ends. Even the philosophical anarchists had swung away from the old "simple life" conception of Bronson Alcott or Robert Dale Owen toward dreams of a highly productive industrial society controlled by workingmen's syndicates.

The nationalists, such as Albert Beveridge, John Hay, and Theodore Roosevelt, influenced among others by Brooks Adams, attacked the existing order from an angle that presaged some of the shifts in opinion of the mid-twentieth century. To them the elements of the "business culture" should be secondary to the fact that Americans were a "conquering race." Continuing this argument Beveridge proclaimed: "We must obey our blood and occupy new markets and if necessary new lands."[15] On another occasion he besought "an English-speaking peoples' league of God for the permanent peace of this war-torn world."[16] Roosevelt said: "No national life is worth having if the nation is not willing to stake everything on the supreme arbitrament of war, and to pour out its blood, its treasure, and tears like water rather than to submit to the loss of honor and renown."[17]

Here were a set of cultural beliefs not included in the Calvinist-frontier-business complex – beliefs that had temporarily intruded before, to be sure, but were not part of the everyday cultural patterns. As implied in Beveridge's phrases "obey our blood and occupy new markets," these nationalistic beliefs were not directly antibusiness. The *necessary* business values could have their cultural niche, as in imperial Germany, but the nation, in Roosevelt's words, should not be dominated by "men with the souls of glorified pawnbrokers."[18] The business virtues and values should be secondary. World War II and the transformation of the United States into a heavily armed military nation were to pose this conflict in values much more seriously.

The Rise of Managerial Enterprise

In the twentieth century forces within the complex that we have called business culture were to bring about changes in practice, if not always in belief, as striking as those caused by the rise of the military virtues and the mid-century sense of world insecurity. Most of the inner changes can be seen as results of the increasing size of corporations that accompanied large-scale mass production, transportation, and finance.

As business corporations rapidly became larger, professional executives became more important than the nominal owners. The new big companies placed executive control in the hands of careerists, selected for their managerial ability. The men needed to own no stock in the enterprise, and if they did buy some it was usually not enough to give them a large stake in the company's profits. In railroads, public utilities, and the new industrial "trusts," ownership was usually distributed among thousands of stockholders, and neither stock nor wealth were necessary qualifications for managerial office.

The resulting split between ownership and control altered business aims and motives. An early fear of loss of initiative and enterprise in such a system, expressed by a prominent professional executive, was that "the average man will not work as closely for the railroad company as he will for himself."[19] But the problem went much deeper than closeness or diligence of work. The profit motive itself, the initial dynamo of capitalism, became altered, and security and personal prestige assumed new importance. The directors of a corporation asked of their executives devotion to duty, loyalty, and cooperation in a hierarchy more than rational hedonism in a market.

Looked at from the outside, the executive of the large corporation came to play a different social role from that of the owner-manager of a smaller competitive business. The professional executive's horizons were expected to be broader than those of the small businessman; he should see business problems in longer range and in their social setting; he should employ specialists to advise him on the probable results of his decisions; he should be the guardian of jobs and savings and the supplier of utilities to thousands of people; he should be a planner seeking to thwart uncertainty by better control of the market. In spite of his free-enterprise language he was part of a closely knit corporate social organization. His conditioning made him a different type from the aggressive, often socially irresponsible small competitor who had built capitalism and industrialism in Europe and America. What the difference might be for both business and the rest of society is a major theme of this book.

2 The Technological and Economic Base

Karl Marx is said to have "stood the great German philosopher Hegel on his head" by applying C. W. F. Hegel's dialectic method to materialistic rather than idealistic premises, and thereby developing the theory of history as class struggle for control of the means of production. But Marx, inevitably lacking knowledge of the future course of advancing industrialism, may unwittingly have made a further inversion, in effect putting the cart before the horse: the *means* of production may appear in themselves to be a more important controlling factor than the class, if any, that owns them. Hence Marx's theory that a class is dominant because it controls the means of production may be reversed to read that the *means* of production determine the character and relation of classes.

Modern social scientists, of course, are not inclined to accept any monolithic causal hypothesis regarding social structure, but they recognize a strong connection between technology and the social organization necessary to use it effectively. Since the twentieth century is the greatest period of technological change in the history of mankind, involving such basic forces as electricity, energy and transportation from petroleum, and electronic computation and communication, the new technology was bound to create different methods of business, and altered mass or class relationships — in a phrase, a new way of living and thinking. This technological pressure, however, was met in every nation by deeply held cultural traditions and limited by geographic possibilities. Therefore, regardless of the uniformity of the technical factors, in each country the results were somewhat different, and each area has its own social structure and business history based on a unique fusion of the elements of change and resistance.[1]

Before 1880 life in the United States was relatively unaffected by electricity, gasoline, or fuel oil, and not at all by airplanes or automobiles. The late-nineteenth-century economy was characterized by the coal-burning steam engine for power, the steam locomotive for overland transportation, and heavy crude-iron and steel machinery for manufacturing. Compared to that of the twentieth century, it was a simple technology and the machines were inexpensive. The uneducated mechanic or executive could comprehend the most complex devices and invent new ones in the course of repairing the old. Lewis Mumford has called this period the paleotechnic phase of industrialism.[2]

By the end of World War I a series of basic changes had occurred that presaged a new stage of business and social organization. Cheap and powerful automobiles and trucks were beginning to remold transportation and living arrangements. Electric generators, distributing power over high-voltage lines to millions of electric motors of all sizes, were displacing the steam engine. Airplanes, mass produced for war purposes, would soon fly mail and passengers. For energy, gasoline, and fuel oil were gaining rapidly on coal. Chemical and electrical processes together with light machinery made of alloyed metals were changing the character of factories. Three- and four-story plants with overhead shafts and belts were being replaced by lighter, cleaner one-story buildings where power moved through wires and materials flowed through pipes or rode on electrically conveyed assembly lines.

Differing forms of business organization, to be sure, may be used to administer a given stage of technology, but machinery makes certain inescapable demands. Big American corporations, for example, differed from Soviet trusts, yet since both ran the same physical type of productive units, the two types of organization had to have much in common. The large-scale complex machinery of the twentieth century could not have been owned or operated by the small business firms of

1850. A steel plant like that of Gary, Indiana, which cost some $50 million in 1907, required a corresponding aggregation of capital, management, and labor. Much equipment, particularly for railroads and public utilities, was so expensive that from a financial standpoint only a monopoly of local markets could justify the investment. In addition, almost all of these large-scale processes showed lower costs per unit of product as output increased, or as the economist would say, they were operations of decreasing cost. The bigger the company grew, the greater its advantage in the market.

Up to the end of World War I, at least, advances in machinery tended to produce bigger plants and bigger business organizations, and in many cases there were no economic alternatives, although shrewd financial operators pushed bigness and monopoly to extremes not demanded by the technology itself. Since nationwide companies in which single plants frequently provided employment for a large part of the population of small cities were necessarily affected "with a public interest" no matter what their product, government regulation and the "welfare state" had their roots in the changes brought about by late nineteenth- and early twentieth-century industrialism.

The managerial system, the major business development of the twentieth century, was also in large part a product of technological change. The system grew up with the railroads and public utilities and moved into manufacturing late in the nineteenth century when the increasing cost of mechanized equipment began to require public sale of securities. The ultimate spread of the managerial system to some of finance, trade, and service may be seen, partly, as a consequence of the demands made upon these sectors by large-scale industry and transportation.

Save in the history of a few individual companies there has been little detailed analysis of the interaction of technological and business change, and here we can only suggest one of the more obvious relationships: the need for more technologists in managerial posts. Twentieth-century factories were best administered by college-trained men, or those who knew when and where to turn for expert advice. Mathematical problems in heat, qualities of metals, and utilization of fuel went well beyond the comprehension of the man not specially educated in these matters. The increasing use of electrochemical processes also helped to push the frontiers of progress beyond the horizon of the "practical" administrator or mechanic. Commercially significant new inventions were likely to require costly application of basic scientific knowledge through group effort to machinery that had already become complicated.

Thus the source of invention and technological innovation moved from the workbench to the laboratory. And research laboratories in general were only to be found in universities, endowed foundations, large business companies, or government agencies. In big companies the pursuit of novelty was normally a group effort, directed by businesslike administrators of research. One leading chemical company came to employ some five thousand people in research activity. Important technological advance was not only institutionalized in the business system, but, to a degree, socialized through the research of countless scientists working for nonprofit organizations.

Better Materials and Processes

Greater productivity frequently came from improvements in the quality of materials or more efficient processes rather than increases in size of machines. Harder metals, for example, were important in increasing mass production. Alloyed tool steels, such as that developed by Taylor, Gantt, and White in 1900, added speed and precision to cutting machinery and allowed more processes to be mechanized. New steel played a key part in the great Ford growth. When Henry Ford saw some French vanadium steel in 1905, he is said to have exclaimed: "That is the kind of material we ought to have in our cars."[3] His engineers, already familiar with the new alloy from reading British journals, used it with great effect in the famous Model T.

Special heat treatment of older steels, such as manganese-carbon, produced better results for many purpose than vanadium or other new alloys. Better furnace control of carbon and other elements made for a wider variety of steels with different qualities, and this change in turn led to far more complex relations between steel companies and their customers. As late as 1927 the introduction of carbide alloys made possible still harder cutting steel, an innovation that again increased precision and led to more substitution of machines for hand processes. The change represented a step forward on the long road to automation, that is, to factories with many managers and few workers.

Machine-made interchangeable parts that eliminated hand-fitting were an important factor in increasing productivity. In the early twentieth century the Cadillac automobile company gave a dramatic illustration of the increasing exactness of the machine process. The mixed parts for three cars were shipped to London and satisfactory automobiles were assembled in the presence of officials of the Royal Automobile Association. Up to the end of World War I, hand-finishing remained superior to machine, but in the twenties better cutting and boring tools, adjusted by the new Johansen measuring blocks, allowed shafts and cylinders to be machined to tolerances that nearly equaled those achieved by hand-finishing.

Interchangeability of parts emphasized the necessarily collective or cooperative character of mass production. In most lines interchangeability was of limited value to consumers until all manufacturers of the particular product joined in standardizing sizes. Reaping the harvest, therefore, was a business rather than a technological problem, and because exclusive parts favored the strong competitive position of some big firms, progress was slow. Led by its president, Harold E. Coffin, the Society of Automotive Engineers in 1910 started a campaign for intercompany technical standards. Coffin held that lack of standards was "responsible for nine-tenths of the production troubles and most of the needless expense entailed in the manufacture of motor cars."[4] At first the big automobile companies were indifferent to Coffin's suggestion, but by 1925 they were participating actively, and by 1930 the battle for standardization in the industry was substantially won.

Meanwhile, Secretary of Commerce Herbert Hoover (1921–1928) had pushed the movement in other fields. Two hundred and ten different shapes of bottles were reduced to twenty; sixty-six shapes of bricks were reduced to seven; nuts, bolts, gears, and countless other common parts were similarly reduced from scores of sizes to only a few. Fewer sizes meant not only easier repairs and replacements, but also higher levels of mass production in each remaining size.

By 1900 many cutting tools had become completely automatic. This permitted one man to operate a battery of lathes or drills. In some cases 150 multiple tools could perform the same operation simultaneously under the guidance of one mechanic, but even before the introduction of more fully automatic machinery, manufacturers had discovered the advantages of a continuous process as well as a more minute division of labor. The bit meat-packers in the 1880s had hung carcasses on trolleys and moved them along a "desembly" line where each worker detached a certain section. Electric power allowed further extension of these efficiencies in time and motion. In the first decade of the twentieth century, brewers introduced electrically run conveyors for the "assembling" of a bottle of beer. Bottles were washed, filled, capped, pasteurized, labeled, and boxed in a continuous process with each worker performing a single operation or merely supervising an automatic machine.[5] When these principles were introduced into the automobile industry by the Ford Company in 1913 and 1914, the savings in man-hours were so enormous, up to seven to one, that in popular imagination the mechanized assembly line, essentially a managerial innovation, came to be practically synonymous with American mass production.

The Electrical Web

In addition to these discoveries and refinements in materials and processes, developments associated with electricity and the gasoline engine brought basic changes in business, the economy, and society as a whole. The use of electricity for communication, power, and lighting had first become widespread in the 1890s. Between 1900 and 1930 electric public utilities, including railroads, created a demand for new capital investment second only to that of housing. The telephone spread rapidly, particularly after the expiration of Bell's basic patents in 1894, and by 1930 this form of communication, nationally organized by the American Telephone & Telegraph Company, had a capital investment of over $4 billion. Still more was put into street and suburban electric railways, which reached the height of their expansion at the time of World War I when 1,280 companies operated 40,000 miles of track capitalized at $5 billion. The downtown sections of cities were a maze of tracks; with sufficient patience one could travel by trolley from New York to Boston. In addition to the spread of rapid transit, the steam railroads spent hundreds of millions of dollars on the electrification of entrances to major cities, and of a few long-distance lines.

During these thirty years an investment numerically as large as that in railroads in the nineteenth century was made in urban power and light stations. Generally built by local interests, but often controlled by big holding companies, these stations by 1930 had a value of some $10 billion. In the nineties progressive entrepreneurs were introducing electrical equipment into industry, in 1895 dynamos were built for a great hydroelectric station at Niagara Falls, and by 1905 it could be said that practically all factories and shops in the United States of any size, constructed in the new century, used an electric drive either exclusively or for most purposes.

Reshaping industrial processes by the dynamo led to new business problems and opportunities. Unlike steam power, which was efficiently produced only by big engines close to their furnaces and boilers, electric power was almost infinitely divisible and could travel hundreds of miles. The current from remote central generators could run small electric motors hitched to each individual tool or machine. Factories no longer needed to be large to be efficient.

Compared to the sums invested in connection with electrical installations, the capital in electrical manufacturing and the annual value of the product were small before World War I.[6] The new equipment was developed chiefly by two firms: General Electric, formed by a merger of the Edison and the Thomson-Houston Electric companies in 1892; and the older Westinghouse Electric Company. These concerns signed an agreement in 1897 to share their patents, and succeeded for several decades in discouraging the rise of general competitors in the field of lighting and heavy equipment.

Two other uses of electricity, for motion pictures and radio, had more important early effects on society than on the business system. Moving pictures, essentially dependent in perfected form on electricity for light and motion, were developed in America and France around the turn of the century and became commercially important after 1905 with the conversion of retail shops to nickelodeon theaters. Distribution of films and outlets for display, rather than production, quickly proved to be the area for business control. By 1930 the technologically mature industry, showing pictures with both sound (1926) and color (1929), was dominated by five vertical combines that owned production studios, film exchanges, and theater chains.

Radio also was developed in the late nineteenth century in Europe, but was used initially only for transmission of telegraphic code messages. After the invention of the three-element vacuum tube by Lee De Forest in 1906, it became possible to broadcast complex sounds without too much distortion. While the three big electrical equipment companies (AT&T, GE, and Westinghouse), by agreement, acquired the necessary patents, no one foresaw the value of network radio as an advertising medium. In 1920, General Electric created Radio Corporation of America, chiefly to sell equipment, which several newspapers purchased and experimented with in broadcasts. Led by Westinghouse, the equipment companies also established local stations.

Since advertising revenue from such isolated stations was small compared with costs, the big three companies saw broadcasting as likely to become a nonprofit community service, with the only hope for revenue lying in the sale of equipment. In 1926, when AT&T decided to sell its station WEAF in New York and rent wire connections for network hookups to all applicants, the situation changed dramatically. Reasonable advertising rates for network time turned out to be profitable to both advertisers and broadcasters. By 1929 the industry had assumed its mature form, with three nationwide networks and advertising agencies leading their largest customers to radio.

The Automotive Revolution

Motor Vehicles

The automobile business, from the standpoint of plant and equipment (including highways), materials of production, and the effect of its needs and products on other businesses, was part of the major twentieth-century industrial complex. Into this new group, whose ownership and products interlocked in such companies as Du Pont and General Motors, may be placed automotive and airplane parts, light electrical machinery including household equipment, synthetic chemicals, products such as fibers and plastics, and older materials that came to be chiefly associated with the automobile such as glass, rubber, and special types of metals. Although the obvious emphasis in this group was on durable and semidurable goods used directly by consumers, these companies also developed new materials, machines, and processes that entered into other types of manufacturing. The development of quick-drying lacquers for use on automobiles, for example, radically altered the production and use of paint and varnish.

The automobile had its origins in France and Germany. Comparison of the French Panhard-Levassor of 1895 with the attempts of American mechanics to build horseless carriages in this same year reveals a striking example of poor technical and business communication across national boundaries. The few men who read engineering journals in French and German were not interested in this apparently useless toy of wealthy playboys, and the practical American mechanics who experimented with automobiles did not read foreign-language magazines. Some other factors, however, help to explain the primitive character of the American designs.[7]

Many of the early American automotive entrepreneurs were men familiar with the large bicycle companies that flourished in the eighties and nineties. American rural roads were of dirt or gravel that would not support a long, heavy vehicle in bad weather. Both manufacturers and potential customers thought in terms of bicycle and carriage in contrast to railroad-car design. Consequently the Haynes, Duryeas,

Appersons, and Popes of the middle nineties designed buggies with bouncy elliptical springs instead of the coiled type used on the railroads, light enough to be pushed out of trouble, and with bicycle-type wheels that would give a high clearance. Such a car did not need the four-cylinder motor, three-speed transmission, and heavy steel frame of the French cars. A single cylinder under the high seat of a wooden buggy seemed enough to provide all the speed that the roads and springs would permit.

Commercial manufacture of such "horseless carriages" started in 1895; in 1899, the first year of large production, some four thousand cars were manufactured by fifty-seven supply and assembly shops. The number of firms involved illustrates a lasting characteristic of automobile production: the company that ultimately placed its trademark on the car was only the final assembler of parts made by a number of specialists. Rubber companies supplied tires, bicycle-makers wheels and other parts, wagon-builders the bodies, and some of the numerous American machine shops began to specialize in motors. Since most of these firms, well established in their other lines of business, would supply the parts on credit, the automobile assembler needed only a large empty building, some simple tools and machines, and a few workers. Entry into the business required little capital. Ford, for example, started in 1903 with paid-in funds of only $28,000.

On the production side, the automobile used suppliers that were already highly developed; on the consumption side, no other nation presented a potential demand equal to that of the United States. The size of the country and its scattered population had always made better transportation a major interest. Doctors, lawyers, salesmen, executives, policemen, firemen, and farmers all needed to get around faster. Good profits for both businessmen and farmers in the years after 1896, as well as generally high middle-class salary levels, gave millions of Americans the ability to speed up their lives with this new thousand-dollar utility.

Although manufacture started on a small scale in both the East and the Middle West, within a decade there was the beginning of concentration in southeastern Michigan. Here there were the necessary subsidiary industries, a good labor supply, transportation, and perhaps most important of all, bankers willing to extend credit. The earliest companies to win a nationwide market, such as Oldsmobile, Cadillac, and Packard, were located there.

In the beginning it was not certain that the gasoline automobile would become the standard type. A number of makers of steam engines put out steamers that had advantages in speed, flexibility, and ease of driving. Still, they were heavier than gasoline cars with equal horsepower, could not be started until steam was raised in the boiler, and if carelessly handled could explode. The electric car, powered by a storage battery, was easier to operate, but heavier in relation to its power and slower moving than its rivals. The latter handicap was gradually reduced; however, the need for recharging the battery about as often as a gas tank would have had to be filled was ultimately fatal to the popularity of the electric.

The Electric Motor Vehicle Company, financed by New York and Philadelphia traction magnates, was not only in a position to push electric cars, but also held an American patent on the internal combustion engine. These big operators did not choose to invest the sums necessary to improve storage batteries and eliminate delays from recharging by establishing battery-exchange stations throughout the country. Since the Electric Company held a weak patent and was not prepared to monopolize the field, it licensed gasoline-car producers on a very low royalty basis until Henry Ford won a court decision in 1911 that held the patent nonapplicable to the type of cars being manufactured. By World War I production of both steam and electric passenger cars had come to an end.

With some companies producing nearly ten thousand cars a year in 1908, mass production – judged by then-current standards – had been achieved. At this point William C. Durant of the Buick Company sought to gain a more secure position in the market by widespread consolidation, and Henry Ford planned to improve the sales of his company by concentrating on a simpler and better product at a relatively low price. Both plans mirrored the background of their proponents: Durant was an experienced executive and promoter from the wagon business, Ford an "engineer" from electrical and machinery companies. According to their own fashion, both plans worked. Without substantial Wall Street aid, Durant combined seventeen companies into General Motors, with stock of a par value of $12.5 million. Included were Buick, Oakland, Cadillac, and Oldsmobile, which had prospered in different medium-to-high price fields, as well as a number of parts manufacturers and less successful makes of cars that were soon discontinued. Meanwhile, Henry Ford, declining a noncash offer to sell out to Durant, planned his famous Model T.

In the beginning the Model T was no cheaper than its competitors, but it was built to stand rough use over country roads and to be repaired by country mechanics. In 1909, the first year of production, it did not lead the industry in sales. Though the assembly process for the new car was carefully planned, it was not radically different from that used by other large companies. It was the popularity and reliability of the Model T over several years that raised sales to a level where price reductions and new plant efficiencies were possible.

In fact, economies in production time were literally forced by the enormous increases in orders. By 1910 the Ford was the largest selling car, and in 1914 of the 560,000 cars sold in the United States, 250,000 were Fords. Reinvesting his profits in expanded production facilities, Ford was able to bring the price of the car below $500, and this in turn built further sales.

The most significant changes in Ford production came in 1913 and 1914. Instead of assembling major parts of the car at various "stations," which meant bringing the unassembled parts to certain points and then carrying the assembled subsections somewhere else, the developing car was routed on a conveyor belt past a continuous line of parts and workers. These parts in turn came from subassembly lines. This arrangement permitted minute division of labor, careful routing of all parts, a controlled speed of operation, and automatic removal of finished products. It cut the time of assembling a Ford by nearly 90 percent. The whole process rested heavily on electrification and precision machinery that permitted complete interchangeability of parts.

Although these innovations in procedure, thought out by C. W. Avery and William Klarin in consultation with Ford, were revolutionary in their significance, they rested on the application of known and tested principles to a complex process. This new development in American mass production was a better ordering or "rationalization" of operations, rather than an advance in technology.

Meanwhile other companies had grown rapidly by manufacturing high- and medium-priced cars. The growth of large-scale parts makers, like Continental Motors, which could supply all the materials necessary for a car at wholesale prices reflecting the economies of mass production, permitted nearly a hundred small-scale assemblers to market under their own names. These small shops, turning out a few thousand cars a year, were still scattered all over the East and Middle West, but the larger operators were concentrated in Michigan, in or near Detroit. While General Motors, into which the du Ponts and their Chevrolet Company came in 1917, was selling an increasing share of the medium-priced cars, the day of drastic competitive pressure on the smaller companies had not yet arrived.[9]

Many things, however, worked continuously against the small company. Although it could turn out its product at a cost that allowed it to compete in the medium-priced range with the biggest companies, it was at a disadvantage in marketing. The larger company could support many more dealers, who not only sold more cars but assured convenient repair service. The big company could also afford larger advertising budgets. Even in 1912, half the cars were produced by seven companies. By 1923, 90 percent originated in ten companies. By the end of World War I, investment bankers reconciled themselves to the continued existence of this "luxury" business and were financing the larger companies — except Ford. The latter wanted no Wall Street influence in his operations and kept virtually complete ownership in his own family.

The 1920s rounded out the automotive industrial complex. In 1925, a group of production men and New York financiers organized a rival to Ford and General Motors built around the executive ability of Walter P. Chrysler, formerly of Buick. He reorganized the waning

Maxwell Company, designed a new line of cars bearing his own name, and then merged with Dodge Brothers, one of the largest producers of moderately low-priced cars. From this time on, in good years and in bad, Chrysler, Ford, and General Motors continued to sell over 80 percent of the passenger vehicles made in America.

From 1918 to 1923, the automobile business had been a major consumer of new capital, but like the trend to closed cars, other changes in the business during the middle twenties were more closely associated with marketing than with major innovations requiring heavy capital investment.[10] Sales were stimulated by the spread of installment buying, long used for goods like furniture and pianos. By 1925, nearly $3 billion worth of new and used cars and trucks, some 60 percent of the total, were sold on time.[11] Together with radios, refrigerators, and vacuum cleaners, automobile installments made "finance company" a household term. The requirement that financed cars be insured also gave an enormous boost to automobile insurance.

As the used-car market grew and old automobiles became more reliable, people with smaller incomes could afford to buy. Now the manufacturer of a new car was not only in competition with other new cars in his own price range, but with used cars of all ages and sizes. This also made it easier for those in the higher income groups to trade their old cars for new ones more frequently, and it put a premium on superficial changes in style.

Style changes, cheap used cars, and installment buying all hurt the sales of the Ford Model T. Even though its price was well under that of its chief competitors in the new-car field, many customers preferred to buy a bigger used car for the same price or, by resort to financing, to pay more for a fancier new car. Furthermore Henry Ford refused to make concessions to changes in style and taste. In 1922 his dealers pleaded with him for more glamour in the Model T. He is reported to have listened without interest and replied: "Well, gentlemen, so far as I can see the only trouble with the Ford car is — that we can't make them fast enough."[12] Meanwhile his chief competitors (General Motors, Dodge, and Chrysler) increased the range of colors, upholsteries, and models available in their cheapest cars. When the falling sales of the Model T finally forced Henry Ford to act, he was quite unprepared to bring out a new car. Production of the Model T was ended in 1927, and it took a year with no production to prepare for the Model A. Ford's abandonment of the Model T ended for that era efforts by the largest manufacturers to sell a small cheap car.

During the next twenty-five years "small" cars grew larger and, from the mid-thirties on, more expensive. This may well represent a normal trend in the companies making complicated durable goods. Rather than reflect manufacturing economies in price cuts, which always threaten competitive warfare, lower costs are absorbed by bigger and more elaborate models.

In the twenties, the motor truck and bus started reorganizing the social and economic life of the nation without attracting much attention from the pundits of the day. Two volumes prepared in 1928 by the National Bureau of Economic Research on *Recent Economic Changes* do not include either bus or truck in the index and have no discussion of automotive transportation. The freight that trucks took away from the railroads at this time was chiefly for short hauls of less than carload lots, and railroadmen regarded such business as generally unprofitable. Not until depression struck in the thirties were railroad economists seriously alarmed.

Trucks first reached 10 percent of passenger-car registration in 1918. Between then and 1930, the number in operation increased nearly six-fold to a total of 3.5 million. More than 75 percent of these were in the service of the owner, and most of them were under two tons. Large trucks available to shippers on a rate or contract basis were still relatively few in number.

As trucks became commercially important, the leading passenger-car companies either bought specialized truck builders, as did General Motors, or, like Ford, started plants of their own. In the case of Autocar and Reo, the truck lines remained after the companies gave up passenger-car production.

Social Effects

Buses produced by the same companies developed more slowly than trucks. In 1925, there were only 18,000 registered, and of the 41,000 in use by 1930 probably more than half were school buses. This last fact underlines the profound social significance of motor vehicles. One of the greatest advances in education, the replacement of the one-room school with its single harassed teacher and short periods of instruction by the consolidated township school, was a direct result of the bus.

Much of the capital investment associated with the rise of automotive transportation was indirect. In addition to highways, bridges, service stations, and new shops, automobiles and trucks were the chief cause of massive investments in the production of oil, rubber, and lacquers. The great upsurge in motors from 1914 to 1929 was reflected in the growing size of these auxiliary industries. The shift to closed cars in the mid-twenties made the automobile the largest consumer of glass and led to new products such as safety glass. The automobile had become one of the chief users of steel. The development in 1927 of the continuous steel-rolling mill, involving the costliest plant investments up to that time, and the development of cold rolling in the 1930s were in large part responses to the demand of automobiles for thin, uniform sheet metal.

By 1930, the effects of the automobile were noticeable in social habits and attitudes. The automobile companies and their leaders became the best-known companies and businessmen. The cost and newness of the family's car began to replace the house as the most universally recognized mark of economic prestige, and like the armorial trappings of the medieval knight the car could always be in evidence. The small village store off the main highway, which could not offer the variety of goods now available in a larger town a few minutes away, disappeared. In cities there was a tendency for new shopping centers to develop along highways that by-passed the old business district. The suburbs grew, and even villages lost people to the surrounding country. Commuters came to depend upon the auto-

mobile as a means of getting to work, and cities like Detroit and Los
Angeles that first became large in the age of the automobile used
highways rather than elevateds or subways. The gasoline shortage of
World War II was to demonstrate painfully that the automobile was a
central element in American life.

No one has or perhaps can reliably estimate the vast amount of
capital invested in reshaping society to fit the automobile. Such a
figure would have to include expenditures for consolidated schools,
suburban and country homes, and changes in business location, as well
as the more direct investments mentioned above. This total capital
investment was probably the major factor in the boom of the 1920s,
and hence in the temporary glorification of American business.

The Airplane

The early social and economic effect of the airplane was far less than
that of the automobile. Up to 1930, neither airplane manufacture nor
commercial air transport had achieved importance as areas for capital
investment, or had affected methods of business. The mention of
planes in this period is justified only because of their subsequent
growth. From the Wright brothers' demonstration of heavier-than-
air flight at Kitty Hawk in 1905 to World War I, planes were in an
experimental stage. European nations, more advanced in the construction of airplanes, developed them at a rapid pace in World War I. In
America a number of leaders of the automobile business invested in
plane factories to meet the war demand, while auxiliary suppliers
added airplane parts and motors.

Still, neither the United States government nor the traveling public
showed much interest in commercial aviation. Up to 1925, the federal
government did little to develop airmail and nothing to establish passenger routes. The Kelly Act of that year marked the beginning of
systematic subsidies for mail. By the next year, with government-
supplied beacons and weather service, municipal airports, and fourteen companies under contract for flying mail, commercial transport
was underway.

Passenger travel was negligible. Accidents were frequent enough to make planes appear dangerous, and fares were higher than first-class rail rates. The air-transport industry received its best publicity from successful individual flights. In 1927 Charles A. Lindbergh flew to Paris alone in an ordinary single-engine plane, while Richard E. Byrd, Bernt Balchen, and others made spectacular polar flights. These were followed by a brief buying wave for private planes, and a slight increase in commercial passengers. Ironically, the great American distances which had caused the railroad to spread more rapidly than in any European country seemed to operate against air passenger travel. Air travel in Europe simplified the crossing of international boundaries and was generally accomplished by short flights over lowlands on routes with many alternate landing places. In the United States there was no need to avoid customs inspection, and major trips often involved relatively long flights over dangerous territory such as the Appalachian or Rocky mountains.

Chemicals Become Important

Far less important in its immediate effect on either business structure or capital investment than automobiles or electricity, the chemical industry nevertheless joined them in bringing great changes in business methods and products. The industry had several nearly separate divisions. Manufacture of pharmaceuticals such as medicines and toilet preparations was old in 1900 and in the hands of many companies whose operations were relatively small scale. The "heavy chemicals" division concerned with the extraction and refining of natural products like potash, carbon, and sulphur, or the preparation of simple inorganic compounds such as acids, alkalies, and carbides, also had a long history in America. Increasing about threefold between 1900 and 1914, these operations conducted by moderately large companies became a major industrial group. Most interesting from the standpoint of business change were the rise of new synthetic processes for such varied products as dyes, fibers, and plastics, the wider use of chemical knowledge, and managerial innovations at the Du Pont Company (to be discussed in Chapter 5).

World War I gave many opportunities to the well-established chemical companies. With military demands for powder and heavy chemicals greatly increasing both production and profits, companies accumulated surplus funds that could be invested in new ventures. A major opportunity came from the confiscation of German chemical patents by the federal government and their sale to American producers. Formulas for dyes were the most immediately important of these foreign processes, and American companies at once attempted to manufacture them. In 1922, the government aided the new industry by a high tariff on dyes. But as a Du Pont official wrote a generation later, this country was a "science Sahara. . . . The job called for a brand of expert technology that existed nowhere in America."[13] Although ultimately successful, Du Pont claimed to have sunk $43 million in dyes before making a profit.

During the years between about 1915 and 1925, the nonpharmaceutical chemical industry acquired its modern structure with four or five big firms doing a third or more of the total volume of business. Recognizing the rapidity of change, these companies safeguarded themselves by making a wide variety of products and supporting a large amount of research. From such efforts in the twenties came the commercial production of rayon, new plastics, lacquers, enamels, and dyes, while research was carried on that would result in new products such as nylon a dozen years later.

As chemical knowledge spread, it revised procedures in other types of business. Oil, steel, glass, and rubber production, cloth and furniture manufacture, are just a few of the activities that were affected by the new chemical processes. So wide was the spread that the limits of the chemical industry became indistinct. Rayon, for example, was considered by the census bureau as a part of chemical production, while oil refining was part of a separate petroleum industry.

Change in Older Industries

Processes and technology changed in the older industries too, although with less important consequences for the business system in general. In many old industries, as diverse as harness-making or domestic steamship passenger service, the new developments put strong or deadly pressure on existing companies, but their passing was of minor significance for the business structure; often the entrepreneur and workers of the older activities could move into new but closely allied fields such as from wagon making to automobile body building.

In the period from 1915 to 1930, intercoastal steamships operating through the Panama Canal, trucks, and passenger cars all hurt the railroad business. The combined effect is shown by the fact that while the railroads in 1929 carried only 50 percent more ton-miles of freight than in 1913 (the best year prior to the outbreak of World War I), the physical volume of manufacturing over the same period increased 80 percent.

While trucks were gradually stealing the freight business, automobiles were robbing branch lines of their passengers. This started a descending spiral: fewer passengers meant fewer trains; and fewer trains led erstwhile passengers to go by car instead. Each year the roads petitioned state and federal commissions to allow the abandonment of certain branch-line services. With the coming of depression new construction no longer compensated for abandonment. The year ending June 31, 1931, was the first one in American history in which there was a decrease in miles of railroad track.

In meeting the challenge of growing competition, the railroad companies were in a different position from other American business. Through the Hepburn Act of 1906 the Interstate Commerce Commission had been given effective power to regulate rates and to prevent railroads from entering into other types of activity. Subsequent acts of 1910 and 1913 extended the powers of the commission to cover railroad finance, accounting, and changes in rates. During these years the Interstate Commerce Commisson, influenced by shippers, viewed its function more as that of a policeman curbing bad actions by the roads than as an authority planning for their ultimate welfare. From January 1918 to March 1920, the needs of war forced the government to run the railroads under a series of lease agreements. Whether or not the roads received what they deserved under these contracts, they at least failed to make the large wartime profits that accrued to many other businesses. The roads faced their first decade of keen competition from other carriers with no large accumulated surplus to finance improvements and many restrictions on what they might do.

One of the least expensive ways of improving railroad efficiency was consolidation of competing or connecting lines. This could prevent much duplication of service and equipment. The Transportation Act of 1920, which codified the existing regulations and made certain new additions, authorized the Interstate Commerce Commission to work out plans for consolidation. Any railroad-initiated consolidations had to be approved by the commission. This produced a virtual impasse. The commission's plans were for the stronger roads to consolidate with the weaker ones to form evenly balanced systems. The private plans were for the consolidation of the stronger roads only, with the weaker ones left out in the cold. As a result few important consolidations took place.

Other lines of approach to lower costs were through development of combined rail, truck, and steamship services, installation of labor- and fuel-saving equipment, and more efficient operation. The first was prevented by law, and the efforts at greater efficiency were often met by opposition from the Brotherhood unions, some of whose members would be deprived of jobs or forced to give up old and favorable work rules. Perhaps a more vigorous and imaginative group of managers would have found ways to make sweeping changes in spite of these obstacles, or possibly a generation of strict government and banker control had sapped the initiative of railroad executives; in any case, change only took the form of gradual improvement in existing types of equipment and ways of doing things.

Nevertheless, the sum of these minor advances was far from negligible. Secretary of Commerce Herbert Hoover said in his *Annual Report* for 1927 that the improvement in railroad service was "probably the most outstanding industrial accomplishment since the war."[14] Steam engines became more efficient, longer trains (both freight and passenger) became the rule, and the hauling of empty cars was greatly reduced. In 1929, 20 percent fewer employees produced about the same operating revenue at about the same freight and passenger rates as in 1920. The improvement in efficiency seemed sufficient in the years of prosperity and might have continued so against a less rapidly evolving competitor than the young automotive industry.

Important changes in technology occurred during the first decades of the twentieth century in the old, well-established iron and steel industry. During the years after the turn of the century a large amount of capital was used to shift from the Bessemer process, which had originated large-scale steel manufacture in Great Britain in the 1860s, to the open-hearth method. Lake Superior ores, which had come to make up three-quarters of the American supply, were particularly well suited to the latter method of smelting. Such furnaces could also utilize scrap of all kinds, as well as a wide range of ores. The process was almost as old as the Bessemer, but the need for more exact temperature control and better furnaces had held back its use until the 1890s. Increasing rapidly each year, it surpassed the Bessemer process in 1900 and by 1914 was responsible for nearly 75 percent of the output.

Adjustment to Superior ore, carried southward in specially designed ships, moved steel plants to cities near the Great Lakes. In the first decade of the twentieth century Lackawanna Steel, for example, moved from Scranton to Buffalo, and United States Steel built a gigantic plant at Gary, Indiana. Cuban and Chilean ore, however, kept other companies such as Pennsylvania and Bethlehem in the East. The rise of a demand for special-quality steels, which had made up about 10 percent of the total in 1900 and constituted 50 percent by 1914, kept small eastern mills operating and even added to their number. The automobile industry, ultimately steel's best nonmilitary customer, also required special grades.

United States Steel, formed in 1901 by a merger of big companies, such as Carnegie and Federal, controlled 45 percent of the ingot capacity in its early years. World War I built up Bethlehem, and a new management after 1928 expanded Republic. By 1930 these three companies supplied 60 percent of the productive capacity, but United States Steel's individual share was less than before the war. During the next generation, in spite of depression, wars, and a record-breaking prosperity, the share of the market held by the dozen leading steel companies did not greatly change.[15]

The old, relatively mature industries still employed the bulk of the labor and occupied the time of the largest group of industrial business-men. Ranking right behind construction, iron and steel, and machinery in employment of workers were three of the first industries to use power machinery: prepared foods, lumber, and textiles. Flour mills had surpassed all other users of water power in the eighteenth century, sawmills had probably first put the steam engine to use, and − in 1814 − textiles had ushered in the modern factory.

In spite of its age the textile business underwent important changes between 1900 and 1930. In addition to changes brought by electricity and relocation, ring spinning and the Northrop loom for weaving in-creased the productivity of cotton machinery and lessened the need for skilled labor. Southern interests promoted movement to their section. When the Pepperell Company was ready to build a mill at Opelika, Alabama, in 1925, "a group of citizens were willing . . . to convey enough land for a mill and its village and to give other induce-ments. In fact, they gave over 300 acres, as well as $62,500 in cash, and promised no taxes for five years and a low assessment there-after."[16] Spurred by such inducements textile plants continued to move southward decade after decade. In 1890, 76 percent of the nation's cotton spindles were in New England; by 1930, only about 40 percent remained there. In general, the cheapest materials were being made in the cotton-producing states, while the finer goods still came from the North.

Because the early lumber business consumed its timber resources with no regard for the future, its shift in location between 1900 and 1910 was even more dramatic than in the case of textiles. In 1899, 70 percent of the timber came from the Great Lakes and Northern Appalachian regions; in 1909, the greatest year of the United States lumber output, nearly 60 percent came from the South and about half of the remainder came from the Pacific Coast. Meanwhile, large firms like the Weyerhaeuser Timber Company, foreseeing the danger of ultimate exhaustion of resources, planned production in relation to the growing cycle of the trees that were cut. As a result some stability was produced in the new location of operations.

Prepared foods, most important of this trio of original industries, also moved and changed, but less than the other two. Factory-baked breads, packaged cereals, and canned goods gained popularity, particularly among the increasing number of city dwellers. Canning became a major business on the Pacific Coast. Railroad refrigerator cars allowed packers to move nearer the cattle of the South and West, to such cities as Fort Worth and Omaha; changes in railroad rates and storage practices brought the flour-milling center back from Minneapolis to Buffalo.

The Onset of Stagnation

While electricity and many special situations led to new factory location and design, automotive transportation, which was to be the strongest force for change in location, had only begun its effect by 1930. The area east of the Mississippi and north of Ohio and the Mason-Dixon Line had lost only a little of its concentration of manufacturing, and its factories and business offices clustered tightly around the major railroad centers.

The last years of the 1920s which seemed so dynamic to businessmen of the time were actually the beginning of a period of stagnation. Only buildings and roads consumed capital at increasing rates. In a study that divided manufacturing into fourteen major industries and one miscellaneous category, the rate of capital change was seen to turn downward in every series after 1925.[17] Businessmen were failing to find enough attractive areas for investment beyond the sterile circle of stock speculation, or the erection of larger office buildings.

The failure of business to expand sufficiently rapidly to ensure full employment between 1925 and 1940 was no doubt the result of many factors. The increasing productivity of capital equipment was one of these.[18] Another may have been that a sort of technological plateau had been reached where no major innovation invited great private capital investment. In any event, businessmen of 1929, exhilarated by the great industrial progress of the twentieth century, were generally unaware of the impending crisis.

3 Big Business and Finance

The rise of the large business corporation in the late nineteenth and early twentieth centuries is one of the major changes in history, comparable to the rise of medieval feudalism or of commercial institutions at the close of the Middle Ages. Relatively unrestricted by political controls or social traditions in the favorable climate of the United States, modern business corporations grew and multiplied prodigiously. Corporate enterprise gradually altered the meaning of property, the circumstances and motivations of much economic activity, and the careers and expectations of many citizens.

The Bases of Bigness

One basis for this precocious growth in the size of corporate business units was, as we have noted, the scale of machinery most economical at this stage of technology for processing and transporting cheap and abundant natural resources to supply the world's largest home market. American technology might occasionally lag from the standpoint of scientific efficiency, but it usually led the world in scale of operations. The rapid increase in the most efficient size for furnaces, rolling mills, multiple drills and presses, and other automatic machinery eliminated the small plant from many lines of activity.

Even with the machines of this period bigness in a single plant had

its limits. Beyond a certain size (varying for different industries) two
or more plants became preferable to one. William Knudsen, the
famous automotive engineer, for example, disagreed with Henry Ford
over the latter's insistence on concentrating all his operations at the
River Rouge plant near Detroit. "If we are going to move everything
down there," Knudsen contended, "some day you will have 100,000
people working there." "That's what I expect," replied Ford. "I think
that is too many people working in one place," Knudsen argued,
"I think we have too many people here in Highland Park. I think we
ought to spread out more. I think the ideal manufacturing unit con-
sists of anywhere from 5,000 to 10,000 people. . . ."[1]

Advances in technology also made it increasingly easy for companies
to spread out. Communication, the essential element in managerial
control, was improved by the teletype, telephoto, microfilm, automobile, and airplane. Mechanized office equipment multiplied records,
and punch cards and filing systems facilitated their use. Such devices,
together with advances in accounting techniques, allowed management
to maintain a head office in a metropolitan center, close to its chief
market and financial connections, and from there to exercise efficient
supervision over plants located in lower-cost areas or closer to raw
materials. More exact scientific controls over materials and processes
lessened the risk of variable quality in multiplant operations. Exactly
the same product, even one as delicate as beer, could be manufactured
in plants three thousand miles apart. By mid-century, companies might
have fifty to a hundred plants located throughout the country. As a
result, although corporations and their managements grew larger,
individual plants were usually kept at the size best suited to their
particular operations.

Therefore, as corporate growth continued, a commanding position in
the market became the major incentive.[2] Since smaller rivals would
not want to risk a price battle with a giant, the big company alone or
with a few competitors could set the price of its products. Larger volume reduced the cost per unit of advertising, public relations, distribution, research, and many incidental expenses.

The New-Style Holding Company

In spite of the important changes in technology, size, and methods of operation, no basically new development in the legal structure of firms took place in the first seventy years of the twentieth century. Proprietorships, partnerships, simple corporations, and holding companies continued to be the forms for carrying on the nation's business activities. But the holding company was used in new ways that promised for a time to be of great significance. The early holding companies, mostly chartered under the New Jersey general act of 1889, were usually of the single-stage variety. The parent company owned stock in a number of operating subsidiaries. In the twenties, however, circumstances led to the piling of one holding company on top of another to form a multistage or pyramided structure.

The pyramid allowed the directors of the top company to control more real assets with the same amount of venture capital, or to attract more capital from the investing public without endangering the insiders' complete control of the system. The mechanics of the structure depended upon the fact that a bare majority, or even less, of the voting stock of a corporation carried control of all of its operations and assets. In Samuel Insull's utility pyramid, for example, each of his dollars invested in Corporation Securities Company of Chicago ("Corps" for short) might control over $2,000 worth of assets in an operating company at the base, such as Georgia Power and Light. This so-called "leverage" depended, of course, on the fact that the public was willing to buy the securities of all the intermediate, nonoperating companies. During the 1920s, investors were not only willing but eager to "get in" on this fast-growing industry without questioning the soundness or practicality of the corporate setup.

The elaborate pyramids were confined chiefly to the railroad and public-utility industries, where investors had faith in the ultimate earning power of the operating units. In manufacturing, one or two levels of holding companies were frequently used as an ownership or managerial convenience, but seldom as a device for drawing in more capital. The argument advanced for the elaborate pyramid was that

managerial and operating efficiency was promoted by bringing companies together. In some instances where public-utility lines crossed
and interwove, or railroads duplicated facilities, the argument
seemed sound; but where the operating companies were remote from
one another, the economies were trifling or altogether absent. In addition, there was a tendency for the top companies to consume the
profits of the operating ones through high management fees and "ex-
tortionate interest rates" on new financing.

In practice most of these structures soon ceased to be orderly
pyramids proceeding from many operating companies at the base
through intermediate holding companies to one parent corporation at
the top. The companies borrowed from one another, bought one
another's securities as well as those of outside corporations, issued
bonds, and often produced a tangle of intercompany ownership that
defied comprehension. Owen D. Young, lawyer and Chairman of the
Board of General Electric, said of the Insull public-utility pyramid:
"It is impossible for any man to grasp the situation of that vast structure . . . . It was so set up that you could not possibly get an accounting system that would not mislead even the officers themselves."[3]

The depression of the thirties, however, discredited pyramided
holding companies. They were shown to be overcapitalized and
financially mismanaged. As a result, they became anathema to investors, and the federal government in the Public Utility Holding Act of
1935 placed many restrictions on such companies. In the sad and
realistic thirties new pyramids appeared unprofitable. After the
spectacular collapse of the Van Sweringen pyramid of trunk-line railroads, the Interstate Commerce Commission also came to frown on
control acquired through complex financial structures.

The abuses of the holding company by empire-building financiers
should not obscure its great value to big business as a legitimate means
of organization. Through its use companies could order their inner
relations in several different ways. They might choose a unified form
of organization, such as that of Du Pont or Ford, where subsidiaries,
aside from those in foreign countries, existed to perform specific
functions. Or they could design a federal type like General Motors,

where considerable autonomy was allowed the presidents of the producing units but major policies were coordinated by committees of the
parent company. A federated type allowing still more autonomy was
the Weyerhaeuser Timber Company, in which the top unit represented
ownership but took little direct part in the management of subsidiaries.

Whatever the type of organization, almost all large companies owned
the stock of operating subsidiaries, just as American Telephone &
Telegraph, for example, held that of the various state telephone
companies. The top subsidiary companies might in turn own the stock
of smaller firms set up for special purposes, but such stages were incidental to the effective control of operations and were not a financial
device for increasing the leverage of some group of insiders in the topmost holding company.

The Rise of Investment Bankers

By the early twentieth century many scholars and journalists
believed that during their lifetime capitalism in the Western world had
fallen under the control, not of giant manufacturing corporations, but
of bankers and financiers. Following a line of reasoning expressed particularly by German economic historians, these analysts saw capitalism
as going through a series of stages. The mercantile stage, in which
America had grown up, was characterized by the importing and exporting merchant as the most important type of entrepreneur. This stage
was superseded in the early nineteenth century by industrial capitalism, with independent small-scale factory proprietors as the dynamic
or formative influence. As business grew larger and more corporate,
the need for raising capital from the investing public brought the investment banker into prominence, until by 1900 he was conceived to
be the most important figure in a stage called finance capitalism.

The last phase of this theory appeared to be well exemplified in the
United States. The rapid growth of railroads and public utilities after
1850 brought an increasing volume of large-scale security offerings in
a market where capital for investment was relatively scarce. Competing with many attractive local uses for money, that could be super-

vised personally by the investor, shares or bonds in remote enterprises were difficult to sell. Only the large investment firm with many contacts at home and abroad could readily dispose of a $5 or $10 million issue.

Consequently, about a dozen large investment banking houses took over the initial underwriting of the financial needs of American big business. As might be expected in a situation where there were many companies seeking money and only a few powerful wholesalers of securities, the investment houses set the rules of the trade. By the nineties it was generally understood that there should be no shopping around or bargaining from one banker to the next.

The bankers regarded their relation to the enterprises that contracted for their aid in much the same light as the family doctor regarded his patients. The investment banker floated the original securities that brought the corporation, conceived in a charter, into actual life. When more money was needed for the growth of the young company, the same banker expected to be consulted about securing the sustenance. He prescribed the arrangements for corporate marriages and the creation of subsidiaries, and when, usually during depressions, the company became financially ill and could not meet its obligations, the banker recommended a plan for reorganization that would restore the patient to health. If corporate death occurred, through liquidation and the sale of assets at auction, the banker attended each phase of the proceedings, usually arranging for purchase of the remains by a group of bondholders.

For the marketing of sizable security issues the underwriting house would associate other large financial firms with itself in a syndicate. Each of the leading investment banks, such as J. P. Morgan; Kuhn, Loeb; Lee, Higginson; or Kidder, Peabody, had a group of "retail" outlets through which most of the securities reached the public. Banks, trust companies, and brokerage houses did the retail selling, but banks and trust and insurance companies also bought for their own investment portfolios. Consequently, it was important for the investment bankers to exercise influence in the affairs of these other financial institutions. In addition, considerable parts of the issue might be sold through cooperating investment houses, "correspondents" in London, Paris, Amsterdam, Berlin, or other foreign money markets. Each of the big American firms, therefore, had to have important European connections or agencies. This somewhat informal world financial network led to the term, generally used invidiously, "international bankers."

The New York Financial Community

In these early years of the century, when the public marketing of securities was increasing the business influence of the investment houses, the concentration of the head offices of large companies in New York City was adding greatly to the size and power of a few commercial banks. From the deposits of oil, meat, and metal producers, the National City Bank, which had always specialized in the financing of raw materials, rose to a leading position in city and nation. With resources of $200 million, a gold reserve second only to that of the United States Treasury, and deposits from some two hundred inland banks, the influence of National City and of its president, James Stillman, approached that of a European central bank. Smaller in size, but almost equal in the financial importance of its chief depositors from the fields of railroads and industry, was the First National Bank of New York, presided over by George F. Baker.

In addition to other metropolitan banks and trust companies, the four major life insurance companies were located in New York. Trust companies and life insurance companies were particularly good customers of investment bankers. Both could legally buy a considerable range of securities, and both were expanding their resources rapidly.

Inevitably the major sellers of securities, the great commercial bankers, and important customers were drawn together, and the vigorous personality and sweeping financial ideas of J. Pierpont Morgan gave a structure and force to this community of interest that it might otherwise have lacked. As early as the late 1870s, he began to display his readiness to undertake big and difficult financial ventures. He had the ability to get rivals to cooperate, and when they would not he was prepared to act by himself. Having failed in the early nineties to get railroadmen to control competition by voluntary agreements, he seized the opportunity offered by the ensuing depression to reorganize several regional railroad networks, and place his representatives on their boards. Believing that cooperation was the life of sound finance, he brought about a number of mergers in the industrial field, creating such giants as General Electric, United States Steel, International Harvester, and International Mercantile Marine.

In some of these activities, other well-established houses such as Kuhn, Loeb and Company appeared as competitors, but Morgan succeeded in creating close relations with Stillman and Baker. He and his partners also controlled the Bankers and Guaranty trust companies and bought strategic shares of stock in the major life insurance companies. Access to these great "pooled savings" gave Morgan and other big investment bankers unprecedented ability to dispose of new securities; anyone denied such connections could scarcely find a sufficient buying public for large issues.

The Morgan–First National–National City financial group and the other old investment houses were not the only big interests in Wall Street. The same upsurge of inland production that had built up the great metropolitan banks had also produced many new general entrepreneurs – that is, men who controlled many companies, but whose occupation was buying, selling, and coordinating such ventures rather than taking an active part in routine management. Great mine owners like the Guggenheims or Thomas Fortune Ryan, and smaller and more speculative financiers like F. Augustus Heinze, Charles W. Morse, or Edward R. Thomas controlled banks and entered into large financial operations outside the more sedate and socially select sphere of the leading international bankers.

In 1907 the Morgan interests had a chance to strengthen their leadership and to weaken the influence of some of these financiers outside the fold. Following a stock-market panic on Wednesday, October 16, centering around the favorite stocks of Heinze, Morse, Thomas, and their allies, depositors started mass withdrawals from the banks of these speculators. Unable to meet these "runs," they appealed to the leaders of the banking community for aid. But the Morgan-First National–National City forces would not approve aid to these banks until their "objectionable" officers or directors were eliminated. As fear spread among all depositors, poorly managed trust companies were in difficulties. Morgan, returning from the annual conference of Episcopal bishops at Richmond, marshaled the resources of the financial group that he considered respectable. When a reliable examiner interrupted him in conference with Baker and Stillman to say that the Trust Company of America, then under heavy pressure from depositors, was solvent, Morgan said: "This, then, is the place to stop this trouble."[4] His word turned out to be the law. He dragooned unwilling bank presidents into subscribing funds for emergency loans, and also used millions lent by the Secretary of the Treasury to supply liquid funds for approved banks and trust companies.

By the end of the two weeks of crisis the elderly Morgan had demonstrated his leadership of American finance. Great individual financiers, such as the Rockefellers, E. H. Harriman, other big investment houses, and the presidents of the two leading commercial banks, had all accepted Morgan's leadership and supported his policies. Furthermore, the cooperative activities of the conservative leaders in the period of crisis appeared to have established a community of interest that continued in later years. In fact, to some outsiders it appeared to be a dangerous money trust.

The Money Trust

Whether or not it could be called a trust, the picture of Wall Street financial arrangements disclosed by the Pujo Committee of the House of Representatives in 1913 showed concentrated financial controls in major areas of the American economy. The influence was exerted chiefly through representatives of the banking group on the boards of directors of various big financial, utility, railroad, and manufacturing concerns. Except where trustees held the stock, as for example in the

Southern Railroad, the group representatives were not a majority of the board, and usually numbered only two or three members. Clearly such control as existed was a matter of influence, not absolute power.

The Pujo Committee decided that the House of Morgan, the First National Bank, the National City Bank, and the two Morgan-controlled trust companies — Bankers and Guaranty — constituted a distinct inner or policy-making group, apart from the broader sphere of financial cooperation which included other large investment banking houses such as August Belmont; Kidder, Peabody; and Lee, Higginson. The firm members or directors of the inner group held 118 directorships in 34 banks and trust companies, 35 directorships in 10 insurance companies, and 193 directorships in 68 nonfinancial corporations.[5] These 112 companies were among the largest in the nation.

Nevertheless, the members of these boards that belonged to the banking group made no systematic attempt to control or direct most big-business policy. Even at the top the group operated with an informality unsuited to governing a business empire. Stillman often stopped in to see Baker and Morgan on the way to National City Bank. Occasionally they lunched together, but irregularly enough so that the meetings were arranged by an exchange of notes. By 1912 Stillman was spending most of his time in Europe. Aside from the chief officials of the separate institutions, each of whom had his regular duties to perform, there was no planning or fact-gathering group, and the lesser men were not called to meet as a joint board of strategy. Many of the 112 companies undoubtedly operated from 1900 to 1914 without any important guidance or restraint from those board members who, on the basis of the Pujo calculations, represented Morgan, Baker, and Stillman.

J. Pierpont Morgan, queried by Samuel Untermeyer for the Pujo Committee late in 1912, denied that he exercised any great power or that such concentration of control existed. But George F. Baker talked more freely about the situation. Untermeyer said to him, "We are speaking of this concentration which has come about and the power it brings with it getting into the hands of very ambitious men, perhaps not overscrupulous. You see a peril in that, do you not?"

"Yes," replied Baker.

"So that safety," continued Untermeyer, "if you think there is safety in the situation, really lies in the personnel of the men."

"Very much."

"Do you think that is a comfortable situation for a great country to be in?"

"Not entirely."[6]

Bankers outside the inner circle were more concerned. President Reynolds of the big Continental and Commercial Bank of Chicago testified: "I am inclined to think that the concentration having gone to the extent it has, does constitute a menace."[7] It seems likely that in most cases the pressure of the inner circle was exerted only in matters involving major financial commitments. The leading members of the group were burdened with too many directorships — partners of the House of Morgan alone held seventy-two — to take any account of the details of operation. But in financial matters the power of the banking representatives was far-reaching. As Charles Mellon, president of the New York, New Haven, and Hartford Railroad said, where Mr. Morgan sat was the head of the board.[8] If the bankers of the country knew that Morgan, Baker, and Stillman were opposed to a certain policy, it might be virtually impossible for a company to finance it. Other bankers and financiers did not want to risk the long-run consequences of the antagonism of this powerful group.

In some instances the financial controls were operated forcefully. Morgan developed certain ideas which he wanted to see applied in important situations. He believed that stable corporate income could be secured by eliminating competition and securing a community of interest. Seeing company financial structure from the banker's standpoint, he was interested in protecting bondholders but relatively indifferent to the welfare of stockholders. In return for accepting lower interest rates, bondholders in reorganized companies were often given large blocks of common or preferred stock. Back of these policies, which increased total capitalizaton, seems to have been the belief that elimination of competition would allow adequate returns on the larger quantity of securities.

Sometimes these principles worked, especially during the prosperous years from 1897 to 1907, but when a region or an industry ceased growing and hard times came around, the Morgan capitalizations could cause new trouble. The New York, New Haven, and Hartford Railroad illustrated a major failure of the Morgan policies. J Pierpont Morgan himself, as a member of the board, dictated a policy of buying competitors of all types, railroad, trolley, and boat, in order to secure a monopoly of through transportation in southern New England. Since Morgan's plans were soon well known, the prices were high. Had the region continued to grow rapidly, the New Haven might have been able to service the resulting additions to its bonded indebtedness. But after the painc of 1907 New England stagnated, and when a deep depression started early in 1913, the New Haven was unable to meet its fixed charges.

Other basic criticisms of the influence exercised by the Morgan-Baker-Stillman group are that it was unorganized, negative, and undemocratic. It did not lend itself to furthering higher productive efficiency or planning for risk-taking expansion. The views of the leaders were more inclined toward financial security than technological progress. Insofar as their influence was exerted in such matters, it was likely to lead to the postponing of improvements. There was no public participation in or control over the actions of the group — with a situation of this nature such control would have been difficult. The men involved acted as private individuals. There was no central organization that could have been regulated effectively, yet as Baker testified, bad policy could be harmful to the country.

On the other hand, J. P. Morgan and Company and the National City Bank were performing many of the central banking functions that the nation required but had never authorized. As in 1907, the group organized the reserves of the financial community and aided solvent banks that were short of cash. To some degree the group policed the otherwise unregulated security markets, attacking the forces of fraud and corruption. Their policies helped to develop confidence that a company financed by these leading institutions would be honestly managed in the interest of the security holders, and thereby probably brought more investors into the public-security markets.

The Federal Reserve Act

The death of J. Pierpont Morgan in Rome in the spring of 1913 and the passage of the Federal Reserve Act in December of the same year mark the end of the period in which the "money trust" exercised its greatest influence. Ever since the depression of the nineties and particularly since the panic of 1907, Republican Congressional leaders had been discussing plans for a new banking system — one that would create a more elastic currency and weaken the hold of big New York banks over the ultimate reserves of cash and specie. Conservatives wanted a privately owned central bank like that of England or France. "The banking interests of the country wanted a change," wrote Democratic leader Oscar W. Underwood, "but they wanted the change so that they might control. The party in power was politically afraid to give them control and therefore did nothing."[9] The progressives in both major parties favored a government-controlled system such as that operated by the governments of Indiana and Ohio in the early nineteenth century.

The Democratic bill, put through Congress in 1913, was a compromise, which probably pleased a majority of the American Bankers Association but not the big metropolitan banks. As a result, the head of the Reserve Bank in New York City felt that "the managers of the new federal reserve banks of the country found that the welcome accorded to them by the banks of the country was, to say the least, cool."[10]

Rather than establishing a single bank in New York, as "Wall Street" would have liked, the new system created twelve Federal Reserve banks, each owned by the banks of its district. National banks had to subscribe to the stock of their district bank; state banks might join the system by subscribing. The unifying control in the system was the Federal Reserve Board with five members appointed by the President, each from a different district, plus the Comptroller of the Currency and the Secretary of the Treasury. The district banks were controlled by boards of nine members, of which six members (three bankers and three nonbankers) were representatives of the stockholding banks, and three more were appointed by the Federal Reserve Board. Of these last, one was designated Federal Reserve Agent and Chairman. Presumbaly the agents would guide the execution of policies decided on by the Federal Reserve Board, but the board of the district bank also elected a governor to be in charge of banking operations.

The Federal Reserve banks did banking business only with members of the system who might rediscount eligible commercial paper, which made up a large part of the holdings of big city banks, in return for Federal Reserve notes. By lowering or raising the interest rate charged for rediscount, the Reserve banks could encourage or discourage borrowing by member banks. Since the Reserve banks were limited to 6 percent return on their stock, they would presumably use their power over rates with a view to market stability rather than profit. The central board also could step in and control rediscount rates.

In addition to attempting to control the volume of bank credit by manipulating the rediscount rate, the Reserve banks might buy and sell government securities. Selling took cash from the money market and added to the reserves of the district bank; buying had the reverse effect. After 1916 the Reserve banks might also advance money to members on government securities.

In theory, the power of government through the central board and their appointees on the district boards seemed so great that many bankers were fearful, and state banks generally refused to join. In practice, however, the local governors — the men actually in charge — soon assumed the leadership. Until 1929 Benjamin Strong, as governor of the Federal Reserve Bank of New York, was the most important figure in the system. By thus relegating the Federal Reserve Board and its agents to a secondary position, the leaders of the New York money market continued to exercise much of their old power.

Other changes from 1914 to 1920 were as important as the Federal Reserve System in changing relations in banking and investment. The intense campaigns of World War I for public sale of government securities, and the forcing of this form of negotiable paper on the banks, laid the basis for the easy money market of the 1920s. This in turn weakened the grip of the "money trust" on the market for new securities and led to the rise of new brokerage and investment houses. No one replaced J. Pierpont Morgan as financial leader, and the men at the helm of some of the most important banks in the 1920s joined readily in the speculative enthusiasm. Thus the Federal Reserve System, the financing of World War I, and the boom of the twenties marked the end of the era of domination of large-scale finance by a few leading houses.

4 The Structure of Business

The spectacular and portentous aspects of the activities of the corporate giants magnified their role in the American economy. To many Americans at the turn of the century, the big bankers together with the Rockefellers, Goulds, Guggenheims, and a score of others, appeared to run the economy and to be gaining rapidly in power. W. J. Ghent, a socialist, predicted that the United States would succumb to a benevolent feudalism run by big business.

For some years the growth of big companies was very rapid. In 1897, there were only eight industrial companies with over $50 million in capital; by 1903, there were forty such giants. On the other side of the picture, in addition to small-scale household units of production, there were over 200,000 factory enterprises and a total of about 1.7 million business concerns. Even if companies with $5 million in capital, whether in transportation, finance, or manufacturing, were considered "big," the total number of such companies in the first decade of the twentieth century was well under a thousand. Their policy-making executive employees probably numbered less than 50,000 men, compared with perhaps 2.5 million proprietors and managers of smaller business.

The Realm of Bigness

In general, the areas dominated by big business (such as railroad and traction companies, public utilities, iron and steel, smelting and refining, farm equipment, electrical equipment and oil refining) were those in which small business either had never existed or had been superseded at an early stage. Furthermore, the rapid growth in bigness that had caused alarm in the late nineties and the early years of the new century slacked off. According to the calculations of Adolph A. Berle, Jr. and Gardiner C. Means, the gross assets of the two hundred largest nonfinancial corporations increased in dollar value only 68 percent between 1909 and 1919, whereas the general price level advanced over 80 percent.[1] In the twenties, the two hundred largest nonfinancial corporations grew more rapidly in assets and income than the smaller companies but still fell far short of being the norm of economic activity in the United States. Even if the next eight hundred nonfinancial corporations were included, which in 1929 covered companies with gross assets of over $20 million, the group did a relatively small part of the nation's total business in dollars, and employed perhaps one man in six. In terms of numbers of enterprises, small- and medium-sized businesses more than held their own. The number of firms listed by Dun and Bradstreet increased from about 1.2 million in 1900 to over two million by 1930, a rate of growth faster than that of the nation's population. Monopoly capitalism or "benevolent feudalism" was developing, if at all, at a gradual pace.

Yet able scholars like Professor Berle held and continued to hold that the two hundred nonfinancial corporations, which in 1929 did only a minority part of even the corporate business, dominated the economy.[2] The basis for this apparent paradox is the importance given to manufacturing, railroad transportation, and public utilities. From 1900 on, these areas had been the realm of big business. However, they did not represent a majority of the opportunities for employment, and the areas open to new enterprise continued to increase. The crucial point in the argument was thus the control exercised by big business over the rest of the economy.

On this question opinions differed widely throughout the first three-quarters of the century, and the real situation was difficult to assess. Were wholesalers dominated by producers? Were mass-produced manufactured goods more important to the economy than food and a hundred kinds of service? Were the few big concerns that did about half the manufacturing or assembling of final products a dominant influence on the thousands that did the rest? Since influence may be variously defined, discussion cannot conclusively answer these questions, but it may prevent stereotyped answers.

Small Business

Below the few hundred giant concerns, at least three distinct levels of business persisted in the twentieth century without much change in pattern. At the bottom, in point of size, were the age-old categories (about one-third of the total) composed of proprietors who did not regularly employ hired help. In 1841 the Earl of Shaftesbury had noted the large number of jobbers, hawkers, and small retailers who had previously been hired workers.[3] As nations industrialized, these occupational transfers increased, affecting even higher levels of entrepreneurship. Both men and women shifted back and forth between working for wages and such self-employment as running a restaurant or a family store, contracting for construction work, making simple products with old machines, or selling special services. For them self-employment was often a recourse from unemployment, as well as an apparent way for the uneducated to rise in the social system. These characteristics were indicated by a larger two-way flow between blue-collar workers and self-employment than in the case of white-collar workers. At the lower level such entrepreneurs had little capital and lacked ability in rational planning and decision-making. A third of their new ventures usually disappeared within a year, and nearly half within two years.[4]

Disappearance might result from such causes as migration, a new job, or death — but financial failure was the major category. In fact, a large number of these enterprises never made a true profit. Still, profit was often not the primary motive in their creation. By keeping a family at work, including children under legal working age, or by contributions from some other job, the enterprise struggled along, much as in the case of a marginal farm. Ultimate failure came when the proprietor could no longer secure supplies or credit, or when returns became too small to repay the effort of tending the store or running the worn and unreliable machinery. Frequently rent was not an additional expense, for the business was conducted in the family home.[5] As with small farms, such business was a "way of life." Poor location was endemic, because it was easiest to acquire space in a disadvantageous area. Even moderately successful proprietors of firms on this minimum level rarely demonstrated the entrepreneurial ability or education necessary to plan expansion, raise additional capital, and take the other steps involved in growth.

Enterprises on the next higher level with only a few employees had, in common with those on the lowest, the making of decisions concerning all aspects of the business by one man or perhaps two or three partners. In 1929, firms with from one to twenty employees constituted about two-thirds of the total, but employed only a quarter of the workers. They dealt with managerial problems on a small scale, might secure bank credit, and might expand to be much larger companies, but few have left any records explaining their decisions.

The third level, "medium-sized" business, employing about half of all nonagricultural workers and including over a hundred thousand firms (4 percent of the total) in 1929, was composed of companies with between twenty and one thousand workers. Such a broad band, to be sure, covered businessmen with very different statuses and problems, from moderate size-shops or plants to big banks, brokerage houses, or department stores, but at this level all the chief entrepreneurs had to deal with the problems of both organizational and financial efficiency.[5] The heads of these firms were the backbone of chambers of commerce, manufacturers' associations, and service clubs, and some joined with self-employed lawyers in political activities. In general, they were probably the group pictured by Americans when they thought of "businessmen."

Yet one must remember that of all business owners these medium to large entrepreneurs were a very small group. Businessmen conceived of as a sector of the American population were typically small, unincorporated proprietors, who in 1929 had an average income of $1,600. Looked at from this standpoint, manufacturing enterprises were relatively unimportant. Seventy-one percent of all firms were in trade and service; of the remainder, building construction alone accounted for as many firms as all of manufacturing.

Commentators of the early century and later historians wrote of the loss of opportunity for the little man in business, but there is no such literature from businessmen themselves. Since the beginning of industrialism there had been a gradual growth in the size of the average firm. This meant that for manufacturing more capital was necessary for a successful start. But this difficulty seems to have been overcome by the increasing level of savings on the part of those in upper-income groups, and greater familiarity with industrial risks by both bankers and private investors. The area in which opportunity was declining was agriculture, not business. In each generation there were more businesses of all types – small, large, and medium – in relation to the population, and fewer people working on farms. Boys interested in business, therefore, not only had an opportunity to go into an increasing number of different enterprises for themselves, but had in addition the choice of a career in a big corporation.

Marketing

While marketing, wholesale and retail, has always occupied the largest number of firms, employees in this sector have been fewer than in manufacturing. In the late nineteenth century the general wholesaler, serving as the essential link between small manufacturers and even smaller retailers, was the key figure in American economic life. By the early twentieth century, however, the domain of the wholesaler was being invaded on the one side by a few big manufacturers who sold their nationally advertised brands directly even to small retailers, and on the other by mail-order houses, big department stores, and chains that ordered directly from manufacturers. By 1929 only about half of manufactured consumer goods went through the hands of wholesalers, but of the products of small manufacturers four-fifths took this route.[7] Yet in spite of the trend toward elimination of middlemen, the growing variety of industrial products marketed increased the number of workers in this sector from 10 percent of the labor force in 1910 to nearly 13 percent in 1930.

With each type of product having its own peculiarities in distribution, the business world of the middleman was an increasingly complicated one. Small-town general stores still bought from full-line wholesalers, specialized shops from specialty wholesalers, sellers of expensive machinery or bulky commodities from jobbers or manufacturers' agents. And in different lines of goods varying names were given to middlemen performing similar basic functions. A man who simply routed goods from producer or central distributor to retailers, without ever taking possession, might be called a broker in farm staples, a jobber in vegetables, an agent in many manufactures, or a drop-shipper or desk-jobber in some types of heavy goods. Generally speaking, the term wholesaler was confined to firms that had warehouses to store the goods. But even wholesaling was primarily small scale and, in some lines, mixed with retailing.

To combat chain stores and more direct methods of distribution, wholesalers, particularly in food and drugs, in the 1920s entered into contractual agreements with groups of retailers for exclusive handling of the wholesaler's products. On this basis the retailers paid lower prices, received credit, and got advice regarding display, inventory control, and accounting. In some cases retailers squeezed by the rise of chain stores took the lead in organizing cooperative wholesale supply. By both methods the rise of chains in foods and drugs was checked in the decade of the twenties.

While isolated instances of chains of retail stores go back to the late colonial period, the modern chains in food and department-store wares were organized in the last half of the nineteenth century. The Great Atlantic and Pacific Tea Company, which started in 1858, was the first big grocery chain, and F. W. Woolworth, famous from 1879 on for Five and Ten Cent Stores, was the pioneer in novelty goods. J. C. Penney, the earliest chain to offer a full line of department-store wares, did not begin operations until 1902. In 1900, there were about 60 chains of all varieties with some 2,500 outlets; by 1928, the numbers had grown to over 600 corporations with about 150,000 stores. Large as these figures appear, the chain stores in 1929 did only about a fifth of the total retail business.[8] In both drugs and groceries the voluntary chains of small retailers were to hold the corporate chains at bay for another generation.

The first two decades of the twentieth century were the golden age of the small- to medium-sized farmer, and consequently for the mail-order houses that grew from his patronage. Sears, Roebuck, the largest of these, begun in a modest way in 1886 and greatly assisted by the introduction of rural free delivery at the end of the century, had sales in 1910 of over $60 million, while its nearest competitor, Montgomery Ward, did around half as much business.[9] Although orders from the catalogue delivered C.O.D., by regular mail, railroad freight, or express, had worked well enough to build these giant concerns, the institution of government parcel post in 1912 added substantially to their market. As farm income leveled off and then commenced to decline in the 1920s, the mail-order houses sought more urban consumers by opening their own retail outlets in the major cities, thus competing directly with the successful chains of department stores.

While in 1910 Sears was experimenting with the granting of installment credit on expensive durables, the mail-order houses were far from pioneers in this important innovation in retailing. By 1900, furniture, pianos, and many other durables were being sold on the basis of installment payments; by 1910, the system had been extended to that most important twentieth-century durable, the automobile. The value to Sears of publicizing installment credit in the catalogue of 1913 is illustrated by a threefold increase in piano sales from $350,000 in 1912 to over $1 million in 1914.[10]

Montgomery Ward in 1905 and Sears a year later opened branch distributing centers. The trend toward distribution through regional branches was also growing in most big companies that sold directly to retailers, some firms using both branches and wholesalers depending on the character of the area. By 1914, for example, Packard Motor Company had a mixed system with factory branches in big cities selling directly to retail dealers.

At about the same time, Ford began setting up regional assembly plants and eliminated all sales through wholesalers. In 1920 Proctor and Gamble, in drugs and cosmetics, divided the country into districts in each of which ten to fifteen salesmen visited all retail drug stores.[11]

During the twenties the management of General Motors, inspired by Alfred P. Sloan, Jr., brought producer control of marketing to a new degree of completeness. In 1923 the Chevrolet division led the way in establishing a standard accounting system for its retail dealers. R. J. Polk & Company were hired by General Motors to collect detailed figures each month on new registrations in each of thirty-one states. These were made "the basis of the most minute checks on the performance of every dealer. . . . It enabled the sales manager to set up bogeys in every department of the dealer's business."[12] The used-car business, for example, was carefully scrutinized by experts in Detroit who analyzed the dealer's stock of cars and the prices paid and received. Instructions were then issued which he had to abide by in order to retain his contract. A good feature for the consumer was that GM insisted that the dealer stand behind his used cars with guarantees and certain free services.

In return for such loss of independence GM gave its dealers a great deal of assistance. Styling was put in the hands of specialists in design, and new models were announced annually with a great fanfare of advertising and displays. Dealer's mark-ups were raised from 17 to 24 percent to give them more leeway in used-car allowances. At the end of World War I, John J. Raskob had initiated the General Motors Acceptance Corporation, which not only provided reasonable installment credit to consumers, but allowed the dealer to finance his new cars with only a 10 percent cash payment and low interest rates on the balance. It was symbolic of the loss of independence by the dealer that GMAC retained title to the new cars until they were sold and the credit repaid. After 1925, another subsidiary, General Exchange Insurance Corporation, carried the necessary policies at rates below those in the commercial market.[13] The whole system of marketing was not unlike the "contracting out" of parts of a process of production, frequently done by manufacturers in the nineteenth century. The producer gained some of the value of private initiative, at the same time securing the highly specialized staff work possible only in a large organization.

At the opposite pole from such close integration of stages was the marketing of raw materials and investment securities. In many agricultural products the processes at the beginning of the century were different from those of the last half. Producers sold to local wholesalers at prices fixed by the market rather than to food processors under contract. The local wholesaler passed perishable goods on to city middlemen and staples to elevator or warehouse men who might also be operators on the produce exchanges of the major trade centers. Although special contracts between refiners and fabricators frequently bypassed the open market, primary metals were also traded on a few central exchanges. Nonperishable staples were traded on exchanges in much the same way as stocks or bonds, with all the devices of long and short selling, scalping, and hedging necessary to orderly, but speculative markets. Once the staples had been collected and resold by the operators in the market, they went through the usual line of middlemen before reaching the ultimate consumer. Security selling, while somewhat similar to commodities at the exchange stage, had its own particular practices; these will be discussed further in Chapter 6.

Advertising

While part of the process of marketing, advertising was in itself a separate business that directly involved the industries of mass communication. The revenue to support this complex came from producers and traders trying to sell products, but the world of agencies and media had different problems from those of the manufacturer or retailer.

By 1900 metropolitan daily newspapers were big-business organizations supported mainly by advertising revenues, and in some cases such as those of Scripps-Howard or Hearst, organized in interurban chains. News gathering, other than local, was in the hands of a few press associations, formed (in order to avoid the antitrust laws) on a stock or membership basis by cooperating dailies. Of these the Associated Press was the oldest and largest, with a volume of business that by 1930 reached $10 million a year.[14]

Magazines such as the Ladies' Home Journal, which had built a circulation approaching a million copies a week by 1900, were the products of large publishing companies more dependent on revenue from advertising than subscriptions. Below these leading "slick paper" magazines in circulation were hundreds of monthlies and weeklies catering to special audiences based on education, status, or business interests, but with very few exceptions dependent for their survival on attracting advertising.

A considerable amount of local advertising, always the mainstay of the newspaper business, was placed directly by the sellers involved, but national advertising, or local advertising assisted by big producers, was handled through advertising agencies. Since in addition to newspapers and magazines, customers might be reached through cards in trolleys, elevateds, and subways, through billboards and electric signs, the planning of a national campaign for a soap, a medicine, or an auto-mobile was a complex process involving different combinations of media for each product.

To sell a product throughout the nation it had to be identifiable by a brand name and perhaps an advertising slogan associated with desir-able features. Companies marketing such goods generally found that additional dollars spent on advertising brought better results than those paid to salesmen. By 1900 many companies were spending up to a half a million dollars a year on advertising, and the Ladies' Home Journal was charging $4,000 for its back cover.[15] For effective use of such valuable space the agencies began to establish art departments and by 1910 were also doing market research.[16] A major consideration in placing ads was, of course, the paid circulation of the publication. To check on this the advertising agencies in Chicago and New York, in 1913, led the way in establishing an Audit Bureau of Circulation.[17]

Meanwhile, emphasis in the agencies shifted to creating new types of demand for a product, and dull descriptions of advantages gave way to appeals to basic emotions such as Packard's "A man is known by the car he keeps."[18] Expressing the new spirit, an editor of *Advertising and Selling* said: "I want advertising copy to arouse me."[19] To this end, academic psychology had offered theories that were talked of by agencies from the beginning of the century, but experience and not theory continued to guide advertisers.[20] In spite of three decades of search for ways to produce "hidden persuaders," many advertisements in 1929 were still conventional, factual, and conservative. Although agency personnel talked glibly of new types of emotional appeal, John B. Watson remembered the agencies and their clients as being "singularly impervious" to the suggestions of psychologists.[21]

The business of handling advertising rapidly reached maturity between 1890 and 1910. From the latter date until 1930, it is estimated that advertising consumed 4 percent of the total national income, a larger part than at any time thereafter.[22] The fact that the social impact of advertising undoubtedly grew after 1945 while its relative cost was less than in the earlier decades is an indication of the efficiency of radio and television.

By the 1920s advertising men, who earlier had been regarded by conservative businessmen as somewhat dishonorable hucksters, began to be respected as vital to the economy. Leading executives of many agencies regarded themselves as economic reformers and prophets of a new order. Standing for higher mass consumption, they regarded producers as steeped in the obsolete doctrines of thrift and frugality. Yet being employing businessmen themselves, they were reluctant to follow their own logic to the conclusion of advocating more pay for the lower-income groups.

Modern public relations was a product of this era of business confidence. Before the war there had been "publicity" men, like Ivy L. Lee, who helped to protect the Pennsylvania Railroad and the Rockefeller family from adverse public opinion, but the term "public relations" was seldom used and the line between advertising and publicity was indistinct. The success of propaganda in World War I increased the belief that public opinion could be molded and led to both public-relations counselors such as Lee and Edward L. Bernays and public-relations departments in advertising agencies and in a few big companies. The steady work of such men or departments was preparation of favorable news items that would be accepted by papers, although occasionally a campaign could be conducted through advertising. Cooperative or good-will advertising for the benefit of industries as a whole, such as the growers of California citrus fruits, public utilities, or insurance, was encouraged by the wartime excess profits tax, but it survived the repeal of the tax in 1922 and by the end of the decade reached $6 million a year.[23] Looking back over the period from the vantage point of 1929, advertising man Ernest Elmo Calkins wrote: "The war taught us the new possibilities of molding public opinion, improved the machinery, and transformed the old-time press agent into the modern public relations counsel, whose clients are colleges, cathedrals, corporations, societies, and even nations."[24]

As a business dealing primarily in public information, advertising had more than the usual need for cooperative organization and promotion of credibility through measures against fraud. The Audit Bureau of Circulation was followed in 1917 by the American Association of Advertising Agencies. Meanwhile, from 1907 on, local groups in the Associated Advertising Clubs of the World were initiating state and metropolitan Better Business Bureaus to prosecute fraud. In 1911, when only Massachusetts and New York had regulatory statutes, the chief trade journal *Printers Ink* drew up a model law against fraudulent advertising, which was ultimately approximated in many states. After 1925, a National Better Business Bureau joined in the campaign of policing the enormous mass and variety of promotional literature that reached consumers.[25]

Services for Business

Advertising agencies and public-relations counselors were among the many types of specialized services available to business firms. For a large number of businesses, the availability of such services was the chief reason for locating in or near a metropolitan center where a medium-sized company could hire all the advice that a bigger competitor might get from men on its own payroll.

The rise of higher education for business, around 1900, at a number of universities provided valuable auxiliary aid through professors of management, business law, accounting, and special fields such as insurance. Management advice was also promulgated through increasing numbers of books and articles.[26] Of this information the most immediately impressive was that set forth by Frederick W. Taylor and his associates[27] on the "science" of plant management (see also Chapter 5).

In the long run, however, the most important auxiliary service to develop at this time was public accounting. Bookkeeping methods had grown more sophisticated in the last half of the nineteenth century, with railroads and some industrial companies making amateurish efforts at cost accounting and departmental or branch comparisons in costs, but the idea of having outside "public" accountants examine the books annually and make suggestions spread from England and Scotland. In 1887 New York practitioners set up the Association of American Public Accountants; within a decade the larger and more progressive corporations were subscribing to the service of such firms as Price, Waterhouse and Company, although for business in general expansion of the practice was gradual.[28]

The federal tax laws of 1909 and 1913 were major events in the rise of United States public accounting. The first law imposed an "excise" tax of 1 percent on all corporate net income above $5,000. Since the Supreme Court had invalidated an "income" tax in 1895, and the penalties for nonpayment in the act of 1909 were limited to $10,000, a number of companies withheld payment while fifteen separate cases wended their way to the Supreme Court. But in a new age, with new justices, the Court chose to adjust the decision to the will of Congress; in Flint v. Stone and Tracy in 1911, the statute was unanimously upheld.[29] The law of 1913, legalized by the Sixteenth Amendment, continued the 1 percent corporate income tax, without the $5,000 exemption, and imposed taxes on personal income — above $3,000 a year for single receivers, and $4,000 for married. Graduated increases beginning at $20,000 reached 7 percent on annual incomes of over half a million dollars.

Thus public accounting was converted from a luxury of big corporations into a near-necessity for thousands of corporate units and wealthy individuals.[30] In 1914 the Federal Reserve Board added to the rush for outside help by demanding certification by public accountants of balance sheets presented for loans on commercial paper. Wartime excess profits taxes and higher corporate and personal income taxes, and in the mid-1920s a tax on the capital value of corporations, all ensured the growing importance of both internal and public accounting. While some companies had quite expert internal accounting, only professional outsiders could keep up with and interpret all the new federal rulings.

With sixteen colleges and universities offering majors in accounting in 1916, leading business and academic scholars of the subject inevitably became involved in efforts to establish uniform principles through forming the Institute of Accountants of America, which included the members of the old association. The profession would have liked a federal statute compelling approved tests for practice anywhere in the country, but they were able to offer only their own examination, beginning in June 1917. Four years later, properly qualified practitioners could become members of a more professional American Society of Public Accountants. By 1924, all states and territories had legislation controlling individual certification, and the big accounting firms had many branch offices.

Inside the firm the emphasis on accounting led to the new office of controller, and in the 1920s to the rise of budgeting or financial forecasting. It seems safe to say that no other type of "staff" or specialized service was so universally necessary to business.

The close connection between legislation, federal or state, and the creation of service organizations was by no means peculiar to accounting. Ever since the 1820s, tariffs and excises had spawned associations. Each regulatory act had always had a tendency to create an organization to inform those affected of how to cope with the law and to support a lobby for desirable changes; as the pace of new regulation increased around the turn of the century, so did the establishment of associations.[31]

Each of these types of business auxiliaries usually had one or more journals, which swelled the number of trade or professional publications available to the business manager to a point where he lacked the time to read them. The rapidly increasing flow of information available to businessmen therefore had a spiraling effect on increasing specialization. As new associations and functions developed and established periodicals, management needed specialists to keep up with them, and ambitious specialists were always alert to the possibilities of subdividing their larger specialty into smaller groups in one of which they could play a leading role. Undoubtedly the net result in the well-managed firm was more informed entrepreneurship, but directing the flows through the right channels, and diminishing their volume before the combined flow overwhelmed those at the top, posed a major problem for management.

The New Competition

Of all the uncertainties faced by the businessman the future movement of prices set by competition was among the most critical. In the last three decades of the nineteenth century manufacturers had tried all the European forms of association only to have each declared illegal by state or federal courts. It now appeared that the only legal and workable alternative was informal price leadership by the strongest companies. If this were done simply by making the proposed price known to all competitors, it appeared that neither the common law nor the antitrust acts were violated.

Highly capitalized concerns particularly wanted price stability, and the growing interest of professional management in long-run security produced wide support for the medieval or mercantilist idea of "just price." This implied the end of secret price-cutting and the adoption of uniform trade practices. As Arthur J. Eddy, a Chicago lawyer, wrote in 1912 in a book called *The New Competition*:

The basis of the old competition is secrecy, the strength of the news is knowledge: the essence of the old is deceit, the spirit of the new is truth. Concealment characterizes all the dealings of the old; frankness is vital to the new.

The old looks with suspicious eye on all associations and combinations; without cooperation the new is impossible.[32]

In industries dominated by a few large companies, informal understandings usually led to satisfactory cooperation in pricing. Steel prices were set for a number of years at annual dinners held by Judge Gary of United States Steel. When rival firms started cutting prices in 1908, they were warned that if they resorted to "unreasonable and destructive competition" they would compel the "application of the law of the survival of the fittest."[33] Licensing of patents between competing companies was another means of controlling prices and conditions of sale. In the group of industries in which competition was not restrained by either large firms or patents, uniformity required some type of group action.

The trade association was the obvious agency for carrying on an "open price policy." By 1912 there were both regional and national trade associations for most industries, although some of them were not very active. To "coordinate competitive forces without relinquishing the fruits that spring from individual initiative," a number of them now started to exchange information about costs, prices, orders, and inventories.[34] During World War I, the government's use of the associations as agencies to estimate, apportion, and stimulate production strengthened the existing groups and aided the formation of new ones. By the end of the war, there were perhaps a thousand trade associations operating on a nationwide basis, and 10 or 15 percent of these were experimenting with open price policy. Under this system each member posted its prices with the association, which in turn circulated them, along with pertinent information, in letters or periodicals.

In the mid-twenties, the Supreme Court held that exchange of information between companies was legal if not used as a means of "controlling" prices.[35] Since in the highly competitive industries the problem was falling prices due to overproduction, the Cotton Textile Institute, for example, tried to get the industry to adopt "the traditional guild objectives of stabilization, cooperation, and control."[36] But in spite of quite complete interchange of figures on prices and production between the leading members of the CTI, profits fell sharply from 1927 to 1929.[37] Voluntary following of "price leadership" appeared to work only in industries with most of the production concentrated in the hands of a few firms.

A Period of Gradual Change

The period of rapid increase in monopoly by newly formed manufacturing corporations ended before the panic of 1907, not only because of federal antitrust action (Chapter 6), but also because big companies had by then occupied most of the industries where "economies of scale" gave an important advantage in the market. In manufacturing, however, industries in which six companies sold half the product or a dozen sold three-quarters decreased slightly as a percentage of those listed in the census to a level of 30 percent in 1929.[38]

Viewing the economy as a whole, the relations between small, medium, and big business altered only gradually. This was less true of the relations of major sectors or areas of enterprise. In 1900, one American worker in three was engaged in farming; by 1929, the ratio was one in five; trade, service, and finance together occupied one of four workers in 1900 and better than one of three in 1929. These changes were manifest in the rise of filling stations, roadside restaurants, beauty parlors, department stores, brokerage and insurance offices; along with the reversion of unprofitable eastern farmland to forest, they symbolized an emerging American society with an economy more dependent on luxury trades and less geared to crops and the weather.

Another type of change from earlier days of American development was in saving and investment. The efforts of individuals to save money, and of businessmen to invest it, are not always in balance. Personal saving depends largely on size of income and social habits, whereas investment depends upon the immediate promise of gains from new facilities and technology, modified by business forecasts of demand in the near future. Thus, although estimates indicate that from 1900 to 1930 the percentage of national income being saved each year tended to increase, the portion invested in real physical equipment declined. Simon Kuznets puts the percentage of national income going into net capital formation during the decade 1899 to 1908 at 12.6, and for 1919 to 1928 at 10.2.[39]

Before 1929 nothing disturbed the business system sufficiently to upset a gradual evolution of ideas and attitudes developed in the nineteenth century. While there were many new regulations, the economy was still believed to be basically self-regulating; while there were more big companies, small firms were doing well and increasing rapidly in number; and while a managerial group with new attitudes was emerging, they still talked the language of the independent entrepreneur seeking profit in the market.

5 Inside the Firm

Like the "short and simple annals of the poor," those of small business seldom survive. A firm old enough and large enough to authorize an informative, scholarly history is invariably at least medium sized. Small proprietorships or partnerships seldom preserve explanatory records such as letters, reports, or clipping books at all, and usually destroy legal records after the expiration of statutes of limitation; hence information comes mainly from brief interviews, trade journals, and various types of statistics.[1] Corporations, which in 1929 numbered about 20 percent of all enterprises, have to preserve certain records such as board minutes noting decisions to take action, but these are seldom a source for information regarding how management saw its problems. Therefore it is impossible to say much from historical evidence about internal management in firms of from one to a hundred employees, which constitute the great mass of employing enterprises.

The Management of Small Business

External records tell chiefly about relations with suppliers, creditors, and customers, not with those between proprietors or partners and their various levels of employees. Prior to 1930 (and even today) the great majority of employers had four or less employees, but for those who employed more, managerial problems arose. The point at which a one-boss system became inefficient varied with the type of business, and until after World War I single men in control of even large operations were loath to delegate power to an adequate number of fellow executives. It may well have been that business failures apparently resulting from lack of capital, inexperience, or poor location were strongly abetted by internal inefficiency and poor morale.[2]

Many small businessmen had their major decisions made for them by suppliers who advanced trade credit. This might vary from onerous restriction, such as a retailer having to buy from a certain wholesaler regardless of variety or price, to helpful organization of the enterprise, as in the case of the holders of franchises in either proprietary or cooperative chains. The latter was not a common arrangement in 1930, but was to become much more so after World War II as food, restaurant, and motel chains spread.

All in all, success for the millions of enterprises that have had less than a dozen employees must have depended largely on the intelligence and personality of the entrepreneur, and much less on the application of the principles of management propounded in books or schools of business. This may account for the fact that the average life of such an enterprise did not appear to change much from the nineteenth to the mid-twentieth century.

Little more is known about the internal problems of the additional millions of firms that have had up to a few hundred employees. James H. Soltow, in studying the origins and endings of such firms in manufacturing, has been able to learn little about the details of internal management in the period before 1930. From his work it appears that many of the entrepreneurs had had managerial experience in larger companies, and often they proceeded on a trial-and-error basis to find a product that was not too highly competitive. A key to success in smaller manufacturing ventures was not so much ability at internal organization as good personal relations with the relatively few suppliers and customers who were the ultimate bosses. Credit was also likely to be secured on personal notes based on some banker's opinion of the entrepreneur's ability and integrity. Few of these firms ever grew large, and a man would often prefer running his own company even though his return was less than a big corporation would have paid him in salary.[3]

Management and the Worker

In these medium-sized companies, labor relations also depended greatly on the personality of the boss. While paternalism was generally the rule, some employers made respected fathers while others were hated. These small employers, who needed to use their workers in many different capacities, feared the rigidities of union regulations with their job specifications; in most cases, outside the big cities they were able to remain open shop. Organizing them was expensive for the unions, and a wise employer would usually offer equal benefits without the cost to the worker of union dues.

In large companies, labor relations were handled on a plant basis, and new ideas regarding management or schemes to reduce turnover in labor met readier acceptance than those affecting the operations of top-level executives. Larger shops run by men at the bottom of the managerial hierarchy presented many new problems in handling both men and materials. The evolving technology in the plant and more complex business controls in the office not only required care and guidance by highly educated specialists, but also group efforts at solving dilemmas that involved many factors. "In the future," wrote Frederick W. Taylor, the pioneer efficiency expert, "it will be appreciated that our leaders must be trained right as well as born right, and that no great man can [with the old system of personal management] hope to compete with a number of ordinary men who have been properly organized so as efficiently to cooperate."[4]

New ideas about better adjustment of men to jobs and higher wages for better production began to appear in the 1890s. When Taylor set himself up as a professional management consultant in 1894, his business card read: "Systematizing Shop and Manufacturing Costs a Specialty." His program soon became known, both at home and abroad, as "scientific management." The basic principle was "that in almost all of the mechanic arts the science which underlies each act of each workman is so great and amounts to so much that the workman who is best suited to actually doing the work is incapable of fully understanding this science, without the guidance and help of those who are working with him or over him."[5]

In Taylor's system foremen had to study the essential motions and minimum time for each job and then instruct the worker. The faster rate that resulted would be maintained by pay increases for productivity. To gain deeper insight, some foremen were required to specialize in supervision of certain functions rather than in complete management of a small number of men. More supervisors might be needed, but they would be paid for by greatly increased output.

Although no company adopted all of Taylor's ideas at once, many started experimenting with them, and still others paid increasing attention to shop management. When Louis D. Brandeis, later a justice of the Supreme Court, told the Interstate Commerce Commission that the railroads could save a million dollars a day by scientific management, "it was a shot heard around America."[6] In the years before World War I, Taylorism was discussed by all types of industrialists and Taylor had many imitators, each with his own system. Henry Ford, for example, said that "starting in 1913 we had time studies made of all the thousands of operators in the shops. By a time study it is possible theoretically to determine what a man's output should be."[7]

A major deterrent to the adoption of such schemes was the opposition of workers. The fear, often realized, that piece rates or other incentives would not be maintained once production speeded up, led labor to disregard the instructions of "efficiency experts." In fact, many workers deliberately slowed down during test periods, and a lasting resistance was set up to management recommendations regarding shop routines.[8]

Interest in worker morale as a factor in productivity came slowly and uncertainly to management, more concerned with technology and marketing. Around 1900 the National Cash Register Company was one of the pioneers in setting up an employment clerk to work on recruitment problems. Other companies established social or welfare secretaries to look after cases of hardship from illness or injury. The welfare title, however, had a bad connotation and by 1912 the positions were being renamed personnel managers. The duties of a personnel department usually included hiring and training of workers, and administration of medical and welfare plans. Some also handled employee grievances and records.[9]

The shortage of labor during and immediately after World War I advanced the new "science" of personnel management. To explain how to find the right man for the job and to keep him working at it, a flood of seemingly learned books appeared and "experts" were hired at good salaries. With the depression of the early twenties and a surplus of workers, the enthusiasm for scientific personnel work subsided, but it rose again in the prosperous late 1920s. In 1928 one-third of the plants with over 250 employees had personnel managers.[10]

The company magazine was another device for improving morale that spread during World War I. National Cash Register was a historic leader with a twelve-page *Factory News* in 1890, which later became a more general company paper, *NCR News*. A survey of such magazines made in 1921 indicated that more than nine-tenths had been started after 1916. A survey in 1924 showed that the number had increased to nearly five hundred, of which over half were devoted to employee interests and the rest more oriented toward sales.[11]

In the 1920s a few hundred companies established noncontributory pension plans and a number made provision for the purchase of stock at below-market levels by small monthly payments. Some large companies also supplied housing and offered training and educational opportunities.[12] It was hoped that such schemes would both add to the worker's interest in the success of the company and discourage his quitting for some other job.

Another approach to reducing labor turnover and increasing productivity depended upon initially selecting the right man for the job. Army psychological testing in the war gave rise to a number of "industrial psychologiests" who claimed that they could measure the aptitude of applicants for different types of jobs.[13] But half a dozen years of testing in industry showed little correlation between use of the system and higher productivity by labor. As Reinhard Bendix says: "The employment of industrial psychologists might do no more than flavor the conventional arguments of employers with the jargon of conflicting schools of thought and to empty the 'pursuit of self-interest' of such simple meanings as it had in the past," which "did nothing to solve the practical problems of management."[14]

Early in the century Hamilton M. Barksdale at Du Pont had unsuccessfully urged hiring outsiders to do research in the motivation of workers.[15] As this idea gained popularity under the pressures of the war period, an article in the *National Association of Corporation Training Bulletin* said: "We must enlist the confidence of the employee in the business and business processes...."[16] Motivation study continued throughout the 1920s but with no important findings until those of Elton Mayo in 1928, which influenced a later generation.

In accordance with the usual pattern, some of the small business firms with under 250 employees, that even in the highly concentrated manufacturing sector composed 96.5 percent of the total in 1923, followed the new practices established by big enterprises. Attempting to survey such firms, the National Industrial Conference Board received data from 4,409 out of a total in the 1923 census of 188,000. Since companies with some interest in new ideas regarding industrial relations probably replied while the others did not, the total of less than 3 percent may bear a relation to the spread of such programs among small business.[17]

While labor turnover was usually more expensive for small plants than for large, plans that required special directors and new facilities were in general too expensive, particularly for the average manufacturing firm, which in the mid-twenties had less than fifty employees. Incentive pay, bonuses, and profit-sharing, however, were popular among the responding small employers – in many cases, no doubt, as a defense against trade unions.[18] Very few companies applied such incentives to management, probably because they were usually proprietary family firms, in which extra reward came from stock or partnership dividends.

In all of this discussion of both large and small firms it should be remembered that the experimenters in industrial relations were in a small minority. Henry Ford spoke for a larger group in saying:

Labour works along under any system. . . . It is not necessary to have people love each other to work together. Too much good fellowship may be a bad thing, for it may lead to one man trying to cover up the faults of another. . . . Ford factories and enterprises have no organization, no specific duties attaching to any position, no line of succession or authority, very few titles, and no conferences.[19]

Regardless of its limited application, the study of worker welfare and morale marks the beginning of the breakdown in labor relations of the simple philosophy of the nineteenth century. In the earlier ideas that justified managerial authority based on the operation of natural laws, success was a proof of virtue, and failure to rise from the ranks of labor showed a lack of either intelligence or proper moral qualities. The inevitable trend of the new psychology was to make management partially responsible for the success or failure of workers, to replace the inexorable authority of natural law with the uncertainties of social relations. Growing as time went on, this shift in justification was to do much to undermine the earlier industrial ethics of both managerial authority and hard work.

In the 1920s, this threat was scarcely recognized. Aided by the introduction of electrical and chemical processes, quality control by scientists, and better understanding of the principles of management, labor productivity increased at the rate of 1.7 percent a year, the highest for any decade for which there are reliable records. In the smug, self-confident atmosphere of the twenties industrial relations had an academic quality of much talk at association meetings and little change in real action.

Ownership and Control

In spite of a few one-man dictatorships such as that of Henry Ford, it was inevitable that as corporations grew larger, there must be an increasing separation of ownership from active control. The good securities market of the early years of the century and of the twenties encouraged families or small owning groups in control of companies to sell stock to the public. Such sales paid for new additions, expanded working capital without borrowing from the banks, permitted the owners to diversify their holdings by buying into other companies, and increased the public interest in the welfare of the firm. By 1930 the management group had come to be much less associated with ownership than in the previous generation.

Increasing the numbers of stockholders diminished the already slight possibility of any group of small stockholders overthrowing management. But also to gain security from raids by big market operators, some companies issued only nonvoting stock to the public. This practice brought down the wrath of reformers such as Professor William Z. Ripley, and numerous journalists. F.P.A. (Franklin P. Adams) in his "Conning Tower" in the New York *World* published "On Waiting for the *New Masses* to Denounce Nonvoting Stocks,"

> Then you who drive the fractious nail,
> And you who lay the heavy rail,
> And all who bear the dinner pail
>   And daily punch the clock —
> Shall it be said your hearts are stone?
> They are your brethren and they groan!
>   Oh, drop a tear for those who own
> Nonvoting corporate stock.[20]

Even the Investment Bankers Association denounced the practice, and it was gradually abandoned. The great majority of stockholders, however, had long since ceased to view their companies as property they could administer, or their votes as instruments of power.

The board of directors also ceased to be an effective representation of ownership. Only a few members of large company boards kept well enough informed to take a hand in guiding the organization, and these members were usually salaried officers of the company. At the end of the nineteenth century, salaried officers had feared the penetrating eye of a Rockefeller, Harriman, or Morgan on the board. In the lush twenties, however, with corporate savings adequate for company needs and new capital easy to acquire, the salaried executives boldly questioned the prerogatives of the outside directors. Management developed the theory that the director's function was merely advisory, that he should not try to form or veto policy or to interfere in the operation of the concern. This de-emphasis of the board as the elected representatives of the owners, as the supreme authority for which management worked as hired hands, reached its extreme in such boards as those of American Tobacco or Standard Oil Company (New Jersey) composed entirely of salaried officers. Still, on all large company boards, officers came to play the leading role.

Was this new assumption of authority a "managerial revolution" and was the new system of big business "managerial enterprise?"[21] By 1930 the answer to such questions was by no means clear. In routine matters the administrators certainly wielded the power, but in questions of financial policy board members representing banks or insurance companies might overrule management. While small stockholders could not by themselves organize to overturn the administration, big financiers who had acquired a large amount of stock might succeed in an appeal to the small stockholders to support their slate of directors. In 1928 John D. Rockefeller, Jr., for example, ousted Robert W. Stewart from the chairmanship of Standard Oil of Indiana, on what Rockefeller regarded as a moral issue, by assembling proxies and overruling the existing directors.[22]

Control, therefore, was generally shared by several of the directors and managers, the locus of authority depending upon the point at issue. The professional manager who, without investing much or any capital, had made his way up through the organization, and the board members who represented financial houses or family trusts were all presumably more interested in a strong, progressive, going concern than in paying unusually large dividends to stockholders. The president of the company, in theory its most important entrepreneur, was apt to be primarily interested in keeping a satisfactory balance between more wages for labor, higher salaries for management, better service for customers, adding to the company's cash reserves, improvement of the physical plant, and dividends for the stockholders. Each of these represented superficially contending interests in that if one got more in any given division, the others received less.

In this situation it was not astonishing that the modern professional manager tended, perhaps unconsciously, to favor the financial claims of those who could bring more constant pressure than could the mass of stockholders. Such a situation meant, among other things, that successful large companies paid high wages and salaries, accumulated substantial reserves against depreciation or depression, and paid relatively low dividends.

The Challenge of Multiplant Management

As some companies came to have thousands of administrators, it became clear that business was encountering the same types of problems that had existed for centuries in public administration. As one well-qualified critic saw it, business growth had "resulted in concentrating in relatively few hands a degree and scope of economic power which transcends the limits of effective administration."[23] Whether or not this was true, business certainly needed its own political science.[24]

A few far-sighted analysts such as Barksdale at Du Pont recognized that quality and systems of management were the keys to success of the large company. As Edith F. Penrose writes: "The services available from management limit expansion regardless of resources available in the market."[25] The history of a firm depends upon the types of opportunities perceived and grasped by its officers. Most American chief executives learned only by hard experience that entrepreneurial services were as valuable and necessary as those of machines.

Pursuit of a science of administration led to better cost-accounting techniques, an increase in middle management, and more use of staff consultants. Alexander H. Church's *Productive Factors,* published in 1910, was one of the earliest books to analyze overhead costs.[26] After World War I, alert companies hired industrial engineers, theoretical economists, and other specialists who might provide new knowledge or perspective on business problems. In order to guard against or prepare for disruptive changes in technology, a few big companies established research laboratories employing scores of scientists. Increasingly complex relations with both government and organized labor necessitated more legal experts to analyze proposed legislation, more trained lobbyists or public relations men to forestall harmful bills, and more reliable analysts to learn or forecast government policy.

The very basis of mass production was the commitment of vast amounts of time and money to a particular way of doing a job. Blueprinting and manufacturing the machinery needed to fashion a new product could take two to four years. The need for careful advance planning, because of inability to change once the process was in motion, applied not only to machines and buildings, but to office work as well. A filing system might become obsolete, but to refile fifteen or twenty million letters in an insurance office was as staggering a task as completely to retool an assembly line. The smooth functioning of a vast organization required established channels of information and control. But such elements introduced a time lag and a chance that an idea for improvement might get lost on the way. Even a well-received suggestion entering at the bottom of the managerial hierarchy might take two years to work its way to the top and then back to the point where it could be translated into action.

Mergers, additional products, and expansion to new territories at home and abroad put more strains and burdens on top management. "Often," writes Alfred D. Chandler, Jr., "it was the rapid increase in the number of administrative decisions resulting from the strategy of expansion that caused executives to bog down in technical detail."[27] The solution was, of course, a rationalized bureaucracy capable of making minor decisions at proper levels rather than having everything rise to the top.

American businessmen were loath to see their problem in these terms. As Charles Francis Adams, Jr. had written back in the 1870s, Americans lacked an administrative tradition in both business and government.[28] From the beginning of industrialism too little management had been a chronic ailment, and the pioneers of big industrial business continued policies of one-man control, often into the 1920s.

In a very few companies mergers and new branches led to thought about managerial structure early in the century. Faced with the addition of large new powder companies, Pierre du Pont and vice-president Barksdale began a series of studies and changes about 1903 that ultimately made the Du Pont company a model for others. The major principle that evolved was that of a top level of management freed from any direct connections with separate parts of the company, a group that would see policy as a whole, rather than several groups negotiating with one another for the benefit of their own divisional interests.

Ideas regarding management on all levels were readily available to those who would read them before World War I. Professional organizations, journals, and meetings devoted to management problems grew from personnel work and college training. The National Association of Employment Managers became, through a series of mergers from 1914 to 1923, the American Management Association, while from 1914 on, variously named periodicals were published that in 1923 became the *American Management Review.*[29] The association grew until by 1930 it had 4,300 members from 1,500 firms and over 100 professors from colleges and universities.[30]

The rise of the university business school was another potential source of ideas and training. The first of these, the Wharton School at the University of Pennsylvania, was founded in 1883; a few others, such as the Graduate School of Business Administration at Harvard, preceded World War I; but the great increase came in the twenties. By the end of the decade most large universities were offering undergraduate or graduate courses both in the essential techniques of management and in academic subjects that might contribute to sounder and broader executive viewpoints.

The reaction to all of this discussion and learning, including publication of the Haskell Committee Report in 1920 charting the Du Pont system, was slow — partly because domineering executives such as Durant and Ford wanted no restraints on their freedom of decision; partly because each company had its own problems that were not always seen by outside management consultants; and partly because experience gained in restructuring government bureaucracies did not always apply well to business. A government agency, for example, has a set job to perform at minimum cost, whereas a business branch has an unknown potential market to exploit at an appropriate cost. George Frazier, for example, an expert in accounting and management who had introduced new systems in state governments in Wisconsin, Illinois, and Ohio, failed to find the right solution for the problems of expansion at Sears, Roebuck.[31] It was the end of the twenties before even a few firms had adopted the ideas originated at Du Pont and perfected by Alfred Sloan, Jr. at General Motors. Consequently, general experience with executive committees and staff and line management will be discussed later (in Chapter 11).

Overexpansion in World War I and the drastic price break in 1920 led medium-sized business also to begin to think about better management controls. Firms doing a few million dollars worth of business a year either saw the need for more top-level executives, or were forced to make such additions to satisfy bank creditors. In the process many one-man family firms started on the road to professional management even though they were not, by American standards, big companies.

Foreign expansion may have been better managed than domestic, simply because the need for new knowledge and new structure was more obvious.[32] American Radiator Company, for example, in 1900 operated its overseas plants through a three-man advisory board resident in Europe, who dealt with plant executives often recruited locally.[33] The same held true for companies such as Standard Oil, but this did not ensure proper utilization of information in making policy at the head office.

The problem of the right amount of management for the production involved was never solved, but the trend was distinctly upward. A study of manufacturing industry puts the increase in administrative employees between 1899 and 1929 at 330 percent, while production employees increased less than 90 percent.[34] Since the increase in the National Bureau of Economic Research's index of manufacturing production rose less than 300 percent, there was probably no saving in cost per unit of output in administrative salaries and expense accounts as company size increased; the economies were from better management and technology reducing the cost of operations.

Promotion and Incentives

On the basis of good flows of information reinforced by accounting controls the inefficiencies of single departments or weak administrators might be detected and eliminated, but how were men to be trained, selected, and inspired to undertake the task of coordinating and directing the enterprise as a whole? How were men to translate power into effective administration? No student of management, inside or outside of business, found a uniformly acceptable formula for choosing executives. Methods of selection remained largely rule of thumb, and as organizations grew bigger, success for the man without influential connections depended on recognition of his abilities by someone in top management, usually through a fortunate conjunction of circumstances. The individual competitive struggle for success in such companies, therefore, took the form of means for attracting attention to one's desirable qualities of loyalty, cooperation, intelligence, and leadership rather than the quest for wealth or market advantages.

The change that had taken place in this branch of the road to success can be illustrated by comparing Andrew Carnegie's instructions to young men of the late nineteenth century with those of a twentieth-century railroad president. "Is there any would-be businessman before me," Carnegie asked a group of Cornell students, "content in forecasting his future, to figure himself as labouring all his life for a fixed salary? Not one, I am sure. In this you have the dividing line between business and nonbusiness; the one is a master, and depends on profits, the other a servant and depends upon salary. . . . I do not believe that even the presidents of these corporations, being only salaried men, are to be . . . classed as strictly businessmen at all." When a man is to be made a partner, "then comes the question of questions, *is he honest and true?*" Among rules for getting ahead Carnegie advised: "Boss your boss just as soon as you can; try it on early. There is nothing he will like so well if he is the right kind of boss; if he is not, he is not the man for you to remain with — leave him whenever you can, even at a present sacrifice, and find one capable of discerning genius."[35]

Two generations later a young boy wrote to a railroad president asking how to get a job like his. The president replied, "Industry and cooperation are very important. . . . Teamwork is as essential on a railroad as it is on a football field. . . . Cultivate and develop a pleasing and friendly personality. . . . Show an interest in other people and what they have to say . . . finish college. . . . " The president concluded: "Of course, opportunity and good fortune also play a part."[36]

Actually, there was nothing new in the evolving big-business situation. Men in the bureaucracies of Egypt, Greece, and Rome had striven for success under somewhat similar conditions, but the turn toward an organizational career for some of the country's most ambitious citizens was a notable departure from historic American conditions and conflicted with a good deal of the nation's cultural heritage. Americans had tended to see themselves as self-reliant, aggressive enterprisers rather than smoothly polished negotiators. The subtleties of approach and fine manners of Europeans had been sources of ridicule; now they seemed to pave the road to success.

While the top executives of the large companies continued to talk the language of earnings for the stockholders and to keep their formal behavior oriented toward profits, many of them had relatively little direct stake in the size of the dividends paid by their companies. Maximization of profits was the orthodox slogan, but one that management accepted with many qualifications. From the earliest days executives of large corporations affected with a public interest, such as railroads, had been in favor of steady but moderate profits rather than maximization.[37] The attitude that secure profits over a long period were more desirable than large and risky returns came to be generally held by the management of companies.[38] While market positions in relation to competitors remained important, executives may have become even less profit motivated than they themselves realized.[39]

What then were the personal incentives of executives once they had reached the probable top of the promotional ladder? A general answer appeared to be "the continual stimulation that derives from the pleasure of immediate accomplishment."[40] The president of a big company, asked why he was working on a holiday, replied: "I'm not working, I'm having fun."[41] The achievements from executive effort were made more satisfactory by the admiration of one's peers in business or by significant groups of the outside public. Thus achievement for its own sake, the wielding of socially accepted power, and personal prestige were generally more important incentives than either increases in salary or company profits, as such.[42]

Many companies, however, sought to substitute for personal profit such financial incentives as bonus plans and management funds, which divided part of the year's earnings among the administrators on either a fixed percentage, or a percentage set by vote of the board of directors or the chief officers. The earliest of these plans antedated World War I, and they were particularly characteristic of periods of high prosperity. In good years, like 1928 and 1929, these payments might greatly exceed the regular salary of the executive, and a few companies paid bonuses even in 1932. Plans for buying of stock by management ran counter to a desire for wise diversification of personal investment in order to achieve added individual security, which was likely to impel officers to hold only a reasonable amount of stock in the companies for which they worked. Despite the fact that some companies adopted bonus and stock-purchase plans and other equally progressive schemes, such mechanisms were not fully accepted solutions to the problem of stimulating energy and devotion to the company.

Intracompany competition and ratings by accounting controls were more positive ways of ensuring efficiency. General Motors cars, for example, were in competition with one another, and their factory and marketing costs could be compared. Success on such a basis could accrue without large profits. During the depression of the thirties the officers of Cadillac won high prestige for not losing money when other cars of the same price range were all showing large losses. "Book" competition could be rigorous in companies like American Telephone & Telegraph, which had similar operations all over the nation. Accountants could check with great precision the efficiency of a local management group, but it was hard to measure the ability of any single individual.

Increasing levels of security and prestige were also incentives for the executive of the big company. Personal recognition could be given through larger offices, more prerogatives, and higher titles that carried prestige in the community as well as in the company. In this way the need for labeling officials in a large formal organization could also be used to improve morale.

Railroads started conferring the title of vice-president on the man in

charge of each part of the business, such as traffic, operation, maintenance, or finance, in the mid-nineteenth century, but other large companies were slow to follow this practice until after 1900. Then spurred
somewhat by ideas of scientific management, and still more by the
demands of increasing size, companies added numerous specialized
officials with titles ranging from assistant superintendent to senior
vice-president. As holding companies spread, there also came to be
scores of officerships in subsidiaries. "In the last forty years or so,"
said the president of International Harvester in 1953, "this system has
developed from what football coaches would call a one platoon system
to something that approximates a thirty or forty platoon system in
industry."[43]

By 1930 a big company might have from five to fifty vice-presidents
of the parent organization and a proportionately large number of assistant vice-presidents as well as assistant secretaries and assistant treasurers. There might also be assistants to the chairman of the board, the
president, and the vice-presidents. Usually these assistants were staff
officers, that is, specialists or roving executives who handled particular
types of problems or else improved communication and knit the organization together. The subsidiaries would have their presidents, vice-
presidents, and other officers. Often the chief officers of the parent
company divided among themselves the topmost posts in the subsidiaries, but the lesser positions were filled by additional officer personnel. Under the officers in rank, but not always in salary, were
managers, superintendents, department heads, supervisors, and their
staffs.

As in the conferring of titles, business needs could be combined with
better morale through officers' clubs. The clubs were generally built
around a comfortable restaurant where the staff could assemble for
lunch and use their leisure time for informal discussion of company
problems. In many companies officers also spent much of their social
life entertaining one another and talking shop over highballs. By such
means the company might become an engrossing interest in both work
and recreation. A later report on the habits of big company officials
noted that, "In many instances . . . executives look upon the office

day as something of an interruption in their actual work."[44] So far did this tendency go in some companies that an opposite danger began to develop, that of losing the perspective of the outsider and viewing problems only in terms of group clichés. The dilemma is inherent in all group activity. The somewhat introverted individualist fertile in new ideas tends to cooperate poorly and to disrupt the smooth functioning of the organization, while the outgoing type, hungry for the friendship and support of his fellows, may cooperate excellently but lack the ability to innovate. Many critics inside the ranks of business thought that the big company tended to advance too many men of this latter type.

Managerial Motivation

The problems of prestige, security, and morale ran from top to bottom of the large company. "You will learn to your sorrow," wrote John L. McCaffrey in *Fortune*, "that, while a drill press never sulks and a drop hammer never gets jealous of other drop hammers, the same cannot be said for people. . . . The man in the middle of the management pyramid, however, neither makes the decisions nor carries them out. He finds it easy to feel that his judgment was neither sought nor honored. . . . He often feels, and frequently says, that he is just a high-priced office boy."[45]

The routine administrator could be given a feeling of added importance in several ways. For lower management and even a few workers the company magazine and company club were means to both individual distinction and closer group cooperation. Company magazines devoted to internal news were probably more important for pleasing administrators than blue-collar workers. By 1925 practically all of the three or four hundred biggest corporations had some type of house organ.[46] These magazines reported promotions, social events, athletic contests, marriages, and other family news. They published fiction and poetry by company employees. Editorially they served as media for indoctrination in company policy and ideals. The fact that there was a company reading public or community also gave a feeling of added importance and responsibility to the chief executive officers.

Company clubs and teams achieved some of these same purposes. Salaried employees were given a chance to build friendships and become recognized personalities within the company atmosphere. In some companies workers and managers mingled at the golf course or bowling alleys, although upper management was inclined to avoid these contacts.

Good organization men were probably less aggressive risk-takers, less active in the quest for profit, than the owner-managers of smaller enterprise. A disgruntled trade-association executive in the mid-twenties remarked, "We are raising a lot of thoroughly drilled yes-ma'ams in the big corporations, who have no minds of their own, no opinions."[47] The salaried professional was particularly disinclined to pursue policies that might eliminate his job, regardless of the profitability of these policies to the stockholders. He might also be reluctant to recommend investments that would upset personnel relations within the organization. For example, the assets of a steamship company became almost completely liquid during World War II through the sinking of its vessels and resulting insurance payments. There was little prospect that the company's normal trade would be profitable for new vessels in time of peace. The chairman of the board, a large stockholder and an independent capitalist, played with the idea of liquidating the operating end of the business and investing the capital in more promising enterprises. Profit considerations pointed overwhelmingly in that direction. But the professional managers in the company, whose jobs would disappear, opposed such a plan. In the end the company decided to continue in shipping. The pressures of personal relations and the momentum of a going concern won out over the policy that appeared to promise maximization of profit for the stockholders.

These considerations, plus that of size alone, and the threat of government prosecution under the antitrust laws tended to make big-company entrepreneurs think more in terms of maintaining a given market position than in terms of radical technological innovation and expansion at the expense of competitors. As Oswald Knauth, himself a managerial top executive saw it, "The life blood of managerial enterprise is a steady demand."[48] Furthermore, if one or a limited number of companies controlled production in an industry, it was possible for entrepreneurs to slow the pace of innovation in the interest of less risk and longer utilization of existing equipment – a process that might increase immediate purchasing power, but delay capital formation, cut future production, and endanger exports. Well-known illustrations of the slowing of innovation in the interests of more complete utilization of existing equipment are American Telephone & Telegraph Company's treatment of the handset phone after 1907, and General Electric's and Westinghouse's relatively slow response to the possibilities of fluorescent lighting from 1896 to 1938.[49]

If complete figures could be assembled, it might turn out that, other things being equal, the larger a firm the longer its life expectancy. Sampling studies point in this direction. But if the longevity was because of size rather than economic efficiency, the prolongation of the large unit presumably hindered new development.

Similarly, size ensured the position of management. "The degree of success that management must produce to remain in office," said Knauth, "is surprisingly small. Indeed management must fail obviously and even ignominiously before the dispersed forces of criticism become mobilized for action. Directors are slow to act. This is entirely proper for they cannot upset the entire organization for every blunder." On the other hand, "honest mistakes may be twisted into dishonesty by the unscrupulous in litigation. . . . Management is curiously lonely in its equivocal surroundings. Its relations with stockholders are as unclear as with directors and employees."[50]

The Uses of Public Relations

Legitimizing or justifying to the public the great power exercised by the managers of big business offered theoretical as well as practical difficulties. The values of managerial trusteeship and social responsibility were common justifications, but carried too far they could be a rationale for socialization.[51] Service to the consumer, based on the theory that consumers exercised ultimate sovereignty and would punish weak managements by loss of patronage, was another justification for the existence of successful ones. But no overall principle as basic and satisfactory as direct competition had been in classic business doctrine was developed by the controllers of big companies.

World War I helped management to see systematic public relations as a way to justify themselves, their policies, and their industries, regardless of economic or ethical doctrines. Many big companies set up publicity or public-relations departments, in some cases headed by what were derisively called "good-will" or "luncheon" vice-presidents.[52] As Colonel Stewart of Standard Oil, Indiana, saw it: "If you don't have the public for you, a seriously large part of it is likely to be against you, and no business can continue to exist successfully unless a large part of the public is for it."[53]

These public-relations efforts of the twenties were still on what later would be regarded as an elementary level. They depended to a large extent on "puff" news items sent to editors, articles signed by important businessmen and planted in mass-circulation periodicals, and advertising designed to create good will. Public lectures, popular company or industry histories, and moving pictures also came into use. The telephone company was a leader in the use of movies. Between 1926 and 1935 the company produced fifty-six public information films. The director of the bureau at American Telephone & Telegraph said that theater managers were willing to show these films because the manager could "see for himself that they are purely informative and educational and will not detract from his program of entertainment."[54] By 1929 the Bell System estimated that during that year 52,932,796 people had attended 131,696 showings of the company films.[55]

In spite of the apparently advanced methods of such companies, the general philosophy of public relations was that of seizing upon some overt act that would reveal the company in a favorable light rather than reforming the basic policies of the company in such a way as gradually to win public favor. The "two-way street" aspect of public relations had not as yet been accepted.[56]

Early in the century business commentators such as Henry Clewes had been unable to pursuade the management of big companies of the value of giving information to their stockholders.[57] Only a few leaders, such as Elbert Gary of United States Steel, became converts to publicity, and some large companies failed even to hold stockholder meetings or publish any type of annual reports.[58]

In the postwar decade, however, the stockholders were recognized by progressive managements as an important group for improving public relations. A few shares might make their holder a loyal supporter against public criticism or government encroachments. As a result, a number of large companies, particularly the public utilities, carried on campaigns to increase both the number and geographic spread of small stockholders. American Telephone & Telegraph, for example, by selling stock to both the public and its own employees through its local offices, increased the number of stockholders owning five shares or less from 50,000 in 1920 to 210,000 in 1930.[59]

Public-relations men turned their attention to giving the stockholder a better impression of the company. Presidents were persuaded to sign letters welcoming new members to the stockholder family; other letters conveyed special news; magazines, previously used for internal morale building, were made more attractive and sent to the stockholders; and annual reports became more detailed and persuasive. The intelligent stockholder might recognize that none of these devices could tell him much about the prospects of his investment in a big organization, but they undoubtedly aroused stockholder interest in the company which in turn produced some degree of identification with company problems. The new public relations demonstrated that more big companies were coming to see themselves as organizations that could not avoid social and political issues.

6 Business and the Nation

In 1900 the people of the country — whether businessmen, professionals, workers, or farmers — undoubtedly believed in both the economic and social value of small, competitive enterprise, and even such well-known economists as John Bates Clark saw no need for tolerating corporate giants. He held that the government could enact regulations that would enable small "mills to produce and sell as cheaply as the biggest establishments can do, but to stop the extortion that trusts practice and ward off the greater extortion they threaten to practice."[1] Political warfare had already begun between the people's representatives and "trusts," with the former somewhat hampered by the paradox of demanding regulation in the name of free enterprise.

In the late eighties the states of Ohio and New York started suits against the trust form of corporate mergers. This was a device initiated by the Standard Oil Company in 1879, whereby the stockholders of a number of corporations turned their stock and its voting rights over to a group of trustees, who then acted as the directors of the merged firms. The New York State Court of Appeals held in the North River Sugar Refining case of 1890 "that . . . it has helped create an anomalous trust which is, in substance and effect, a partnership of twenty corporations. . . . It is a violation of the law for corporations to enter into partnership."[2] In the Standard Oil case two years later the Ohio Supreme Court, going further, said that the object of the trust "was to establish a virtual monopoly . . . throughout the entire country. . . . All such associations," it held, "are contrary to the policy of our state and void."[3]

Meanwhile, the Republican members of Congress, in return for Western support of the protective tariff, had passed a strongly worded antitrust law. The Sherman Act of 1890 prohibited "every contract, combination in the form of trust or otherwise, or conspiracy, in restraint of trade or commerce among the several states." This strong and sweeping federal language, in conjunction with the attitude of the state courts, might seem to have imposed barriers to mergers or monopolistic corporations.

This did not prove to be the case. "The trusts wriggled out of the court's grasp."[4] Even before the New York and Ohio courts rendered their decisions against the trustee device, New Jersey had made the trust unnecessary by passing a general incorporation act for holding companies. This New Jersey Act of 1889, legalizing what had been universally prohibited in general incorporation acts, hindered state antitrust prosecutions. By 1904 the seven biggest industrial companies had New Jersey charters. Meanwhile the United State Supreme Court seemed loath to apply the Sherman Act against big unified manufacturing companies. In 1895 the justices ruled that a monopoly of manufacture was not directly a restraint of trade.[5] "The effect of this decision," wrote Theodore Roosevelt, "was . . . the absolute nullification of the anti-trust law."[6] On the other hand, the Court ruled in 1899 that a contract between medium-sized companies governing conditions of interstate sales was a violation of the antitrust law.[7]

The lesson seemed fairly clear. Merger through a holding company was permissible because it involved no contracts or agreements between competitors. The Standard Oil Company adopted this form. Buying up of rivals and merging them into one big company was also legal, at least in manufacturing, while efforts by small companies to control markets by cartels or agreements were illegal. Because of the judicial interpretations the Sherman Act has been referred to as the "mother of trusts."

Business and Progressivism

In the period from the 1890s to World War I both big and small business became involved with different aspects of the varied but rather

steady pressures for social and regulatory legislation called the Progressive movement. In reality this was a series of initially unrelated movements aimed at controlling unwanted by-products of advancing
industrialism and its corollary, urbanism. On the one hand, big
business was steadily attacked by the organizations representing smaller
business as the symbol of both ruthless competition and too-great concentration of power; on the other, small business was even more
harassed by some regulatory legislation and the increasing power of
organized labor. The upper middle class, in general, alarmed by the
rapid increase of immigrants, turned to urban reform designed to
reduce the power of the slum wards and make city administration
more businesslike.

Just as the highly varied reformers lacked unity of aim, different
types of businessmen lacked uniform reactions. Big business had relatively few contacts with small- and medium-sized enterprise. The
really big companies had offices in the major metropolitan areas, and
in the decade 1900 to 1910 had relatively few branch plants. In most
cities medium-sized local enterprises dominated the business scene.
Trade associations and organizations like the National Association
of Manufacturers were supported by small business and neglected by
the "trusts." As a result small business was pleased by attacks on the
trusts and worked also for railroad regulation, while big business
appears to have favored some regulations that would force higher
standards on small competitors.[8]

The battle against, and the minor effects of, regulatory "social legislation" on small business are hard to estimate. Uneven state regulation
was always a problem for local enterprise. As the advanced industrial
states led with laws for compulsory workmen's compensation insurance, the movement was endorsed by companies that had to run the
risk of large damage suits and initially opposed by many others; but
by 1911 the National Association of Manufacturers was advocating
a model workmen's compensation act that they hoped all states would
adopt. This phase of social legislation, at least, appeared to be supported by both unions and employers.[9] Laws limiting hours, or for-
bidding child labor, became forces driving some manufacturing to the
South where such legislation scarcely existed before 1914, while

working against this trend were higher freight rates in the southern area and loss of close contact with customers and suppliers.

The period 1897 to 1903 was the most important in United States history for industrial mergers and consolidations and many people, fearful as to where the trend was leading, launched new attacks upon the trusts. Professor C. J. Bullock of Harvard wrote in 1901: "If experience ever demonstrates that the arguments of many economists are correct then we shall be confronted with the grim fact that competition is dead and that monopoly is inevitable in most important branches of manufacturing industry."[10] Desiring to prove the government's power to deal with the situation, President Theodore Roosevelt ordered his attorney general to start prosecutions against some of the larger monopolies. The resulting Supreme Court decisions in the Northern Securities and Standard Oil cases led to further exposition of the meaning of the Sherman Act of 1890.

In the first of these cases (1904) the Court ruled that the intent and result of the formation of the New Jersey holding company for Great Northern and Northern Pacific railroads were an illegal combination in restraint of interstate trade, and that no state, simply by creating a corporation, could prevent Congress from exercising its power to regulate commerce. "The power to deal with industrial monopoly and suppress it," exulted President Roosevelt, "was thus restored. . . . "[11]

But what did the law mean by "restrain" and "monopolize?" In the Standard Oil case of 1911, the Court abandoned the doctrine that a monopoly of manufacture was not directly a monopoly of commerce, as had been set forth in 1895 in the American Sugar Refining case, and held that it must use its own judgment in deciding whether monopolies were in harmful restraint of trade. Applying this "rule of reason," the Court ordered Standard Oil to be broken up into certain constituent companies. Justice John Marshall Harlan dissented from the assumption of discretionary power by the Court. "This statement," he wrote, "surprises me quite as much as would a statement that black was white or white was black. . . . One thing is certain, the 'rule of reason,' to which the Court refers, does not justify the perversion of the plain words of an act in order to defeat the will of Congress."[12]

Equally incensed by the legal doctrine, Progressives and Democrats demanded a stronger law. As a result the Clayton Act was passed in 1914. Whereas the Sherman Act had used general and sweeping language, the framers of the Clayton Act sought specifically to prohibit the practices that led to the control of markets. The law condemned price discriminations, exclusive selling or leasing contracts, the aquisition of stock in one corporation by another or the combination of two corporations through stock ownership, or interlocking two corporations through stock ownership, or interlocking directorships in two or more financial corporations any one of which had over a million dollars in capital. Still, each prohibition was limited to cases where the result would be substantially to lessen competition or tend to create a monopoly. Denounced in the Senate as "the greatest victory of a legislative nature that has been won by the trusts and combinations within the lifetime of any man," the bill nevertheless added somewhat to the restraints on corporate activity.[13] Another act of the same session created the Federal Trade Commission, charged with enforcing the Clayton Act and preventing unfair competition. This commission was expected to enforce the antitrust laws in the same way that the Interstate Commerce Commission enforced laws relating to the railroads.

The Clayton Act specifically exempted trade unions and farmer cooperatives, in the proper pursuance of their functions, from its provisions. Later laws such as the Capper-Volstead Act of 1922 and the Cooperative Marketing Act of 1926 strengthened the immunities of agricultural organizations, while the Webb-Pomerene Act of 1918 also placed combinations for foreign trade beyond the reach of antitrust laws.

The federal court decisions from 1914 to 1930 continued to emphasize the fact that the antitrust laws were to be seen as barriers against the continuation of overly oppressive forms of monopoly rather than criminal legislation for the effective punishment of those who conspired to restrain trade. In 1912 a district court handed down prison sentences for flagrant violations of the Sherman Act by officers of the National Cash Register Company, but higher courts set the judgment aside and the company settled by paying some insignificant costs and promising to be good in the future. In the United States Steel case, which dragged on for a decade and finally brought about a Supreme Court decision in 1920, it was ruled that size in itself did not violate the law if the big company appeared to act in the public interest. Opponents of the decision held that this sustituted the "rule of business expediency" for the "rule of reason." In the subsequent series of trade association cases in the early twenties, the Supreme Court ended up, it will be recalled, by ruling that exchange of prices and other information among competitors was legal if not carried on for the explicit purpose of raising prices. During the twenties, Republican attorneys general instituted relatively few antitrust actions, and as Republicans opposed to regulation came to dominate the Federal Trade Commission, Professor William Z. Ripley accused it of trying to commit hara-kiri.

Forty years of antitrust laws had failed to restore anything approaching "pure" competition. But except in some agricultural markets, pure competition had only existed in the theories of the economists. The federal laws had served to define certain rules for "monopolistic" competition. A few companies could share a market and fix prices as long as they did not do this by written agreements or take overt action to prevent new competitors from entering the field. The laws dictated a live-and-let-live policy among the largest firms, since attempts by them to devour one another might lead to prosecution. Although such arrangements lacked the efficiency of monopoly, where advertising and duplicated services could be reduced, and probably produced prices higher than under more effective competition, the situation seemed on the whole to satisfy the public. It was doubtful whether most Americans in 1930 wanted to see General Motors or General Electric broken up into smaller units, and even more doubtful that they wanted a single automobile trust with the concomitant need for strict federal regulation.

Business and World War I

World War I began in Europe during a deepening depression in the United States. In 1914 the nation was a net debtor on the balance of international security holdings to the extent of about $2.5 billion. With the likelihood of war many Europeans temporarily preferred cash to securities and tried to sell on the American market. So heavy were the selling orders on Monday, July 31st, a few minutes before the opening of the exchange, that according to the president of the New York Stock Exchange, "A half-hour's session . . . would have brought on a complete collapse; a general insolvency in brokerage houses would have forced the suspension of all business. . . . It is idle to speculate what the final outcome might have been."[14] The Board of Governors voted not to open the exchange. Other exchanges took similar action, and unrestricted trading in stocks was not resumed until April 1915.

Instead of producing a flood of orders, the first effect of World War I was to cut the demand for American goods. Civilian orders dropped, and the governments of both sides regarded their supplies of matériel as sufficient. To prevent drains on the American gold supply, the House of Morgan organized the leading bankers in a pool to limit the export of gold. Not until the spring of 1915 did European orders begin to come in sufficient volume to relieve the depression and reverse the flow of money.

The Allies foresaw the ultimate need for credit in the American market and at once approached the House of Morgan for a loan. Somewhat reluctantly the American House took the matter up with the State Department, with the result that President Wilson on August 15, 1914, made a statement against any loans to belligerent nations. As the needs of the Allies became more pressing, Robert Lansing, the legal counselor of the State Department, opposed Secretary of State Bryan's strict ideas regarding financial neutrality. In October 1914, Lansing persuaded Wilson to issue a statement that short-term bank credits for facilitating trade were not to be subject to the ban on loans. Since such notes were sold by the seaboard banks as acceptances (paper endorsed by a bank) to banks in the interior, and renewed when the notes came due, the distinction between credits and loans was tenuous.

The managing of a vast amount of ninety-day credit which was in fact not self-liquidating became increasingly awkward. Following the resignation of Bryan over the severe presidential attitude toward Germany in the Lusitania sinking of May 1915, the banking leaders of New York pressed for government approval of Allied loans. Lansing, who had become Secretary of State, urged this policy on Wilson and, in September of 1915, the President relaxed his opposition.

J. P. Morgan and Company now undertook the syndicate leadership for a $500-million Anglo-French loan. The leaders had unusual difficulty in placing the securities. The general attitude on the part of the public that was pro-Ally appeared to be one of supreme confidence in the ultimate victory of their side, and they felt no great pressure to buy bonds. In marketing this and subsequent Allied loans, the House of Morgan became a major factor in sustaining the Allied cause, adding still more to its enormous prestige as the leader of Wall Street.

By 1917, Allied credit was breaking under the strain of what then seemed massive creation of international debt. Some $2 billion in bonds and $1 billion in theoretically short-term paper had been absorbed by the American market, and the financial houses doubted their ability to market large additional issues. It was at this juncture that Germany solved the problem by bringing the United States government to the assistance of the Allies. Liberty loans by the government removed the pressure from the banking community, at the same time making the leading investment houses less important both in the war effort and in the postwar market. By 1920, $21 billion worth of government bonds made all previous bond-selling efforts appear insignificant.

Possibly there was no politically viable policy that would have been able to keep the United States out of war. The country was deeply involved economically with the success of the Allied cause, with continued prosperity dependent on the sale of supplies to Britain and France. The House of Morgan had been the leader in financing the Allies, and neither it nor many other important American firms were neutral in attitude. It seems almost certain that Wilson's neutrality would not have stretched to the point of standing aside from an Allied defeat. When all of this has been said, the fact still remains that Germany deliberately took the risk of war with the United States by resuming unlimited submarine warfare in February 1917, and Wilson had merely to implement his previously announced policy of arming American merchant vessels to have war inevitably follow.

In spite of some advance efforts by government councils and a few business leaders, plus some military "preparedness" bills — that by diverting production in wrong directions such as battleship construction were worse than useless — neither government nor industry made substantial economic preparations for war.[15] The War Industries Board, finally set up at the end of July 1917, lacked power or clearly defined policies, and throughout the year mobilization was "an intensely decentralized, fragmentated, haphazard process."[16]

Back of the confusion was an American resistance to organizing bureaucracy and long-range planning, as illustrated in the internal management of big business in this same period, intensified by a President unwilling to delegate power and unequal to the task of wielding it himself. It is ironic, although understandable on the basis of political institutions, that the presidents of a nation chiefly notable for its economic achievements usually have lacked training and interest in such matters.

War and Mass Production

The United States contribution in goods to World War I was largely in raw materials and semifinished products; relatively little finished war material emerged from American factories before the armistice. As early as 1916 the demands of England and France had brought the United States economy to the normal level of full employment. Since additional labor had to be found among those not ordinarily counted as employed, it was possible during 1917 and 1918 to add only about three million workers, or about 10 percent, to total employment including military, and nothing to the 1916 level of national product. The disappointing immediate results of the productive effort were partly caused by bad harvests, but shifting workers to new tasks or attracting women or retired workers to jobs was a wasteful process.

American business leaders also realized fully for the first time the rigidities of mass production. As Grosvenor B. Clarkson, one of the directors of the Council of National Defense, explained: "A group of French workmen who had been making automibiles could almost on a day's notice begin making ariplanes, and might have one done within a few days. The process of making standardized parts for final assembly into a whole is incomparably different."[17] A changeover from auto-mobile to airplane motors, for example, meant months of work on blueprints and specifications, then the manufacture of new machine tools for new purposes, and finally elimination of unforeseen, but al-most inevitable, miscalculations in the actual production operation. The placing and execution of orders for goods became inextricably snarled. There was not only that general congestion of the northeastern section, but there were innumerable local entanglements . . . orders were many times placed where they never could be filled."[18]

In the winter of 1917 to 1918, one of the most severe on record, the war economy threatened to break down altogether. With each of the armed forces and private industrial suppliers bidding against the others for scarce labor and materials, production was highly uncertain. Even if the needed goods were produced, railroads — prohibited under threat of antitrust prosecution from greater cooperation — were unable to move and unload the vast quantity of freight unwisely assigned to the Port of New York. At the beginning of 1918, the government was forced to take over the administration of railroads and wire communi-cation, and in March financial operator Bernard Baruch was made chairman of the War Industries Board with new powers. Baruch still lacked control over military procurement and preferred to use his power over prices as a lever in concluding voluntary bargains with suppliers.

In estimating productive possibilities, Baruch's staff relied heavily on industry trade associations, and the whole effort at coordinated nation-al supply brought the war contractors closer together in their business relations. Some companies bid for unfamiliar war work in order to keep their peacetime staff employed.[19] It was thought at the time that this cooperative atmosphere and limited partnership with government would continue after the war, but antitrust laws, prosperity, and the size of the competitive market all worked in the opposite direction, and the war had little long-run effect on the business structure.

A Decade of Overconfidence

Even before the Republican landslide of 1920 the liquidation of wartime boards, commissions, and mixed corporations (those partly owned by government and private stockholders) had proceeded rapidly. The atmosphere was one of seeking a return to some mythical period in earlier decades when laissez faire had presumably been the rule. Presidents Harding and Coolidge, with Herbert Hoover as their Secretary of Commerce, gave businessmen the most reliably friendly national administration they had enjoyed since the time of William McKinley.

After a brief but severe downward readjustment of prices in a depression from 1920 to 1922, the remainder of the decade was one of high prosperity for those benefited by profits, particularly in the larger companies. Much of the prosperity of the decade was based on an average annual increase of 4.6 percent per man-hour in industry, a peak for the twentieth century.[20] Until 1926, the upswing followed the usual pattern of increasing investment in durable goods and real estate. After the mild recession of 1927, however, heavy involvement in foreign securities and speculative recapitalizations produced an unprecedented type of upswing.

In addition to large funds attracted to the New York stock market from Europe, the security markets were supported by a great upsurge in domestic saving. Raymond Goldsmith puts real per-capita savings from 1922 to 1930 about 50 percent higher than in the preceding decade, and on a current money basis the peak savings of these years ran three times the prewar maxima.[21] Such sudden increases from larger high-level incomes would have been hard to utilize in any case, but with net capital formation 15 percent less in relation to national income than in the first decade of the century, surplus funds flowed into all sorts of uneconomic channels, not only in the financial world, but also in the old standbys of real estate and overoptimistic building construction.[22]

In spite of Henry Adams' belief that his generation was "mortgaged to the railroads," the chief capital-consuming activity of Americans for three hundred years had been the construction of buildings: homes, barns, sheds, stores, schools, meetinghouses, mills, factories and offices. The construction business directly employed two and a half million workers in 1920, more than any other manufacturing activity except iron and steel, and indirectly employed a million more in factory production and transportation of building materials. For the half-decade 1925 to 1929 the cost of new construction averaged nearly $11 billion a year. A part of these totals duplicates sums counted in the capital expansion of other industries, but even so, the money going into homes was larger than the new capital invested in any general type of transportation or industry. The next largest consumer of capital, aside from government investment in streets and roads, was the rapidly growing electrical industry.

The easy money market tempted all types of operators, from the main-street office building promoter to the utility holding-company tycoon, to think up new schemes for marketing securities. Big mortgages, often based on optimistic estimates of the value of hotels or office buildings, were broken up into $500 or $1,000 units and sold to small investors. The readiness of the public to buy stocks and bonds encouraged, as we have seen (in Chapter 3), the formation of inefficient pyramided holding companies. The role of the holding company in the boom of the twenties, however, was dependent not upon its efficiency or inefficiency, but upon the popularity of its stock as a speculative security. The Middle West Utilities Company, Electric Bond and Share, and other similar stocks soared to heights that bore no relation to the earnings of the operating companies. And at these inflated values the stocks were used as security for loans with the proceeds of which other properties were purchased.[23]

Another of the devices that flourished in the easy money market was the investment trust. The investor with small savings could not directly achieve the security that comes from diversification of holdings, but he thought he could accomplish this by buying a few shares in the trust, which would invest in a wide range of securities. By 1929 there were nearly four hundred investment trusts. As in the case of the pyramided holding company, there was nothing wrong in principle with such an arrangment; the trouble came from speculative and unwise use of the funds. Instead of making diversified purchases as disinterested investors, the officers of the trust often bought large blocks of stock in order to gain control of companies, in effect perverting their trusteeship for personal power. Later, some trusts were used as dumping grounds for large blocks of stock that insiders wished to dispose of. The Senate committee investigating stock-exchange practices saw the investment trust as "the vehicle employed by individuals to enhance their personal fortunes in violation of their trusteeship, to the financial detriment of the public."[24] As a result, the stocks of investment trusts declined more during the depression than the average of the market as a whole.

Meanwhile the character of American banking was changing to fit the new relationships of credit, saving, and investment. With good rates of profit and a slackening in the rate of real capital expansion, successful companies found themselves relatively independent of banks. Before 1914 many companies had used most of their savings for expansion and provided for working capital, and even some fixed capital, by bank loans. In the twenties they tended to retire such loans from profits, and if additional capital was needed, to turn to the security market rather than the banks. Commercial banks, therefore, did less lending on sixty- or ninety-day renewable paper or open credit lines. When big businesses came to banks for money, they were likely to offer stocks and bonds as securities for sizable loans. This gave the banks less paper that could be rediscounted, and so reduced the ability of the Federal Reserve System to control the money market through manipulating the rediscount rate. The change also produced large loans secured by thousands of shares of common stock which could not be sold readily on a declining market.

The urban real estate and stock market booms brought prosperity to metropolitan banks, and the larger ones grew still larger through mergers. But in many country districts land values declined and small local banks, unable to collect their loans, failed by the hundreds: nearly a thousand went down in the prosperous year of 1926. As a result of mergers and failures, the total of nearly 31,000 banks in 1920 had fallen to 25,000 by 1930.

Boom and Bust

In spite of agricultural depression, a leveling off of the market for most forms of capital goods, and no general increase in salaries or wages, financial mechanisms created a runaway bull market in 1928 that ended in the crash of 1929. The older and larger houses cannot be absolved from whatever blame attaches to being caught in the general wave of overoptimism of the late twenties. While bonds sponsored by the House of Morgan, for example, stood up better and had fewer defaults in the thirties than the average of those marketed by others, nevertheless the Morgan name was attached to some of the vulnerable holding company issues, and Morgan credit supported unwise financial operations such as those of the Van Sweringens. The record of the National City and First National banks and their security selling affiliates, which had been formed before the war, was much the same. In fact, by 1928 even conservative men of Wall Street came to believe that the old-fashioned business cycle had been eliminated. "With the assistance of the Federal Reserve System," wrote Paul M. Mazur of Lehman Brothers, "we may expect freedom from the unwarranted and annoying financial panics of the past."[25] All but a handful of financiers were won over to the speculative enthusiasm. "There was a great deal of atmosphere," recollected President Albert H. Wiggins of the Chase Bank.[26]

To some extent this market was a product of salesmanship. Charles E. Mitchell, chairman of the National City Bank, trained young men and women to sell securities and then sent them out to find the investors. They and their counterparts from other leading banking and brokerage houses rang the doorbells of prosperous-looking citizens and urged them to increase their commitments in order to share in the speculative gains. Margin accounts were carried legally with as little as 25 percent equity, and temporarily with much less; homes and businesses were mortgaged to buy common stocks; and with this inflow of money the market rose higher and higher without regard to underlying economic probabilities.

The widespread frenzy for easy profits literally pulled itself along by its own bootstraps. Buying on installment or by discounting stock market profits, through increasing loans, produced record-breaking consumer purchases in 1929. Four billion dollars in European money and cash from domestic corporate reserves, attracted by high interest rates, flowed in to support stock market margin accounts. Employment in finance rose to a point where the salaries and wages of such workers exceeded those in mining and agriculture combined. But such a process had its limits. Customers became loaded with securities, the effective demands for housing and luxuries were temporarily met, and the fact that capital-goods investment was not proceeding rapidly threatened unemployment. By mid-1929, before the stock market peak, the more sensitive business indexes were headed down.[27]

The more cautious Wall Street operators, noting the decline of automobile sales and new housing, began to doubt the stability of high security prices by the late summer. In spite of withdrawal by such cautious insiders, and contracting broker's loans, stock prices advanced into September and maintained high levels until October. People who had come to depend on stock market profits for their new clothers or automobiles could not affort to withdraw from the market. By October 1, 1929, the value of listed stocks on the New York Stock Exchange, which had been $27 billion on January 1, 1925, stood at $87 billion.

The collapse of the speculative structure came in a series of breaks that started on October 15 and reached serious proportions by Thursday, October 24, when nearly 13 million shares were traded. Prices underwent the greatest decline, up to that time, in the history of the stock exchange. Some issues dropped many points before any bid was forthcoming. Brokers frequently sold the stocks of their margin accounts without giving the "owner" time to supply more cash.

At this juncture the House of Morgan and other important banks tried to stem the panic as J. Pierpont had in 1907. Early in the day, leading bankers met conspicuously at 23 Wall Street, the Morgan "corner," and early in the afternoon, partner Thomas W. Lamont announced that they would support the market. Later Richard Whitney, representing the House of Morgan on the floor of the exchange, walked to the post where United States Steel was about to fall below 200, and dramatically bid 205 for 25,000 shares. All such efforts did not greatly exceed the success of King Canute with the waters of the sea. The pressure for liquidation was too strong to be arrested, and unlike previous market crises where the break had been over in one day, this "panic" became a recurring one.

The Monday following the bankers' reassuring action, the market again broke with orders to sell unmatched in many stocks by any to buy — or, as brokers said, there were "holes" in the market. A major trouble on these days of unprecedented activity was that the ticker fell far behind and no one knew how many margin accounts were being closed out, producing a delayed flood of additional stock. The bankers, in spite of reassuring statements, were too strained by partially compensating for European withdrawals of money advanced for brokers' loans to support the market, and the net losses for Monday were much larger than those of the preceding Thursday. With confidence in any stabilizing force gone, Tuesday, October 29th, became the worst day of selling — 16.4 million shares — and John Kenneth Galbraith thinks "it may have been the most devastating day in the history of markets."[28] The New York Times average stocks fell 43 points and stood lower at the end of the day than in 1928. Many stocks lost over half their value.

Even this dreadful day failed to end the liquidation. The market went up again sufficiently to wipe out most of the losses of Black Tuesday and then started a downward slide that only reached bottom on November 14th, with the Times average at half its height on September 3rd, but still high in relation to where it had stood in 1927 or would stand in 1932. Hence, in spite of serious declines in basic economic indexes, it was possible to say that only speculators had been wiped out. Not even the bankers themselves realized the total number of large bank loans no longer adequately secured, with the deficits constituting legal charges against the banks' capital that would ultimately undermine the whole structure.

For the present, however, neither business leaders nor politicians discerned the underlying financial weakness, foresaw its long-run effects, or gave sufficient attention to the increasing recession in demand and employment. In 1907 the greatest service of J. Pierpont Morgan and his associates had been in saving banks from failure as the result of runs. In the successive market breaks of October and November 1929, the failure of metropolitan banks was not a serious issue. For the time being the Federal Reserve System cushioned the shock and the depositors were not panicky. For these reasons it was possible for President Hoover to call it a speculative panic and to reassure the public that the sound productive processes of the country had not been impaired.

The End of the Old Order

The stock market boom of the late twenties appears in retrospect to have been a time when the people of the country temporarily lost their sane judgment. But how many people? Perhaps five to eight million out of nearly fifty million people with incomes had any stock market holdings, and there were only half a million margin accounts. To control such a small group in the interests of national stability would seem an obvious solution. Unfortunately, however, the small group comprised the most influential citizens not only in finance, but in industry, trade, and politics.

In the middle of this period of increasing interest in stocks and bonds the country had acquired a banking system designed to break the control of Wall Street over ultimate bank reserves and to provide a more elastic currency and credit. The Federal Reserve System partly achieved these purposes. It might also have produced greater financial stability if international monetary problems of the mid-twenties connected with the gold standard had not encouraged an easy money policy, or later if the deflationary views of the central board had been more acceptable to the political and business communities.

Commenting on the role of the Federal Reserve System in the runaway stock market boom, Winthrop D. Aldrich of the Chase National Bank testified: "The rediscount rate of the New York Reserve Bank remained unchanged from July 13, 1928 to August 9, 1929. . . . This long postponement . . . has come to be regarded as quite the most conspicuous failure of the Federal Reserve System since its inception."[29] John Maynard Keynes's view that there was a fundamental incompatibility between correct management of internal and external monetary policy best explains the dilemma of the Federal Board.[30]

In the light of earlier history, perhaps no amount of Federal Reserve action could have prevented some break and ensuing depression. American business had never made the transition from a period of high optimism to one of caution or pessimism without severe financial difficulties. Basic to the situation was a declining rate of real capital formation that was undermining the stock market boom, and no plans for new major areas of investment appeared in 1929 or 1930 to alter the trend.

The cataclysm of 1929 did more than temporarily ruin the reputation of financiers; it undermined public faith in the basic philosophy of American business. The business leaders of the late twenties believed in the nineteenth-century idea of a self-regulating capitalist economy based on natural economic laws. The theory called for a society in which government limited its functions to those necessary for physical and legal security; it assumed that natural laws operated in such a way that the able man who worked hard would benefit society and be financially rewarded; it regarded business depressions "as passing interruptions of progress."[31] Influenced by these beliefs, neither political party held the federal government responsible for unemployment relief or support of the aged. The prevailing philosophy of both major parties in the twenties was unchanged from that expressed in Cleveland's Second Inaugural Address: "While the people should cheerfully and patriotically support their government its functions do not include the support of the people."[32] Pursuing the idea of a limited government, the Republicans held both federal employment and expenditures roughly constant from 1923 through 1929.

Compared with later decades, the old order was an economy of lower wages for workers and higher incomes for the middle and upper classes. According to rough estimates, the share of the national income received by the top 10 percent had been increasing since at least 1910 and reached nearly 40 percent of the total by 1929, while that of the lowest 10 percent had been falling.[33]

In the late twenties the belief that any man could succeed by intelligence and hard work had been given additional force by the stock market boom until it seemed that every man could become financially secure by modest saving and investment. John J. Raskob, chairman of the Finance Committee of General Motors, and also of the Democratic National Committee in 1928, wrote in the summer of 1929: "If a man saves $15 a week, and invests in good common stocks and allows the dividends and rights to accumulate, at the end of twenty years he will have at least $80,000 and an income from investments of $400 a month. He will be rich. And because income can do that, I am firm in my belief that anyone not only can be rich, but ought to be rich."[34]

The ensuing depression that erased some common stocks altogether and left other speculative favorites at 4 or 5 percent of their former value abruptly ended the era that inspired Raskob's soliloquy. Still, basic social change is seldom as sudden as it appears to be on the surface of events. The wholly self-regulating economy and the wholly self-reliant individual had been myths born of wishing. Although government activities had reached low points at various times in the nineteenth century, the states had never completely refrained from regulating and assisting business or owning enterprises. Effective federal regulation of railroads, prepared foods, and drugs had appeared in the first decade of the twentieth century. During the period that federal expenditure was being held down by Coolidge and the Republican Congressional majority, state and local expenditures for paving, public buildings, and other improvements were skyrocketing. The automobile era needed far more public equipment than did the railroad age.

Airplanes and electricity joined the automobile in calling forth both federal and state regulation and support. Airlines and interstate transmission of electric power soon came under federal regulation. Large airports, and the system of beacons to guide flights, were publicly owned. Highways and bridges, destined to be the biggest single type of investment other than building construction, fell into the hands of government without protest from private enterprise.

In a long view of United States economic growth, the brief period of relatively uncontrolled industrial business may be seen as coming to a gradual end between 1870 and 1935 and the aphorisms of the twenties may be heard as parts of a swan song.

Part Two
An End and a Beginning, 1930–1945

7 The Great Depression

In no previous period had the American economy swung so violently from prosperity to deep depression and back again as it did in the years 1930 to 1945. The shifts were so extreme that they deeply affected not only business but the national culture as well. The United States of the early thirties, with a quarter of its workers unemployed, its business leaders in despair, and its intellectuals thinking in terms of fundamental political and social change, was very different from the self-satisfied nation of the late twenties, or the new government-underwritten society of the postwar decades.

In viewing the performance of the economy, with the graphic profiles of dollar volume of business, employment, or stock prices suggesting the ups and downs of a roller coaster, a prime question is bound to be, why did it happen this way? Why in a relatively mature and stable society should real national income be cut nearly in half in only three years?

Except for the height of the stock market boom, the twenties were not superficially different from other prosperous decades in American history, but the depression of the thirties was unprecedented in its severity. According to standard series the dollar volume of business sank from 16 percent above normal in July 1929 to 49 percent below normal in July 1932, and the descent describes a fairly straight line between the two points, save for a slight rise in early 1931.[1] No previous depression, according to the same series, had ever deflated the dollar

volume of business by more than 35 percent, but this drop amounted
to 56 percent. Furthermore, the level of the late twenties was only
briefly reached in 1937. During the thirties economists and businessmen perforce addressed themselves to the question of what had hap-
pened to the business system.

Responsible economists and political leaders talked of economic stagnation and the mature economy. The American dream of an ever-higher
standard of living appeared to have ended. Some thought that Thorstein
Veblen had been right: the captains of business had strangled the economy.

Businessmen, of course, thought differently. One group who were
not economic theorists supported the views of the President. "In the
large sense," wrote Herbert Hoover, "the primary cause of the Great
Depression was the war of 1914–1918. Without the war there would
have been no depression of such dimensions."[2] Briefly and oversimply,
the argument was that the war left the Western world with intergovern-
mental debts too large for repayment by normal exchanges, as well as
with currency problems that were never settled. For some years the
situation was nursed along with further American loans, but since the
United States tariff precluded collection of interest and principal
through the necessary surplus of imports over exports, a day of reckon-
ing had to come.

From a Western-world standpoint, the war was unquestionably an
upsetting factor of great magnitude; from the standpoint of the domestic affairs of the United States, the argument is less convincing. American participation in the war was brief, and even in 1918 the economic
drain did not rise above 25 percent of the national income. It appears
doubtful whether this short-term shift to war production, or the building up of what was, in relation to the national income, a moderate
debt should have caused such violent movements in the economy a
decade later or seriously weakened its ability to recover from depression.

Another argument of businessmen, resting on adverse governmental
activity, was the complaint that government regulation had already
progressed so far by 1930 that enterprise was discouraged and the self-

adjusting character of the economy largely destroyed. This school of
critics usually dated the beginning of the difficulties from state railroad
legislation in the 1870s, or the federal Interstate Commerce Act of
1887. The Progressive movement, state and federal, added many more
laws regulating working conditions, business combinations, railroads,
and public utilities. The conservatives' fear of the effect of these laws
was similar to that in the New Deal period. Mark Twain wrote in 1907,
"Mr. Roosevelt has done what he could to destroy the industries of the
country, and they all stand now in a half-wrecked condition and waiting in an ague to see what he will do next."[3] In this same period corporation and graduated personal income taxes had their beginning. Later
there was a widespread fear that the necessary growth in federal power
during World War I might lead to socialism. While these fears were
proved groundless by the postwar political regimes, it was nevertheless
true that business was somewhat more regulated than before the war,
and considerably more so than in 1900.

Carrying on the same line of reasoning it was argued that "normal"
recovery would have started at a rapid rate in August 1932 had investors not been scared by the probable election of a liberal Democratic
president in November. "I do not think there is any question," wrote
Paul W. Litchfield of Goodyear, "that America would have worked its
way out of that depression if the Hoover Administration had remained
in office. . . . But the new administration which came into power in
1933 had a different idea. It did not talk about hard work, thrift,
resourcefulness. The government would fix things."[4] After the election
things went from bad to worse, and after the Roosevelt inauguration,
new reforms, regulations, and taxes continued to inhibit the risk-taking
activity of entrepreneurs and investors.

There was another facet to this "strait-jacket" argument that was not
emphasized by big businessmen. The rigidities blamed on government
regulations and the discouragement of new enterprise attributed to
taxes or controlled rates could also be regarded as unwanted by-
products of big business itself. By the 1920s about half of the
industrial production of the United States was in the hands of large
corporations. In railroads and public utilities the giant company was

practically the rule. No matter how carefully they studied management and operation, these big companies could not preserve the flexibility, speed, and daring of smaller business. New risks were assessed from the standpoint of management's fiduciary obligations to thousands of stockholders; changes were slowly and carefully examined in the light of their effect upon a complex organization; markets were well enough controlled as to both price and production to permit delay in the introduction of upsetting innovations. No one has found quantitative measures that could weigh these various deterrents to recovery but obviously the problem was one involving many forces.

A widely believed explanation for the falling off of the rate of economic advance was found in the closing of the West and the "maturity" of the economy. President Franklin D. Roosevelt and other New Dealers made much of this argument. The buoyancy and drive of the American economy had depended, they claimed, largely on the development of new western lands by farmers or ranchers, and the exploitation of western lumber and mineral resources by private capital. Speaking in San Francisco in 1932, Roosevelt said, "A glance at the situation today only too clearly indicates that equality of opportunity as we have known it no longer exists. Our industrial plant is built; the problem just now is whether under existing conditions it is not overbuilt. Our last frontier has long since been reached, and there is practically no more free land."[5] Many scholars argued that European economy had expanded in the nineteenth century because of the exploitation of the more temperate and habitable areas of new continents, and the chance for further enterprises of this kind had also greatly diminished. Meanwhile, the "mature" industrial nations had built their basic equipment to a stage where little more investment was needed at home. "Our task now," continued Mr. Roosevelt, "is not discovery or exploitation of natural resources, or necessarily producing more goods. It is the soberer, less dramatic business of administering resources and plants, already in hand."[6]

True as the argument may have been from the standpoint of contemporary psychology, it proved false economically and historically. The "maturing," if it existed at all, was obviously a temporary plateau resulting merely from the prevailing distribution of income and stage of technology, and if technological change were in truth progressing at either a constant or accelerating rate the "maturity" could not last. With the overwhelming majority of the people of the world, including many in Europe and the United States, living in essentially preindustrial conditions, it seemed far too early to talk of lack of rather routine possibilities for further expansion.

The apparent lack of opportunity may have been partly the result of business attitudes toward risk-taking and investment that were maladjusted to the technological level of the economy — that is, to the *kind* of opportunities offered. Replies from a questionnaire sent by a government committee to large manufacturing corporations in 1928 showed that about two-thirds would not invest in new equipment unless it promised to pay for itself within three years, and no firm would risk a six-year amortization.[7] With equipment becoming more complex and expensive, such short-range decisions may well have impeded growth. In any case, the replies show how psychological factors affected the course of business activity, and the failure to exploit either American or world-wide opportunities to the utmost had, as we shall see later, social-psychological causes.

The explanation of the depression that ultimately appealed to the largest numbers of professional economists was put forward by the British theorist and statesman, John Maynard Keynes. His hypothesis regarding reasons for "irregular" performance of the economy were the most exciting and important modifications in classic economic theory since its comprehensive exposition by Alfred Marshall in the late nineteenth century. He started from the established fact that national income was chiefly spent on either producer or consumer goods. He then argued that whereas consumer expenditure depended mainly on the size of the national income and the character of its distribution between the poor and the rich, and for all practical calculations varied only as these elements varied, producer-goods expenditure, or investment, depended not on the rate of saving but on business expectations of increased demand.[8] The next step in Keynes's argument was that the national income could only increase if investment increased and vice versa, a proposition with which most businessmen would agree. He concluded that "the duty of ordering the current volume of investment cannot safely be left in private hands"[9] — left, that is, to "business sentiment."

He deduced a further theorem that was to form an important justification for progressive taxation and government subsidy or aid to low-income groups. He asserted a "fundemental psychological law that men are disposed, as a rule and on the average, to increase their consumption as their income increases, but not as much as the increase in their income."[10] Obvious corollaries of this law were that more even distribution of income would increase consumption, and that depression could be caused by too much of the national income going to wealthy individuals who neither consumed sufficiently nor invested their surplus in activity employing labor.

Applied to the situation of the thirties, the argument ran that poor income distribution had produced oversaving and underinvestment, and hence underemployment of resources. Already acted on by practical politicians, Keynes's book in 1936 gave these ideas the appeal of the fine logical mechanisms of classic economic theory. Although it gained few converts on this side of the ocean before 1940, the theory fitted snugly with the American data. As noted in Chapter 6, the share of the top tenth of income-receivers had probably been increasing since at least 1910. Simon Kuznets' figures, prepared for the National Bureau of Economic Research, indicate that the share of the 1 percent who received the highest incomes increased over 18 percent between 1919 and 1929.[11] Since practically all of the net saving available for risk-taking investment was made by the top tenth and most of it by the top twentieth,[12] this shift in income distribution could allow a great increase in saving with no proportionate increase in consumption. According to Harold Moulton of the Brookings Institution: "If, in consequence of wide variations in the distribution of income, the proportion of the national income that is saved expands rapidly there results a maladjustment which retards rather than promotes the expansion of capital."[13]

With wages and consumption staying nearly the same, the investor's

money went into real estate ventures or the stock market; there it encouraged speculation, mergers, and recapitalizations, which in turn
increased the general level of security prices, while new investment in
labor-employing enterprises failed to keep pace and by mid-1929 was
actually declining. In 1924, financing that resulted in additions to
physical equipment was 76 percent of the net total of new financing;
in 1929, it was only 35 percent. Furthermore, the dollar total was lower, standing at $3.2 billion in 1929 as against $3.5 billion in 1924.
Somehow or other, in spite of continuing changes in technology,
and a well-sustained demand by the consumers with higher incomes,
American productive investment had reached a nearly static level, one
too low for the expansion of the economy at its old rate. With the collapse of demand in the depression there was little incentive for investment in new equipment.[14]

Keynes's theories explained the fallacy in the classic "Say's Law"
that supply creates its own demand, and hence that unemployment
had to result from slowness in the readjustment of the labor supply to
new opportunities, but with these theories he inevitably undermined
the whole Puritan ethic that unemployment was voluntary, the fault of
the unemployed. According to Keynes, if businessmen failed to invest
enought to create reemployment, government could take up the slack
either by more spending or by tax reductions that would lead to a
deficit. Theoretically, as far as employment was concerned it did not
matter whether aggregate demand was increased by business or government spending, although politically and psychologically there was, as
we shall see, a considerable difference.

Keynesian policy, properly implemented by large and continuous
programs for badly needed public works such as express highways,
bridges, schools, and housing, could have benefited the nation while
curing the depression, but neither Hoover, Roosevelt, nor other leaders
of the Republican or Democratic parties had any more grasp of such
ideas than had American businessmen. With the exception of a few
professional economists such as Harold Moulton or Rexford G. Tugwell (an adviser of Roosevelt), who were thinking along the same lines
without as much theoretical acuteness as Keynes, influential people in

the United States did not urge a deliberate spending policy prior to the deep depression of 1938.

Unfortunately, the forces of reality worked in exactly the opposite direction. All governments from local to federal economized by discharging employees and cutting salaries. The federal government made a moderate increase in public works appropriations, but state and local governments, lacking funds, cut back drastically on all unnecessary expenditures. After reaching a peak in 1930 because of contracts already let, total public construction declined steadily to mid-1933, when it was at a rate one-third below that of the beginning of the depression.

Loss of Business Prestige and Morale

Such an unprecedentedly violent contraction of all activity would have severely shaken the business system at any time, but following the euphoria of the twenties it was psychologically devastating. In 1929 business, particularly big business, had enjoyed a degree of public approval unique in American history. The "robber barons" of the last century and the "malefactors of great wealth" of the Progressive Era were the leaders of the nation. Brief biographies of successful businessmen had helped to sell the ubiquitous *Saturday Evening Post* and other American magazines. In 1928, when the Democratic National Chairman was also a chairman at General Motors, both major party candidates had pledged their faith to Wall Street and the self-regulating economy. Bruce Barton, a leading advertising agent, had taken the final step when he pictured Christ in the image of the businessman.

The transition from this high point of public belief in the American business system to an attitude of greater distrust of both business honesty and ability than had characterized any previous period was cataclysmic. As late as June 1930, the panic of November 1929 was being written off as past history; in the words of the President, prosperity seemed "just around the corner." Instead there came mass unemployment, bank failures, and the exposé of spectacular business scandals. Within less than two years the results of a generation of public relations work lay in ruins, and the "puff" stories and planted news by which good will had been built were being ridiculed by journalists and other public leaders. The well-educated members of the public, now acutely conscious of the pitfalls of propaganda, were determined to view things realistically.

Furthermore, by the summer of 1932 many businessmen themselves had frustrating inner doubts about the self-regulating nature of the economy and its continued expansion. Labor and materials were obtainable at bargain rates, perhaps never to be reached again, yet few entrepreneurs decided to buy and build. The most advanced business thinking ran more along the line of cooperative arrangements to raise prices and stabilize production at low levels than toward freely competitive efforts to seize new opportunities. Some conservative journalists talked in terms of Hoover's assuming dictatorial powers or transferring authority to twelve dictators of the nation commissioned to revive the economy.

At first many business executives, influenced by the encouraging statements of the Hoover administration and the press, continued previously planned expansion, but a steadily declining volume of sales indicated by the spring of 1930 that a depression was imminent, if not already in progress. Seen in perspective, while 1930 was a year of growing uncertainty, with new construction contracts both public and private falling off and orders for heavy producer goods very small, 1931 and 1932 were years of disaster, in which every firm reduced its expenses to the barest minimum necessary for survival.

Business Adjusts to the Depression

Staff activities such as specialized consultants, personnel departments, and public relations were eliminated or reduced to token size. Skilled workers were kept on the payrolls by working only three days a week, while managers took periodic reductions in pay. Allowances for depreciation were trimmed to unrealistic levels, so that other charges, often including small unearned dividends, could be met. The impact was, of course, highly uneven. Manufacture of heavy producer goods such as steam locomotives practically ceased. Other firms in production goods found it necessary to close many plants, leaving unemployed most of the people in towns dependent on such works or on one heavy industry. By the end of 1931, as public construction slowly declined and private fell to less than a quarter of its 1929 level, this chief form of investment sank too low even to maintain existing physical structures adequately.[15] All types of declines ultimately affected financial houses. As new issues shrank, stock trading fell away and bank deposits dwindled.

Only food, some drugs, and essential services such as lighting, heating, and automobile repair continued to resist great contraction. While imprudent or unlucky retail operators might fail, landlords needed tenants for their stores and producers and wholesalers required outlets, so that rent and supplies were extended on credit to proprietors who seemed to be doing as well as could be expected under the circumstances. Thus, while the decline in the number of business enterprises from 1929 to 1932 was up to 35 percent in manufacturing, construction, and finance, the declines in trade and services averaged 3 percent or less.

Perhaps the volume of business at the end of 1931, marking the greatest two-year drop in American history, might have been the low point of the depression had the financial structure remained stable. By April of 1931, however, the cessation of American lending to Germany and Austria had broken the artificially supported circle of payments which went from the United States to central Europe, then to France and England, and finally back to America to purchase exports. When French bankers, foreseeing trouble, called in their Central European credits in April and May, Austrian and German banks were unable to continue the circular flow. A world-wide "liquidity panic" ensued, with the Federal Reserve System doing nothing effective to prevent contraction within the United States.[16] In 1931 over 2,200 American banks closed their doors. In one way the situation was worse than before the creation of the Federal Reserve, because then the strong banks through clearinghouse committees helped the weak; now everyone relied on the "Fed," which failed to rise to the emergency.

The continuing uncertainty as to whether business loans could be

secured or renewed, as to whether long-run contracts would be ful-
filled, or over the liquidity of bank deposits, made recovery impossible.
Reluctantly President Hoover abandoned his insistence on voluntary
measures and in December 1931 endorsed a bill for a government lending agency, the Reconstruction Finance Corporation. Unfortunately
the aid, about $2 billion, was too little, too late, and too narrowly dis-
tributed. In 1932 over four thousand banks failed, and on March 5,
1933 – the day after his inauguration – President Roosevelt declared a
national bank holiday.

Much familiar political and economic history has been omitted from
this simplified account in order to emphasize three of the chief causes
of the great disaster: the decline of government expenditures, particularly for public construction; the failure to take the imaginative and
drastic steps necessary to reconstruct the American banking system;
and the failure to make emergency foreign loans, particularly to Germany. While the ordinary businessman could well feel himself the
victim of great forces beyond his control, in accord with the economic
thinking of the day he sought to curtail production and maintain prices
rather than rebel against government by men whose knowledge and
tactics belonged to a past era.

From the standpoint of government policy the shift from Hoover to
Roosevelt was from an administration that was ineffective but left
business alone, to one that was slightly more effective but harrassed
business with new regulations. Until 1939, with some ups and downs,
the dollar volume of business averaged a level equal to early 1931, and
business adjusted itself to continuing depression. Within this dismal
period, however, some interesting experiments by government were
attempted and some lasting and important laws were enacted.

Business and the New Deal

The most comprehensive plan for semivoluntary regulation of all business ever attempted in a capitalist economy was put into operation by
the National Industrial Recovery Act of 1933. Each "industry," including retailing and service, was to have its members sign a code of

fair practices and set up a code authority. The bill initially had the support of distinguished business leaders, the National Chamber of Commerce, the American Federation of Labor, and President Roosevelt. In effect it aimed at a partnership of government, labor, and business in which the latter was granted suspension of the antitrust laws so that price-fixing and production could be controlled by the code authorities, who were often the chief members of the industry's trade association. In return business had to grant labor the eight-hour day and recognize the right of collective bargaining.

The regulatory part of the NIRA was to be administered by an ex-manufacturer, General Hugh Johnson, who had the confidence of business. A large public works appropriation in the second part of the act was to be spent by Harold Ickes, who was so careful and frugal in granting contracts that this part of the law was practically inoperative in 1933.

Industries such as cotton textiles, that were harrassed by cutthroat competition, entered into the plan for controls over prices and production with enthusiasm, hoping that they could in some way avoid the labor provisions. In the less competitive automobile industry, a code was finally agreed upon that did not contain the labor section. Some industries that failed to agree upon a special code accepted the President's Reemployment Agreement, which dealt chiefly with conditions of work, while others, such as the Ford Motor Company, refused in spite of strong government pressure to enter the system at all.[17]

General Johnson may have wanted to deal objectively with both business and labor, but doubting the constitutionality of the act, he sought to avoid legal action. Consequently the industry code authorities usually dominated by the more substantial firms, got along fairly well with Johnson while failing to live up to the labor provisions. After his resignation in September 1934 and the shift of administration to a small board, neither business nor labor was happy with the law. When it was declared unconstitutional in May 1935, NIRA had few friends.

The failure of this elaborate attempt quickly to restore prosperity by voluntary self-regulation suggested to some that a completely regulated capitalism would lack much of the vigor of free enterprise with few compensating advantages; others thought that the law was too hastily conceived and too loosely administered to fit the needs of a complex economy; while later observers could contend that the whole apparatus had little to do with the upswing in the volume of business that began late in 1934 and continued with only minor setbacks until 1937.

Opposition to the New Deal

The NIRA and most of the other legislation of the spring of 1933 went through Congress with nonpartisan majorities. Investment was divorced from commercial banking, either cutting Wall Street firms like the House of Morgan in two, or forcing the company to drop out of one type of business; bank deposits up to $5,000 could be insured by government; and a large amount of accounting information had to be supplied in order to list new issues of securities on the exchange. At this time financial leaders regarded opposition as hopeless, and the legislation as mild compared to demands by liberals for the nationalization of banking.

The President's effort to raise prices by monetary inflation, however, revived the traditional struggle over the gold standard. Having behind him a sweeping Democratic majority, and supported by a group of economists who believed essentially in the quantity theory of money, Roosevelt obtained cancellation of gold payment clauses in federal bonds and other loan contracts, the power to devaluate the dollar up to 50 percent in relation to gold, and ultimately a silver purchase program. He aimed to provide "the kind of dollar which, a generation hence, will have the same purchasing and debt paying power as the dollar value we hope to attain in the near future."[18]

Because of the belief of his advisers in the stimulating effects of inflation on the domestic economy, at an International Monetary Conference held in June 1933 the President refused to enter into any fixed exchange relations. He ended his experiments with the value of the dollar in January 1934 when he fixed its gold content at 59.06 percent of the previous amount. In spite of great changes in prices and international exchange rates, until 1971 no revaluation was attempted. The country never returned to free and unlicensed exchange of paper money for gold. Since no foreign country did either, the United States could be said to have returned to the modern version of the gold standard, that is, gold issued by special application to pay international trade balances.

Some critics have blamed the inflation of World War II on the expanded gold base for American currency provided by devaluation. Yet the price changes in the North during the Civil War and in the World War I period were of about the same magnitude as in World War II and its aftermath. More immediate effects of the monetary policies were to hinder international agreements regarding convertibility of currencies, and hence to discourage international trade, and to drive silver standard countries (such as China and Mexico) off a metallic base by raising the market price of silver.

Offsetting the reduction in trade caused by monetary readjustments was the government's policy of reciprocal trade pacts. By the Act of 1934 Congress allowed the executive to negotiate with individual nations special agreements that might lower tariffs by as much as 50 percent. Before World War II such agreements, affecting about a third of American trade, had been negotiated. Since many countries had treaties specifying "most-favored-nation" treatment for their goods, the tariff reductions spread beyond the new trade pacts but the total economic effect in the thirties was not large.[19] In spite of the efforts of tariff lobbyists, these policies were still in effect in 1970.

Although early business opposition to the New Deal centered on the abandonment of the gold standard, it is probable that most businessmen were opposed to all of the reform, as distinct from relief measures. Herbert Hoover spoke for conservative businessmen when he said in 1934 that the New Deal represented "a vast shift from the American concept of human rights which even the government may not infringe to those social philosophies where men are wholly subject to the state." But faith in a self-regulating economy led inevitably to a negative position. Business leaders had no positive program of their own to oppose the Roosevelt formulas for curing the abuses of the twenties.

During 1933 a Senate committee investigating Wall Street practices aroused the already critical public with exposures of dishonesty by important financiers that led to a demand for more regulation. The stock exchange appeared to be a private club run by a group of specialists and floor traders at the expense of small investors.[20] Two of the largest corporations listed on the New York exchange, for example, made no annual reports, and even the stockbrokers who brought the market its business felt they had little to say about how it was transacted.[21] By the spring of 1934 an administration bill requiring further disclosure of information regarding all listed securities, and control of market practices including margin requirements, by a Securities Exchange Commission was before Congress. From April until the passage of the bill by substantial majorities in June, important business interests waged a more concerted battle against the administration than they had over gold, and again they lost.

The following spring the war was resumed over the Holding Company Act designed to break up the pyramided companies that controlled nine-tenths of the nation's electric power. Again business suffered defeat in the heavily liberal Congress, but the final version of the act was so weak that by 1946 the thirteen largest systems had only reduced the number of their corporate entities by one-third.[22]

In practice, the financial acts from 1933 to 1935 probably had little effect on recovery. That the majority of private or investment banking houses elected to give up commercial banking led to no shortage of bank facilities, and it produced a healthy competition for the customers of the firms that took the opposite course. Accountants and lawyers profited greatly from helping their clients to meet the new requirements. The real burden of the law of 1934 fell on firms desiring to float new securities, who had to pay for the information needed and go through a twenty-day waiting period before permission to sell. Yet, in all, qualified observers doubted that the new system had much effect on the small amount of new financing.[23]

In the long run the banking and security legislation became acceptable to most businessmen, as did other measures such as social security and reciprocal trade agreements, but the labor policies of the New Deal aroused lasting and nearly unanimous business opposition. Up to 1929 big business leaders and smaller entrepreneurs in trade and service had always hoped that unionism could be restricted to diminishing sectors of the old handicrafts such as carpenters, masons, and plumbers. Initially, the depression gave hope that even in these areas union strength would become ineffective. In 1932 the American Federation of Labor had just over two million members, about the same percentage of the labor force as at the beginning of the century.

Ironically, the fact that President Roosevelt was not much interested in labor matters led him to go along with his liberal advisers such as Frances Perkins, Rexford G. Tugwell, and Robert F. Wagner. The latter, both in the Senate and as chairman of the National Recovery Administration labor board, was the chief architect of labor policy. In 1933 and 1934 he learned the weaknesses of the law, and corrected them as chief author of a National Labor Relations Act, which had passed the Senate in May 1935 when the NIRA was declared unconstitutional.

Business attacks on the administration over the Holding Companies Act led the President to support the NLR or "Wagner Act." Although the evidence can never be unearthed, one suspects that a large number of the supporters of the act were appealing to the labor vote while holding an inner conviction that the law was bound to be held unconstitutional. Basing its right of jurisdiction on the fact that some of the products worked on were shipped in interstate trade, the act imposed severe restrictions on employers and gave unusual privileges to unions. Yet the Supreme Court had currently shown its unwillingness to accept a broad interpretation of the commerce power. Even labor leaders doubted that they would gain much from the law, while employers were advised by their lawyers to disregard it.

The really crucial engagement in what had now become a war between the President and most of business was the election of 1936. Well in advance, a group of business and conservative political leaders formed the Liberty League to protect the Constitution and American liberties from the assaults of New Deal legislation. Two former Democratic presidential candidates, John W. Davis and Alfred E. Smith, joined with leading businessmen and lawyers in the work of the league. Anti-Roosevelt publicity was easy to secure, since by 1935 most of the nation's newspapers had turned against him. Roosevelt was attacked for extravagance and consequent increase in the national debt, as well as for infringement of personal liberties.

These charges had a basis in reality. The President was a loose administrator and Americans were relatively inexperienced in creating bureaucracy. Deficits were continuing, and there was a widely held fear of public debt even among those who supported the New Deal. Businessmen, unaccustomed to government forms and regulations, bitterly resented the new burdens of paper work, legal advice, and federal supervision.

To the ordinary citizen, however, who never came in direct contact with business regulations, who saw in public finance an unsolved mystery, and who felt that his savings, his home, and his income were all better protected than ever before, the appeals of the Liberty League had little force. Furthermore, the businessmen's informal campaign of vituperation against the President went to lengths that appeared ridiculous to the wage- or salary-earner. In upper-class circles he was referred to as "that man," and a steady stream of malicious jokes about the President emanated from clubs and offices.

In the fall of 1936 a *Literary Digest* poll indicated that a majority of those rich enough to have telephones favored the Republicans, yet the President was reelected in one of the greatest landslides in American history, polling 60 percent of the vote and carrying all states except Maine and Vermont. It was this sweeping political triumph in both Washington and the state capitals that set in motion the chain of events that created a new and powerful American labor movement.

Still hoping that the courts would declare the new law unconstitutional, employers resorted to all the traditional devices such as espionage, special police, and black lists to prevent the spread of organization. But three powerful forces were working against them. Late 1936 and early 1937 was the one time of returning prosperity in the gloomy decade that followed 1929, and manufacturers wanted to maintain or increase production. Secondly, the federal administration and the governor of what turned out to be the key state of Michigan were in favor of unionization. And thirdly, the new industrial union movement had an imposing national figurehead in John L. Lewis, and some dedicated young leaders at lower levels.

The key strike occurred at the General Motors works of Flint, Michigan, in late 1936 and early 1937, near the peak of the business upswing. It was not the Wagner Act, but the practical, physical support of Governor Frank Murphy, who refused to enforce three court orders, that allowed the union to win a limited victory.[24] The unionization of most of the automotive industries led to a peaceful settlement by United States Steel, so that by April of 1937 the rank and file of workers in some major large-scale manufacturing industries had been unionized for the first time in American history, and the dream of a dwindling or vanishing labor movement was at an end.

The situation was given permanence by a startling reversal in attitude by the Supreme Court. Harrassed by the President's Court Bill to add as many as six justices to the Court, the tribunal on April 12, by a 5 to 4 vote, upheld the National Labor Relations Act. Companies such as "little steel" and Ford Motor continued to resist organizers by use of force, but before World War II they all had to bow to court orders.

The law prohibited the employer from taking physical, verbal, or written action designed to prevent the activities of union organizers. When the organizers were ready they could ask the National Labor Relations Board to hold an election within the company (the employer was denied this privilege) and the group winning a majority would then represent all the workers. Dues to support the winning union had to be deducted by the employer from all paychecks.

In a chapter of his memoirs entitled "Fascism Comes to Labor — with Consequences," Herbert Hoover wrote: "In violation of the whole spirit of American justice, the Board was judge, jury, and prosecutor. There was no effective appeal from its decisions. . . . The Board appointed by Roosevelt presents a prime exhibit of the collectivist character of his officials and also of the collectivist character of the regime."[25] A more objective historian writing nearly a generation later has called the Wagner Act "probably the most bluntly anti-corporation legislation the United States has ever known."[26] The long arm of government touched the plant at two of its most sensitive areas, cost and authority. For the employer this was by far the most intolerable act of the New Deal.

Thus by government action one of the weakest labor movements in the industrialized world had been suddenly raised to one of the most powerful. It had, however, an inherent weakness, a division between the old American Federation of Labor and the new Congress of Industrial Organizations made up of unions expelled by the AF of L. Had World War II not temporarily postponed most union problems, this rift might have been a serious deterrent to the effectiveness of organization.

Continuing Depression

While unions were winning victories in the courts and before the National Labor Relations Board, workers were losing their jobs. Between August 1937 and April 1938 the dollar volume of business dropped 35 percent, the fastest drop in American history, and unemployment rose again to the ten million level.

The basic problem, as seen by business commentators, was lack of any consistent economic policy on the part of the administration. In 1935, over strong business opposition, Congress had begun a policy of providing jobs at rates of pay higher than unemployment relief to workers with special skills. The aim was humanitarian, and when possible a preservation of the skill involved, but no project was to spend over $7,500 in capital. This turned out to be the greatest spending program of the New Deal, $11 billion by 1941, yet because of its limit on capital expenditure it did not provide any important demand for producer goods. Furthermore, since the appropriations were usually on an annual basis, it did not even promise a reliable level of consumer demand, and this was soon demonstrated.

In 1936, the only full year of rather steadily mounting prosperity (although there were still six million unemployed), Congress — over the President's veto — paid $2 billion in cash to the holders of veterans' bonus certificates originating in World War I. This made federal spending nearly 25 percent higher than in any previous peacetime year and produced a $3.5 billion deficit. In addition, a short-lived experiment in heavy taxation of undistributed corporate profits was initiated that led to an unusually large payment of dividends.[27] The result was a buoyant consumer demand that if nourished with a large federal deficit might have made 1937 a truly prosperous year; but at the beginning of the year the President completely reversed his policies.

Claiming fear of a runaway boom, although stock market indexes of neither price nor volume were approaching 1929 levels, and unemployment was still high, the Federal Reserve Board raised the reserve requirements for banks and tightened money, while the President promised a balanced budget. Since Roosevelt was trying to win conservative support in Congress for his Court bill, it could be charged that he made the economy a political football; however, it should also be remembered that he had never ceased believing in the moral worth of a balanced budget and that he had no theoretical conception of the relation of government spending to aggregate demand.

As a result of this gyration in policy the federal budget for July 1, 1937 to June 30, 1938 was practically in balance, in fact the total intake showed a surplus over outgo, and the nation was back in a deep depression. While this brief account necessarily casts the President in the role of villain, or bungler, aside from asking for greater consistency, his business critics had no solutions to offer. When he turned to them for advice in the grim winter of 1937-38 the general answer was "sit tight and economize."

There was a return to deficits in the two following annual budgets, not only to relieve obvious suffering, win votes, and satisfy liberal critics, but also for a new purpose that was eventually to restore prosperity: military expenses. Business, as judged by articles in its publications, was not reassured by the new turn of events. "Activity of this kind," said the *Guaranty Survey,* "obviously cannot be regarded as constituting normal business recovery.... Such outlays ... can represent only an economic burden in the long run."[28] Business sentiment was also disturbed by a large-scale investigation of monopoly by the Temporary

National Economic Committee of Congress and a wave of antitrust prosecutions.

The decade ended, with business at what might by then be termed average depression levels, and with few optimists foreseeing great improvement in the near future. While war in Europe led to some rearmament expenditure and a small increase in exports of manufactures, these were practically balanced by a decline in those of agriculture. The unemployed numbered 9.4 million, or 17 percent of the civilian labor force, and many theorists were reconciled to an economy that would continue to operate with high levels of unemployment.

The financial sector of business was at its lowest ebb. The volume of shares traded on the New York Stock Exchange in 1939 was under half that of 1932 and falling lower every week. New capital issues were less than a billion dollars and stock prices were at about 1932 levels, with railroads and industrials up slightly and utilities much lower. Only a mild upturn in private construction was a feeble light in the gloom that overhung Wall Street.

The New Deal in Perspective

In spite of loud protests and mutual distrust, the New Deal forced business and government to work more closely together, to form a kind of partnership which grew in importance in later years. Business firms had to assign special employees to the tasks of understanding new federal regulations and of dealing with new agencies. One company framed a set of extracts from relevant statutes and hung it in the front office as a reminder of how much it had come to be regulated. In most big companies someone at a high executive level had to spend much time in Washington learning to know the operations and personnel of important bureaus and commissions. Small businesses that could not afford to have specialists in federal relations dealt with these matters through trade or other associations.

Early in 1951 the editors of *Fortune* collaborated with Russell W. Davenport in an issue of the magazine, published later the same year as a book entitled *U.S.A.: The Permanent Revolution,* in which they compared the bad old days with the happy, prosperous United States of mid-century. The factors that they saw as responsible for the better society, such as higher real wages, fairer labor relations, greater security, more honest financial dealings, and greater social responsiblity by corporation executives, stem largely from the days of the New Deal. One cannot help but conclude that unpleasant as this period may have been, many big-business executives at least came to see the reforms as inevitable adjustments to changing economic conditions.

Except for the Wagner Act, which was subsequently replaced by the Taft-Hartley Act more favorable to employers, the enlightened executive of mid-century might conclude that his objection was more to the way Roosevelt talked and to the uncertainty of his policies than to the lasting things which he did. The propaganda of the New Deal against "economic royalists" and the "greedy" was highly offensive to most businessmen; the legislation, in retrospect, appeared more moderate.

8 Business and War

In the depressed years of the 1930s a few big businessmen had seen military expenditure as an aid to prosperity, but the general political climate was strongly against "munitions makers."[1] Isolationist and pacifist sentiment among the public was increased when a Senate committee headed by Gerald P. Nye exposed many questionable activities by munitions makers in World War I and the succeeding years. Hence, while there was a War Policies Commission created by Congress in 1930 and staffed by outstanding business leaders, nothing of importance was planned or accomplished. As war seemed closer in 1939 the President appointed a War Resources Board, but when it appeared to be unpopular he dismissed it. The rearmament bill passed by Congress in the fall of 1939 provided for more hardware, but no organization.

During the twenty-six months between the invasion of Poland and Pearl Harbor businessmen welcomed the end of New Deal legislation, but did not become trusting supporters of President Roosevelt. While, like all Americans, manufacturers recognized the need for greater national defense, they still regarded the administration as unreliable and antibusiness and hesitated to become deeply involved in government contracts for armament.[2]

The period after the Fall of France in June 1940, when it became obvious that the United States would either have to make large-scale efforts to support England or put itself in readiness to fight Germany, divides into three nearly even periods: eighteen months from Dunkirk to Pearl Harbor, during which time the President hesitated to try to force conversion of the economy by law; an equal period from the beginning of war to satisfactory production levels of matériel in mid-1943; and a third interval from the peak of war production in September 1943 to the beginning of continuous reconversion in mid-1945.

The Period of Voluntarism

In the situation as a whole, and during the first period in particular, there was, in spite of the protestations of Bernard Baruch (head of the War Industries Board in World War I), little to be learned from previous experience. As seen in Chapter 6, in 1916, in the face of continuing bad harvests, the work force of the nation had been fully employed producing food, other raw materials, and some component parts for the French and English. Existing national defense legislation was geared to long-range objectives only. The declaration of war gave President Wilson plenty of power but nothing new with which to work. Consequently there was no dramatic change in national productivity, and the war was over before retooled mass production lines began to supply large quantities of finished matériel. Germany and Japan looking at the 1917 and 1918 record, without subjecting it to careful analysis, could well doubt the ability of the United States to convert to war production within any reasonable length of time.

In 1940 all these factors were different. In that year the unemployed were conservatively estimated at almost 7 million. By 1944 these 7 million had been put to work and the total employed workers had increased from 47 to over 63 million. This 35-percent increase in the number of employed workers almost exactly coincided with the percentage increase in real national product or income for the same period.[3] In contrast to the time covered by United States participation in World War I, the period from 1940 to 1945 was long enough to yield the fruits of mass production. In addition, more than in the earlier war, the Second World War needed the kind of automotive equipment that the United States was best fitted to produce. To look at international comparisons of 1939 and conclude that the United States

had about 40 percent of the world's industrial capacity greatly under-
estimates its superiority. America had far more than half the peacetime
capacity of the automotive industry, and that was what would count
most. With new technological resources in agriculture and less of Europe to feed, basic grain products were not a problem as they had been
throughout World War I.

Therefore, until the spring of 1941, the "we can have both guns and
butter" argument made sense to most businessmen. The amount of war
production called for could easily be added to an increasingly prosperous civilian business without running into shortages in either labor or
materials. During this period it was the President's policy to involve big
business in the war effort through voluntary pursuit of profit. Only with
the massive congressional appropriations that followed the passage of
lend-lease in March 1941 did material shortages begin to appear and
some allocation of priorities become necessary.

Although the war demanded what America could do best and production continually increased, the organizing of the war effort was a period
of bitter struggle and internal confusion. In this dreary and complex
history it is easy to single out villains and to accuse the President of a
lack of administrative ability, but in a long view trouble seems to have
been inevitable. Even without ambiguities in ultimate authority or conflicting pressures, it had taken a generation, as described in Chapter 5,
to develop effective bureaucracies in big business. To set up a bureaucratic structure composed of separate and often hostile interests, with
vaguely defined lines of power, yet so large that it could administer over
$50 billion worth of business a year within fifteen or twenty months,
was obviously a human impossibility.

Two basic and probably unavoidable factors produced conflict from
beginning to end. The top-level business executives who headed the
various agencies were conditioned to treat their counterparts in other
organizations as competitors and to seek first and foremost a good
record of accomplishment for their own operation. For this reason
Roosevelt would have preferred cooperative politicians in these positions, but until the appointment of James Byrnes as head of the war effort in May 1943 he thought it safest to work through businessmen who

understood production. The other, much more serious conflict was that the Army always wanted the maximum possible war production and therefore gave only grudging acquiescence to civilian efforts at balancing economic claims. In the long run the armed forces, as we shall see, essentially won and by early 1943 were largely in control of their own supply.

The Council of National Defense, provided for in World War I, was the initial agency for war preparation, but since it was composed entirely of Cabinet members it needed an operating body, which was provided in May 1940 through a presidentially appointed Advisory Commission. The member of this commission in charge of production, William S. Knudsen (formerly president of General Motors), became the first organizer of industry for war.

For this stage of preparation Knudsen was a wise choice. He had a firm, practical grasp of the needs of mass production. He knew the retooling time would be more than a year and he was able by his knowledge and experience to convince the President and impatient military men that if they wanted great productivity in the future they could expect little in the present. Airplanes, tanks, and ordnance put together on moving assembly lines required big plants — only components could be made by small companies — but the majority of the 225,000 manufacturers complained that Knudsen thought chiefly in terms of the automotive complex, so thoroughly familiar to him, and in fact quite capable of providing all that was needed in most sectors of supply. As Knudsen expressed it to the President: "What I think we should do . . . is to bury the automobile manufacturers under defense orders — three times as much stuff as they can make with their present facilities."[4] If a manufacturer were a regular supplier of the automotive or airplane industry he was likely to be kept busy; if, however, he was one of the majority who were not, it might be hard to get into this stage of the defense effort.

In the period when war was highly uncertain, industry in general feared creating excess capacity. Big companies preferred to build new plants with either government funds or loans from the Reconstruction Finance Corporation, rather than to disrupt their normal assembly facilities. The steel companies particularly had no desire to pay for increased capacity that they thought would be useless in time of peace. In October of 1940, Congress encouraged new construction with borrowed money by granting a five-year period for depreciation, which could be apportioned as a contract cost. If large companies could by such means readily make all the elements necessary to fulfill a military order, they were disinclined to subcontract to smaller firms.

In January 1941 the loosely knit Advisory Commission was superseded by the Office of Production Management, with Knudsen as director and Sidney Hillman of the Amalgamated Clothing Workers, who had represented labor on the commission, as associate director. The President insisted that the two men were equal in power, but at this point labor troubles were not acute, whereas production problems were about to become so, and the dominant role was clearly Knudsen's. With $30 billion in congressional appropriations following lend-lease, the maladjustment between the distribution of materials, contracts, and components that was to become chaotic by 1942 began to set in. The OPM issued its first priority order on March 22, and by August allocation of material was becoming the major issue.

During this period, while Knudsen was doing a good job in securing production and handling the military, he was not doing well with business in general, with Congress, or — by late 1941 — with the President. Knudsen was a single-minded production man who did not enjoy conversation about broader unfamiliar problems. Invited by Harry Hopkins to confer more often with the President, he failed to do so; meanwhile pressure mounted for a more generally acceptable administrator. In addition, there was much friction between the Office of Price Administration and Civilian Supply, headed by Leon Henderson and staffed largely by New Dealers, and the staff of the OPM, whose members had come chiefly from business. Applying one of his usual methods in such instances, in August 1941 Roosevelt placed a Supply, Priorities, and Allocations Board, with Donald Nelson of Sears, Roebuck as executive director, over both the contending agencies.

The relationships in this troika were poorly defined and Pearl Harbor necessitated further revision. By a War Powers Act of December the

President was given very large scope to delegate and reassign powers. Accordingly he abolished the OPM and SPAB and placed the ultimate power over priorities in the sole hands of Donald Nelson as chairman of a War Production Board. The board itself was merely advisory and the Army-Navy Munitions Board had to report to the President "through the Chairman of WPB."[5]

Nelson had been involved in the preparedness effort from the beginning, first as Coordinator of Defense Purchasing on the Advisory Commission, and then in addition as Director of the Small Business Activities Office, before becoming Executive Director of the top-level SPAB. His appointment was thought to represent the victory of the liberal, socially minded businessmen over both the hard-headed big-business conservatives and the military.

The Average Businessman and the War

From the middle of 1939 to the middle of 1941 business as a whole enjoyed returning prosperity. As the depression ended and employment spread, people turned in their old jalopies for new cars, and automobile sales were up 30 percent within a year. Families also bought washing machines, refrigerators, and all the other expensive durable goods. Local retailers in almost every line gained from bigger household expenditures. After mid-1941, however, as priorities became necessary for metals and rubber, retailers and distributors of consumer goods began to feel the pressure. In part, the hardships and closing of a number of trade and service establishments reflected not only the cutting off of supplies but also the drafting of young proprietors.

The actual war period was not one of high prosperity for the great majority of businessmen. Some, such as automobile distributors, tire dealers, and various types of sellers of durable goods lost all but a trickle of their normal trade. Construction, except for military bases, war plants, and attendant housing, came to a virtual halt; while the workers in firms without war contracts were drafted or moved to other jobs, the older proprietors found it difficult to maintain their standard of living or even to preserve their enterprises from bankruptcy.

In industry, small business — that is, firms with under 500 employees, and particularly the majority that employed less than 20 — found trouble in either fitting into the war effort or getting material for their usual products. On the other hand, some of the tens of thousands of small companies that won prime or subcontracts found ways of eluding the excess profits taxes and making very large sums, a process impossible for big, closely scrutinized contractors.[6]

The problem of spreading the war effort to utilize the extra capacity of smaller plants was an extremely difficult one. Such plants generally lacked engineering staffs and machine tool designers who could inspire confidence in the men letting the contracts for the Defense Plants Corporation and the armed forces. The small companies could seldom underbid the larger ones. Interested chiefly in reliable maximum production, the armed services regarded subcontracting as the responsibility of the prime contractor. Trade associations played little part in World War II, and most individual small businesses could not afford a man in Washington to let them know what they should bid on.

Obviously, if the half of the industrial labor force employed by the 200,000-odd small manufacturing plants were to be brought into war contracting it would have to be by some special intermediary agency. In October of 1940 the Advisory Commission made Robert L Mehorney, a Kansas City furniture maker, Deputy Director of Small Business Activities under Donald Nelson. But it was not the commission that let contracts, and Mehorney failed to convince the military purchasers of the reliability of many small manufactureres. From June to December 1940, 86 percent of the $11 billion prime contracts went to 100 companies, and by late in 1941 three-quarters of Army and Navy contracts had gone to 56 companies.[7] Since manufacturers without contracts had difficulty getting material, priority unemployment was becoming general in the fall of 1941 and exciting many Congressmen.

At this juncture the President, without notice to the OPM, superseded Mehorney by lawyer Floyd B. Odlum, president of the Atlas Corporation of Jersey City, who launched the most determined effort of the period to include the majority of manufacturers in the war effort. He toured the country in a red, white, and blue special train showing manufacturers what was needed and what they might bid on. Without Nelson's approval he tried to get the President to set aside 2 percent of critical materials for plants employing less than twenty men. In the crucial metals industry this would have meant 18,000 out of 28,000 firms. He also tried, with more success, to get small contractors to form pools. By January 1942 some thirty such pools had received $100 million in contracts. By this time he had also had analyses made of 70,000 plants potentially available for contracts.[8]

As Nelson himself saw the situation, there was no reason why small manufacturers should be uneconomically or arbitrarily favored when the far more numerous enterprisers in trade, service, finance, and transportation enjoyed no such advantages. He preferred urging the services to make advantageous allocations, but not making the program "a form of WPA."[9]

The presidential order of January 16 establishing the War Production Board, with Nelson as its head, gave the latter broad and undefined powers. He could have transferred all contracting, subcontracting, and control of materials and schedules from the military services to agencies of the board, but for reasons we shall discuss presently, he refused to assume this overall control of the war effort.[10] To make sure that he acted in the interests of the majority of businessmen, Congress backed up the WPB, in June, with a Small Business Act under which Nelson created the Smaller War Plants Division. By this time Odlum had left the scene and the directorship was given to Lou E. Holland, then head of the Small War Plants Corporation. The additional apparatus made no real difference. During 1942 Holland arranged for $250 million in orders to 3,700 prime and subcontractors, but the real spread of contracting to some tens of thousands of medium-sized manufacturers came from increasing knowledge of the possibilities for supply by prime contractors and the General Munitions Board of the Army and Navy.

In all, the period from 1940 to 1945 marked a reduction in the total number of business firms of about 5 percent, from 3.29 million to 3.11 million, in contrast to a growth rate of 13 percent from 1931 to 1940 and 35 percent from 1946 to 1955. The largest losses were in construction and service, whereas the number of manufacturers increased 14 percent, underlining Nelson's contention that this group needed help less than other businessmen.

Although the excess profits taxes from 1940 through 1944 were far too complex to explain here, some of the increase in small manufacturing may have been due to the tax laws which gave advantages to companies whose net incomes were less than $500,000. Up to the end of 1942 profits from increased income on war business could be partly balanced against losses on normal business. The taxes rose on a progressive scale, from 1940 to 1941 to a maximum of 50 percent at $500,000 net income, from 1941 until October of 1942 of 60 percent, from then until early 1944 of 90 percent on all excess profits, and 95 percent after that. Such taxes encouraged deductible expenditures for research, goodwill advertising, expense accounts, and special services, while they discouraged companies with exhaustable natural resources from depleting their reserves at almost no profit. Yet no nation found any better solution for taking some of the profits out of war, and more of the cost of World War II was met by taxes than in any previous major American conflict.

Production and Its Control: The Critical Years

Production of durables, of which automobiles were the major part, had been cut back to 26.5 percent in August 1941, but while the motor companies were willing to fill contracts by building new plants with quick write-offs of the expense, or by using surplus facilities, they were not willing, in time of peace, to convert the main assembly lines. The industry contended that only automobiles could be efficiently manufactured in their plants, and the OPM accepted the situation.

"The period between Pearl Harbor Day and the beginning of WPB on January 15th [sic], 1942" wrote Donald Nelson, "was one of great writhing and thrashing around on the part of the automobile magnates and the functionaries of government who were trying to prepare the nation for war. The industry, without opposing conversion, had wanted to use up certain raw materials and parts for a final splurge in passenger car production – and the truth of the matter is they made out a very good case."[11] But on January 20, 1942, Nelson's WPB stopped further production of passenger cars and light trucks, and the vast power of the automobile industry was concentrated on war supply. "Historians who wade deeply enough into the facts and figures, the cold engineering statistics of World War II," Nelson wrote, "may some day come to the conclusion that our automotive industry could, alone, have produced almost enough to lick the Axis."[12]

In spite of Nelson's firmness in shutting down production of consumer goods, Senator Harry Truman blamed him for failure to use his full authority over the economy. Unquestionably he preferred to delegate authority rather than make decisions himself, but there was much to be said for his restraint. He recognized that while it was necessary to keep up morale in the civilian population, only the military could know, on the basis of secret strategic plans, what was to be needed and when. To be sure, they did not know exactly and were seldom able to make any estimates that would satisfy a business purchasing agent – for one thing they lacked trained personnel for such forecasts – but if they were unable to estimate, neither could any one do it for them without endangering the war effort. The working compromise that gradually took shape by mid-1943 suited both prime contractors and the military better than rule by a WPB czar.

In the first six months of 1942 over $100 billion in contracts were placed by the agencies having power to do so – that is, the armed services, the Maritime Commission, and four corporations to aid expansion established by the Reconstruction Finance Corporation. Since no such increase in production was possible, chaos resulted. The agencies fought one another for materials and components, and in the scramble "all semblance of balance in the production program disappeared. . . . After a tragically slow start, many a plant was changed over to war production when its normal product was needed more than its new product. Locomotive plants went into tank production, when locomotives were more necessary – but the Tank

Division did not know this."[13] Factories were built which were not needed and could not be used, and many more priorities were issued than there were materials to go around.[14]

The basic problem was relations between the WPB and the Army and Navy Munitions Board. The latter was composed of representatives of the agencies that determined needs, resources, and supply for the Army and Navy and allocated the contracts for the armed services. It was headed, after December 7, 1941, by an aggressive and efficient investment banker, Ferdinand Eberstadt. Compromises on the part of Nelson and action by the President during the first half of 1942 had transferred to the ANMB complete control over priorities, without proper regard for civilian requirements. In effect, the ANMB and its chairman stood between Nelson and the heads of the armed services, making for friction and poor communication. Supported by the military, Eberstadt offered plans to prevent too much bureaucratic centralization of decision-making in WPB headquarters in Washington.

The solution worked out during the summer was to transfer Eberstadt to the WPB, to a position in charge of operations and programming, in order to work out a more decentralized system of materials control.[15] The result of a series of conferences in September and October was the adoption of the system regularly used in the automobile industry, already introduced into machine tools by Eberstadt, and publicly employed by the British government for the control of steel. The plan required contractors to supply accurate schedules of the materials needed; it thus gave the WPB "more detailed information as to the amounts of metal going into particular products than had ever been gathered together in any one place before."[16]

An equally important feature of this controlled materials plan, particularly in Eberstadt's view, was to shift "the detailed administration of allocations from the WPB to the claimant agencies, chiefly the Army, Navy, Air Forces and Maritime Commission, and to delegate the secondary power of allocation to the prime contractors, who passed allocations on down through the industrial system."[17] Thus the services and their big contractors won control of the flow of materials and exercised it with general efficiency, but with an understandable tendency toward overestimates, until the end of the war. As might be expected, the controlled materials plan was hard to apply to the smaller contractors, but Nelson regarded it "as an absolute necessity at the time and the best mechanism we could think of to speed up production."[18] The new plan was partially put into effect late in 1942 and completely for aluminum, copper, and steel by June 1943.

By early 1943, distribution of manpower and scheduling of components were becoming even more serious problems than shortages of materials. In late 1942, Charles Wilson of General Electric was put in charge of scheduling at the WPB; although he also represented the conservative big-business-Army view, he and Eberstadt proved incompatible in their necessarily closely associated tasks. As a result Nelson asked for Eberstadt's resignation early in 1943 and Wilson emerged as the chief coordinator of metals and components until his resignation in July 1944.

From Scarcity to Surplus

All of this in-fighting had concerned only materials and production schedules on war contracts and critical components. By May 1943, with those matters tolerably in order, the President felt the need of some man with a broader politicosocial view of the economy to coordinate price controls, civilian needs, and labor problems. He created the Office of War Mobilization with ex-Senator and Supreme Court Justice James F. Byrnes in charge as an "assistant president," superior to all other civilian directors.

Byrnes was unquestionably an able administrator, but between September and November 1943 war production in some items was becoming excessive and he presided chiefly over the problems of labor supply, reallocations, and reconversion. All of which proved fully as difficult, and of more long-run significance for business than the problems of conversion to defense contracting.

After the fall of 1943, the labor problem was not one of overall scarcity, but of maladjustment in regions and types of workers. Defense contractors with plenty of work ahead of them could hoard labor, whereas low-wage industries not offering overtime (such as cotton textiles) could not keep an adequate supply of workers. Areas where defense contracts had been cut back developed pools of un-employed, while in other areas, particularly the Pacific Coast, labor was scarce. The pools could not be dried up by moving the unem-ployed, both because no government agency wished to use such arbitrary power and because the skills needed in one area usually failed to coincide with those that were in surplus supply elsewhere.

Obviously businessmen below the level of the great prime con-tractors were anxious to mop up these pools of unemployment by resuming production of civilian goods, for which there was high demand. The services, spearheaded by the Army, on the other hand, wanted to maintain reserves of unemployed in case military production suddenly had to be increased. These differences were, of course, mirrored in Washington in the WPB, Congress, and the War Department.[19]

At a high level of generalization, the business aspects of the bitter controversies over reconversion can be seen as a contest between big manufacturing companies assured of war contracts, who wanted to preserve the prewar competitive structure in their industries and therefore opposed selective reconversion on the one side, and smaller or newer manufacturers, plus most of trade, service, and transporta-tion on the other. Any such contest fought politically would be likely to swing in favor of the vastly more numerous latter group, but the armed services were at this time the nation's most important agents of power and since to them the big contractors seemed more likely to guarantee adequate supplies, they favored that side.

Hence when in June 1944, based on studies by his own men and Bernard Baruch, Nelson announced that the WPB would offer a four-point reconversion plan, it was immediately brought under effective military attack. Briefly the points called for were (1) the end of priorities on magnesium and aluminum, (2) testing of a single model of any postwar product, (3) advance retooling for civilian production

if this were possible by nonpriority orders, and (4) "spot authorization" by WPB regional directors for resumption of civilian production
that did not interfere with war contracts. The services objected to the
whole concept of war-industry planning for peacetime production,
fearing that management would divert the best engineering brains
to such problems at the expense of improvement in munitions.
They objected most strongly of all to spot authorization for reconversion, which they claimed would drain the best labor from defense
work. As a result OWM Director Byrnes postponed spot authorization until mid-August, and in fact relatively little reconversion had
taken place when the Battle of the Bulge, in December 1944, forced
practical suspension of reconversion until late in April 1945.

Nelson, coming from a nondefense consumer-oriented business,
seemed to the Truman committee and probably to the average
businessman to be a heroic defender of the people and to the Army an
insensitive dictatorial supporter of oligopolistic business – the later
"industrial-military" complex. In retrospect Nelson wrote, "The
lesson taught by these recent years is clear: our whole economic and
social system will be in peril if it is controlled by military men."[20]

Yet the Battle of the Bulge, indicating the possibility of stubborn
German resistance, justified in part the Army's fear of premature
reconversion. From first to last the Army found the WPB a difficult agency with which to deal. It seemed to some businessmen
as well as to the services to be unwilling to use its power energetically
in support of the war effort. When in August 1944, for example, the
labor force required redeployment, and labor hoarders needed to be
cracked down on, the WPB did nothing until late December and then
issued a weak statement "that neither delegated powers to the
War Manpower Commission, nor . . . agreed to act automatically on
receipt of a request from the Commission for invocation of WPB
powers."[21]

Reconversion

By April of 1945 the end of the European phase of the war was in
sight, and after the massively destructive bombing of Tokyo on June

19th there was little doubt that the Japanese phase would end soon. Yet up to April at least, reconversion was about where it had been the previous fall. A change in the situation came, not only from military events, but from the resignation in March of General Lucius M. Clay as deputy director of the all-powerful OWM. With military caution less well represented, it was easier in April to reinstate spot authorization for reconversion, but the need for approval by the OWM, WPB, and War Manpower Commission made effective action still difficult and progress was slow. Until after V-J Day civilian goods actually became scarcer.

Early in 1945, with the government still buying about half of industrial production, rapid reconversion presented problems almost as great as had initial conversion. Small plants that had been re-equipped rather than expanded for war work faced the problem of removal of government machinery and other inventory as well as raising working capital to see them through the period of change. To ease the situation, the RFC extended loans and Congress passed a law requiring removal of government equipment within sixty days of notification. Once they could get spot authorization from a WPB field agent and approval from the WMC, reconversion went better for small manufacturers than had war contracting. Such firms were usually high-cost producers, likely to secure early cancellation of war contracts, and since the RFC and the Surplus Property Board found storage space, sometimes in unused plants, the sixty-day clause worked in all but 6 percent of the cases.[22]

From V-E Day on, when rapid reconversion in the near future was being demanded by all parties involved except the military, a new business-government issue arose. The Smaller War Plants Corporation wanted reconversion controlled by the WPB to prevent a scramble for labor and materials. Fearing that such free competition would bring inflation, the Office of Price Administration took a similar stand. But the former OWM, now the Office of War Mobilization and Reconversion, headed after July 23 by ex-banker John W. Snyder, and the WPB under Julius A Krug, primarily a government specialist, both favored the relaxing of all controls on "freedom of action".[23] One factor strongly favoring this laissez-faire approach was that the

WPB and other agencies were rapidly losing the businessmen who had headed their divisions, and large-scale new activity would be difficult. When the WPB was succeeded by the Civilian Production Administration on November 4, 1945, less than 10 percent of all wartime controls were still in effect.

Wartime Developments

While in both World War I and World War II the major business problems may have been the running of the emergency boards and bureaus, the greatest success may have come in the organization of shipbuilding. From 1936 on, the United States Maritime Commission had been subsidizing the construction and operation of vessels for approved foreign trades. This had provided a small number of up-to-date ships, but in general the merchant marine capable of navigating rough water was composed of leftovers from World War I or an earlier period. Between 1939 and 1945, American shipbuilders, using many new processes, such as subassembly of large sections at secondary plants, electric welding, and a high degree of standard-ization, turned out over 56 million dead-weight tons, an amount about equal to the prewar steam tonnage of the British Empire. In the course of this achievement Henry J. Kaiser's shipyards reduced the time of building a Liberty ship, the standard slow freighter of World War II, from nearly two hundred days to seventeen.[24]

The war also accelerated certain business developments already in progress. The need for efficient use of all transportation and labor led to new branch plants in undeveloped areas. On the economic side, the new factories brought lasting industrialization to parts of the South and West. On the business side, new centers presented problems in executive coordination, in managing a team whose players were separated by thousands of miles. Such problems plus close contacts with government administrative agencies led business to put greater emphasis on good communication for the control of large sprawling corporations. For smaller business, contracts and taxes also led to improved methods of accounting. Difficulties stemming from the war led the giant Standard Oil Company (New Jersey) to reconsider its entire administrative structure from 1941 on.[25] The result was not only the creation of new departments, but almost complete adoption of the principle of policy formation by committees. As Frank Abrams, its later chairman, explained: "It stands to reason that if you get five men together and one man is wrong, the mistake is going to be picked up. Or if one man has a good idea, the others will contribute to it and develop it."[26]

Comparison, from the standpoint of business, of the effectiveness of the organization of production in World War I and World War II is made difficult, if not impossible, by the real differences in the situation, and the differences in the chief published accounts. World War II placed twice as great a strain on the economy, and because of advances in technology much more than that on the supply of some materials. The chief accounts from World War I, which lasted only nineteen months, are, from January 1918 on, written by major participants and full of praise for accomplishments. Those for World War II, covering a couple of months short of four years, are by professional historians attached to certain agencies, who tried to be objective. Furthermore, in contrast to Bernard Baruch's satisfaction with the War Industries Board, Donald Nelson was severely critical of the pressures brought to bear on the WPB.

As said at the start of this chapter, the needs for new hierarchies of administrative power and nationwide bureaucracies in World War II were simply greater than could be met, here or abroad, in such a short period of kaleidoscopic external change. Each of the major agencies seemed to make unnecessary errors, but each cooperated well enough to release a large part of the enormous potential for war supply. Small business and the civilian economy may have suffered to an unnecessary degree, but helped by reconversion loans and a vast backlog of demand both recovered phenomenally in the first five years of peace.

Shortage of labor and a government friendly to collective bargaining produced a sharp wartime rise in real wages that led to both higher consumption and higher production in the postwar years. Since in the postwar inflation that followed the early abondonment of controls and rationing, wage rates outran price increases, and the value of inherited wealth and incomes of people on relatively fixed salaries lagged, it can probably be said that the war brought an advance in economic democracy.

Part Three
Toward a New Order, 1945–1971

9 A New Environment for Business

The general structure of business was not greatly changed by depression or war. The so-called "degree of monopoly" remained fairly constant; small enterprises continued to proliferate faster than the population as a whole; auxiliary aids in accounting, management, or engineering grew more numerous but played their customary roles; marketing followed established trends; and trade or professional associations, banks, and exchanges all performed the same basic functions as in earlier decades.[1] Yet the system operated with such different relations in technology, types of location, financial practices, relations with organized labor and the federal government that, as Arjay Miller of Ford said, "The emphasis these days is on opportunism, on a more nimble response to a shifting environment."[2]

Research and Technology

As usual, technology was a root cause of much of the institutional change. Quick results from large-scale research financed by the government during World War II convinced many entrepreneurs in industries where technology was advancing rapidly, such as chemicals, petroleum, airplanes, electronics, and some types of machinery, that it paid to invest in research and development. Such investment not only improved machines and processes, but as a by-product created new types of business and brought the sponsoring firms into new markets. By the 1950s management had become "research-minded." Whereas in earlier years such expenditures had often been hard to justify to bankers or boards of directors, now research came to be regarded in some lines as the most promising form of investment. By the mid-fifties 3,000 companies had research facilities employing 500,000 workers.[3] From the efforts of these workers, carefully oriented toward marketable products or improvements, came an unprecedented demand for new capital.

Nearly half the money spent for research by private business in 1955 came from federal agencies. This amount steadily increased as both aerospace and military operations became more important. By 1970 it was hard to separate federal and private support, since much aerospace research, privately funded, was for government contracts. The total in 1969 had risen to $27 billion, with the directly paid federal share still about half. Only about $4 billion was classed as "basic research" of which colleges, universities, and federal agencies did about two-thirds.[4] Although perhaps only a temporary result of depression, in 1970 business and government expenditures for research fell drastically.[5]

Whether basic science would progress rapidly enough to open new areas for application when old ones reached stability remained a question. In general, business money was not directly spent on basic scientific experimentation from which wholly new lines of procedure might emerge, but in perfecting and protecting existing processes and ways of doing things, or in a search for improvements that would soon be salable. There were of course exceptions, such as the interest of chemical companies in basically new products even if development costs were high, but the tendency was to work for the ultimate refinement of existing equipment or methods. Automobile companies, for example, wanted better performance from gasoline-driven vehicles, not a substitute for the automobile.

From corporate research came major improvements in electrical machinery, chemicals, and synthetic materials that affected nearly every aspect of daily living, altering the character of factories, business offices, homes, communications, and transportation. As mechanical operations gave way to more reliable electrochemical processes and natural products were replaced or modified by synthetic substitutes, there was usually a saving in the demand for labor. All types of new devices meant that, on the one hand, nearly every factory and home operated with less manual work, while on the other, they usually expanded the variety of products and services, opening new areas for both investment and jobs. To the consumer, the synthetic fibers used in many articles of clothing were the most obvious of the new products.

From the standpoint of massive achievement and demand for new capital investment, the most important single area of chemical alteration of natural products was in petroleum. Various fractions of crude petroleum became the raw material for a large part of the chemical industry, and chemical advances such as catalytic cracking completely altered oil refining. Although listed separately from the chemical industry by the census bureau, the high-octane gasoline that led in turn to high-horsepower gasoline motors was the product of complex chemical processes.

The elimination of manual operations took many forms. Processes controlled by central panels of electrically operated valves and meters were a step toward the automatic factory. Almost every new electrical or chemical process required fewer workers and allowed for more efficient operation than did older methods. Many of the new communication devices within the plant depended on the electronic vacuum tube developed before World War I. Operations involving sorting, counting, starting, or stopping were made automatic by the photoelectric cell, and cutting operations were replaced by stamping, pressing, and ultimately, in some cases, by lasers. In construction, labor-saving electric welding appeared, and prefabricated synthetic panels began to reduce the need for masons, carpenters, and plasterers. In transportation the steam locomotive was rapidly replaced by the diesel engine, which applied its power through electric motors. Atomic energy development, relying heavily on electrical processes, promised public-utility plants eventually operating at large savings in man-hours. Pipelines and conveyor belts, old in principle, were extended in the forties and fifties to reduce human handling of materials.

The vacuum tube, and in the 1950s the transistor, were the basis for new types of electronic enterprise, particularly in radio and television (which greatly affected advertising) and in "miniaturizing" or further automating many processes. The computer, an adaptation of the same technological advances, promised to affect all types of business operations.

A result of academic research just after the war, the electronic digital computer was commercially available in the 1950s. Applied to mass data problems such as inventory control, sales figures, re-production of complex specifications, and more elaborate accounting, it became after some years of trial and error a valuable aid to the management of lower-level operations. By 1971 there were about 70,000 computers in use and perhaps half a million specialists of high or low degree trying to design ways of making them work better. "We have a long way to go," said a management consultant, "before the computer can talk the management language, and managers can talk the computer's language."[6] Special companies arose to sell computer time or programs, and big corporations, such as those in aerospace, rented the use of idle equipment so that small companies could gain the benefits of mass data-processing without a prohibitive investment in capital or labor. Computer costs in many businesses, however, were still running much higher than the old methods of operation, and were only justified by hope for future efficiencies.[7] They were also, as we shall see in Chapter 11, threatening to submerge higher management in a sea of facts and figures.

Apart from their effects on management and the economy, the results of scientific and technological research made the United States less dependent on Europe for knowledge and new processes. In fact, by World War II the United States was abreast of or leading the other nations of the Western world in most areas of applied science. In the 1940s the traditional pattern was noticeably altered: instead of Americans rather uniformly going to Europe to see what was new, European business leaders now sent observers to the United States. Yet in the practical effects of research on productivity, America fell behind its own record of the 1920s and from 1950 to 1970 behind Japan and, except for Britain, behind the leading nations of Europe in the rate of increase of industrial production.[8] In part this lag per capita came, as with England before World War I, from having more capital invested in old equipment and hence finding it harder to adapt to new technology; in part it was because the Japanese and some of the European rates were very high; and in part it may have resulted from the effects of affluence on lessening the drive for work and wealth.

The Shift from the Cities

Growth in production alone could not measure the changes in ways of life and business that took place first in America and soon all over the industrial world. Despite the dramatic governmental growth inaugurated by the New Deal and World War II, or the social and economic importance of the maturity of the giant corporation and its managerial system, or the potential cultural effects of the rise of radio and television, later historians may characterize the period from 1925 to 1960 as that of "the motorization of the United States." The Rooseveltian concept of the welfare state would no doubt be of major importance in times of business recession, and the changes in management and electronic communication would, in time, profoundly and subtly alter human relations, but the effect of the automobile was immediate. Like the steam railroad from 1840 to 1880, it changed the face of the nation.

Because of automobiles people not only traveled and sent goods differently, they lived and thought differently. As noted in Chapter 2, the motor industry continued to be the greatest stimulant to American investment, drawing private capital into rubber, glass, electrical equipment, steel, and other metals; while indirectly it was responsible for millions of new suburban homes, stores, offices, and factories, and for massive government expenditures on highways, bridges, and tunnels. During the twenties government construction of roads for automobiles had become, except for buildings, the largest type of investment. By 1940 the network of paved highways represented a capital outlay as big as that in railroads, and larger than that in public utilities. Following World War II building construction again became the greatest consumer of capital, but much of the new investment was in locations made accessible only by continuously large expenditures for roads.

From the standpoint of the businessman, the automobile and truck had joined with electricity in offering economies from relocation. The nineteenth- and early twentieth-century pattern of plant location had been dictated by rail transportation for materials, products, and workers. Factories had been built at trunk-line junction points, both to gain the lower competitive rates and to be assured of an adequate supply of labor. Within a metropolitan area the tendency had been to locate at central points where railroad lines converged. Here goods could easily be shipped or received from the various roads, and workers from all parts of the area could reach the plant by train and trolley. These advantages had to be paid for, however, in high land prices and taxes.

By 1950 trailer trucks with oil-burning diesel engines could compete effectively even with long-distance rail service. Although it cost more per ton-mile to haul the load on a concrete highway, the savings in time, loading, terminal charges, and overhead costs might make the total expense less than by rail. Furthermore, to gain the essential economy of even carload shipments to particular markets was difficult for some medium-sized producers, while trucks gave them a means for economically shipping small quantities at any time. In all the major industrial sections and in many rural areas, reasonably priced electric power freed manufacturers from the need for access to cheap coal. Combined with the efficiency of small-scale use of electric power, these factors enabled smaller enterprises to live in competition with larger ones. Furthermore, country or suburban locations relieved managers of some of the problems connected with hiring blacks or other urban minority groups.

More and more Americans thought of travel whether for work or play in terms of the automobile. By the forties industrial plants, except those in the biggest cities, provided parking facilities and with some use of other people's cars practically everyone who wanted to could ride to work "privately," which usually made a suburban or even a country location more attractive to employees than one in the central city. Since prestige was attached to driving rather than by going by bus, some transportation companies found waiting buses, ready to start at the end of the shift and go to within a short walk of workers' homes, virtually unoccupied. Meanwhile, as the truck freed many companies from the need of rail connections, it was possible to use cheap land for large plants.

Office work not directly connected with outside personal contacts responded to the same influence. Increasingly, record-filing, calculating, planning, drafting, and laboratory work accompanied manufacturing in its move to the country. While central cities remained the chief meeting place for financiers, brokers, special consultants, jobbers, and wholesalers, the retailers and service suppliers followed their customers to the country. In order to survive, big-city department stores found it necessary to open rural or small-city branches, and motion picture displayers built country "drive-ins" or theaters in shopping centers.

The term "country" exaggerates the usual shift, which was from a central city to its more thinly populated suburban fringe. There was still an advantage in being near the large quantities of labor, the big banks, the suppliers, and the distributors of the metropolis. Distant sites near country towns were likely to be occupied by plants that needed only a moderate amount of labor, run by concerns that could supply managerial and skilled employees from other offices. The head office would ordinarily remain in its original city, from which by telephone, teletype, and airplane it could manage branches in areas of cheap land and often nonunion labor.

New developments, such as the general spread of electric light and power lines to country districts, reliable electric pumps, quick-heating electric stoves, radio and television, higher real wages, and federal mortgage credit for homes, aided the automobile in dispersing population. Workers and managers were not only willing but anxious to leave city apartments to become suburban or country homeowners. Analysis of the movement for the 1960s showed a more rapid rate of growth in employment for cities in the twenty-five thousand to one million group than for larger ones, with old industries such as textiles, apparel, and woodworking seeking static or declining regions where poorly skilled labor might be in surplus, and the younger expanding industries, more in need of auxiliary services, moving to the big metropolitan areas. Unfortunately, blacks leaving the South also migrated to these big centers where unskilled labor was often not in demand.[9]

Movement of all types continued the building construction business as one of the most important in the nation. Without any significant new machinery beyond improved bulldozers and gasoline shovels, contractors managed to effect some economies by building many houses at once and thereby getting more continuous productive work from each of the numerous types of specialized labor. Some progress was also made in factory prefabrication of house panels and units of equipment. As a net result, mass builders like the Levitt brothers could produce houses in large developments near New York and Philadelphia for about two-thirds the cost of individual construction. By 1971, mobile homes made in attachable units provided houses of up to 24 by 60 feet or more, at about half the cost of conventional construction and their sales were rising rapidly.

Such economies still would not have put new houses within the reach of average families whose income was under $4,000 a year in 1950 and whose cash savings were insignificant, had it not been for government-guaranteed mortgages on small homes. Under the Act of 1950, the government guaranteed practically the whole cost for veterans. Furthermore, mortgages could run up to twenty-five years with payments of interest and principal arranged so that a uniform amount was paid each month. For the first time in American history the white working man with a job but no savings could buy where he chose on reasonable terms. Thus the government partially underwrote the housing boom and the relocation of business that followed World War II. By 1954, 20 million government-guaranteed loans had been made, covered by $30 billion worth of mortgage insurance.[10] Federal policies also had an important effect on private lending institutions, which dropped the idea of first and second mortgages repayable only in large amounts and adopted the "packaged" form with a uniform monthly payment, even when no government guarantee was involved.

In spite of the fact that most of these factors were operating as early as the 1930s, the shift to the country was not rapid in the period before World War II. In addition to depression, difficulty in disposing of existing plants or offices except at a large loss in terms of their cost of replacement, and fear of a poorer labor supply in the suburban or country areas, were among the factors retarding movement from the older central cities. When it came to moving to or establishing a branch plant in another section of the country, the problem of administration was often a serious deterrent. Unskilled labor might be available in an agricultural region, but the important nucleus of highly skilled or managerial labor would be lacking. If the plant needed a lot of such labor, a move from an older industrial area presented difficulties, and subsequent skilled-labor turnover would be a menace to production.

The government offer of quick amortization of the cost of new plants as a deduction from taxes or of construction of plants for lease to operators in World War II, however, spread industry into the South and the West. Most of the states west of the Mississippi River gained industry at an increasing rate because of the war and kept many of their plants in operation afterward. Nevertheless, the movement away from the older sections is easy to exaggerate. While the value added by manufacture increased almost fourfold in California and Texas between 1939 and 1947, the same figure rose threefold in Ohio and Illinois, and nearly that much in New York and Pennsylvania.

Of the ten major metropolitan manufacturing areas, ranked by value added by manufacture, Boston, Pittsburgh, and Buffalo each dropped one place between 1939 and 1947, and Los Angeles,

Cleveland, and San Francisco-Oakland advanced one place. The position of the big four — New York, Chicago, Detroit, and Philadelphia — remained unchanged. Twenty years later the first ten included the same manufacturing centers except for Rochester having displaced its neighbor Buffalo.

Business in Family Machines

Families of the nineteenth century had prized big homes, fine furniture, and good horses, none of which were made by big business. Before the middle of the twentieth century the most valued possessions, for both convenience of living and social prestige, had become electrical household equipment, television, and automobiles, all products of giant companies. These new durable consumer goods had much in common with one another and nearly the whole range of products might be made by one big company. The automobile, by far the most important single product, probably exemplifies the general character of the entire business.

The great depression demonstrated the maturity and stability of the automobile business. It ceased to be among the most rapidly growing, but it continued to sell cars to people who lacked money for what an earlier generation would have regarded as necessities of food and housing. Instead of falling to near zero, as bankers had feared they might, automobile sales about followed the average for all business.

The automobile emphasized particularly the aspects of mass production associated with direct public consumption. By the middle thirties the industry comprised some thousand factories owned by over eight hundred companies, as well as thousands of smaller subcontractors and distributors. The producing end of the business used about half the nation's malleable iron, a fifth of the steel output, and around three-quarters of all glass and rubber. Large-scale operations and large capital investment characterized the final manufacturing stages of this and other mass-production businesses. The main manufacturing plants of even the smaller companies were very large, normally employing upwards of five thousand workers,

and representing investments of over $50 million each. The industry
continued to be dominated by General Motors, Chrysler, and Ford,
who produced 80 to 95 percent of the domestic total, and General
Motors came to be the nation's largest industrial company. Even the
specialized manufacturers of parts usually operated very large plants.
While technological improvement continually increased efficiency,
there was presumably no place in the whole productive operation
where added size would lead to any considerable saving in direct
manufacturing cost.

As a result of many years of engineering effort, the final products
and most parts were highly standardized. This, however, presented
one of the dilemmas of mass production for the consumer market.
To keep down costs it was desirable to make very few changes in
design. By never changing a simple model, Henry Ford had sold cars
in the twenties at incredibly low costs — for less than $800 retail in
terms of the 1971 value of money — whereas no new car in the
latter year, even after taxes were deducted, could sell for nearly so
low a price. But ultimately even Ford was speared on the other horn
of the dilemma, failure to appeal to a changing public taste.

The problem for the manufacturers was to make each year's
products different enough so that those who could raise the money
would be coaxed to buy, without incurring large costs at the factory
for retooling the assembly lines. Although the same situation existed
in principle for other high-priced, mass-produced durables, it proved
undesirable for several reasons to pay for as rapid a stylistic obsoles-
cence as occurred in the case of passenger automobiles. The other
durables might be concealed within the owner's home, but he
appeared in public in his automobile; newness and cost, therefore,
became matters of obvious social prestige.

These considerations put a premium on automobile advertising and
selling. Since the number of producers was small, and a rapid approach
to monopoly by any one firm would undoubtedly have been met by
antitrust prosecution, price competition at the factory was minimized.
Wholesale prices were adminstered, as in a monopoly, to seek the
level that in the long run would show the largest total profit. All

producers either reached about the same conclusions or followed the lead of one of the big three as to price.

On the retail front, the situation was different. Here, in automobiles and other consumer durable goods, thousands of dealers competed strongly with one another. In years when demand was slack, the wise buyer demanded and received large discounts. The entire single-price structure of American merchandising, built by the big retailers of the late nineteenth century, was crumbling. In 1971 it was still too early to see the ultimate trends of this new stage of retail price warfare.

Because of their high cost and long life, consumer durables in general and automobiles in particular spread the practice of installment selling. By the late forties installment sales had put durable-goods purchases largely on a "pay-as-you-go" basis. Late in 1954 a newspaper cartoon showed a banker admonishing a teller arrested for embezzlement, "If you wanted nice things, why didn't you get them on installments like the rest of us!"

Institutional Capitalism

Installment selling, packaged mortgages, and deductions from pay for pensions, medical plans, and social security were all aspects of a new organizational or institutional form of capitalism in which the individual had his saving mandated by claims against his already heavily taxed income. The average man might never become the owner of much disposable personal capital, and even successful business executives could be well into middle age before they started appreciable voluntary saving.

The decline of the independent capitalist was, of course, reflected in the character of capital markets. From World War II on, most of the new capital came from corporate reserves; about half the rest came from long-term bank credit; of the remainder, raised by public flotations on the security markets, about three-quarters was supplied by various funds. This left the old-fashioned "risk-taking" individual investor responsible for only about 5 percent of the total. These estimates, stemming from the Federal Reserve Bank, could not take account of all the millions of forms of individual investment of time or money in home improvement or small business ventures. But undoubtedly most of the estimated twenty-five million stockholders of 1971 owned shares in investment funds and eschewed the risks of new issues of securities. Or looked at another way, the market for new securities was so small among the upper-income group that individual solicitation on the pattern of the 1920s no longer paid.

Since there was a shortage of capital for business purposes throughout most of the period after World War II, various organizations tried to make up for the lack of individual investors. In addition to pension and general investment funds, commercial banks entered the long-term capital market more openly than ever before, with five- to fifteen-year loans. Insurance companies, freed to make limited investments in equities by modification of state laws, represented another immense pool of saving. In addition, from 1954 on the Small Business Administration would guarantee a limited amount on loans, and some local organizations (such as chambers of commerce) offered long-term loans to build business in their communities.

By the middle sixties twenty-five years of tolerably continuous prosperity and inflation had built some large new personal fortunes, particularly in real estate and oil. Using the credit of one company to buy control of another, ambitious financial operators were putting together "conglomerates," reminiscent of the old pyramided holding companies except that the associated enterprises were often in widely diverse types of business. Incentives behind such expansion, usually carried out with a large amount of borrowed capital, included balancing the tax losses of one firm against the gains of another, tapping unused corporate reserves for new investments, cutting costs by firing or retiring apparently unnecessary managers, and a faith that modern accounting and management theory could provide a guide to success. As of 1971 the movement had resulted in more spectacular failures than successes. There still seemed to be truth in the old belief that each type of business had its own problems, particularly in marketing, whose solutions required some experience and specialized knowledge.

This new environment of institutional investors and predatory big capitalists offered a threat to management in all but the very largest companies. Officers of one or more of the funds could decide to buy control of a company by "overhead tenders" (direct offers to the stockholders) and the existing management, lacking comparable resources, had to abide by the results. At best the new owners might alter the control of the board, at worst they might replace the entire top management.

In one sense the new world of finance was not unlike that of the early era when Morgan; Lee, Higginson; or Kuhn, Loeb might juggle boards and management. But in the sixties less power rested with the investment houses and much more with the funds, which had been a negligible influence before World War I. While the situation marked a revival of the power of private finance, it was on a different basis than in the days of J. Pierpont Morgan, George F. Baker, and James Stillman. There was a money influence composed of banks, funds, and insurance companies rather than a "money trust." Groups of these controllers of pooled capital would lend money to, or buy securities from, individual corporate operators such as James Ling or Howard Hughes, but the initiative or leadership appeared to be with the operators rather than with the bankers or executives of the funds.

Business and Government in Partnership

In another area capitalism also became a more closely knit web. In spite of loud protests and mutual distrust, the New Deal and World War II forced business and government to work more closely together, a relationship which grew in importance in later years. At the close of his book *Laissez-Faire and the General Welfare State*, Sidney Fine chooses the Employment Act of 1946 to symbolize the final blow to the idea of a federal government of closely restricted powers, separated from the activities of business. This law established the President's Council of Economic Advisers with responsibility for reporting the measures necessary to preserve economic stability and full employment. In the words of President Truman, the act specifically rejected laissez faire and asserted that "our economy within reasonable limits will be what we make it, and intelligent human action will shape our future."[11] Later presidents continued to make active use of the recommendations of the advisers, but usually to support policies regarded as politically desirable.

Business firms had to assign additional employees to the tasks of understanding new federal regulations and of dealing with still more agencies. More than ever before, Washington was the home of large numbers of legislative counselors, or lobbyists, representing all varieties of business activity. Agencies such as the Federal Trade and Securities Exchange commissions found it valuable to seek the advice of business. For this purpose conferences were held and advisory committees of businessmen appointed. If business and government were both to be held socially responsible for the general welfare, there had to be real communication between them.[12]

Taxes, contracts, and legislation made men who knew their way around Washington, such as ex-government officials, valuable employees. A man who had just left a government agency not only knew how to deal with it from the business side, but also had friends among its personnel. Defense contracts made retired military or naval men useful corporate officials. Big companies were also glad to have one or two of their executives take leave to work in government departments where a sympathetic understanding of the business side would be of use. "Time and again," wrote E. Pendleton Herring, "our commissions have been run by officials who are merely the pale reflections of the very interests they are supposed to regulate."[13]

Higher personal and corporate taxes led to changes in business structure and procedures. High taxes on earnings encouraged prosperous companies to merge with money-losing firms that could be built up, rather than pay what they regarded as unwarranted returns to the government. Wartime excess profits taxes worked in the same direction. Companies that currently showed losses but might expect good earnings in the future, when it was hoped that taxes would be lower, were valuable investments for firms with large profits. Both of these pressures led to more product diversification by large companies. Since a maximum personal tax of only 25 percent was paid on capital gains, it was better for the receivers of large incomes to make additional money from property manipulation rather than from salaries or dividends. If a small business achieved great success, the best way to make "after tax" money was to sell it. The tax laws, therefore, were an incentive toward the business concentration that the government was trying to prevent.

War contracting also tended to make big business bigger. Of $18 billion worth of war plants built by private companies between 1950 and 1953, three-quarters were units with values exceeding $50 million. Of plants built directly by the government, about half — over $7 billion worth — were constructed and operated under contracts with only thirty-one corporations.[14]

Government contracts continued to provide a large part of the income of big manufacturing companies. In the fiscal year 1950–51, during the Korean War, one hundred corporations received over $18 billion in defense contracts.[15] While at that time General Motors led with $2.4 billion followed by United Aircraft with $1.2 billion, by the later stages of the war in Vietnam the airplane companies were the leaders. The Korean War brought a renewal of the excess-profits tax, so effectively employed in World War II, but fast write-offs of depreciation drew much of the sting for those companies that needed to expand. During the period of the Korean War $17 billion of new plant expenditures were rapidly written off, allowing the companies involved to acquire large tax-free reserves. Prime contracting for military supplies remained largely in the hands of some 150 big firms, which passed subcontracts on to their usual suppliers.

As military spending continued at high levels throughout the 1950s and 1960s, companies in a few industries such as uranium mining or aerospace came to be, like the older city paving contractors, private businesses with the government as their chief customer. In the case of airframes, for example, with the government buying over 85 percent of the product and aiding in financing its very costly development, and with business-trained technologists on both sides of the bargaining table, the real location of entrepreneurial decisions was hard to determine.

Medium and small business gained from federal activity in other ways. The Small Business Administration was established in 1953 to make or guarantee loans that otherwise would be hard or impossible to place, and also offered various kinds of advice and research. Small business was defined for assorted purposes as up to 100 or 1,000 employees, and thirteen regional offices had authority to make loans for as much as $150,000. In spite of a jurisdiction covering the operations of the vast majority of American businessmen, and nearly all blacks and recent immigrants, the administration never developed much drive, or political leverage. By 1971 it had authorized only a little over $2 billion in loans and, under a new administrator, was seeking a higher limit on lending.[16] Much of the contracting for urban construction was financed by federal renewal programs and the construction of educational facilities was aided by federal grants.

Medium- and large-scale farmers also profited, sometimes greatly, from agricultural benefit payments. Thus there was not only a continued big-business – military interest in national politics, but also a political alliance between many other businessmen and commercial farmers, made potent by the control of key congressional committees by southerners, who often personally represented both business and farming activities. In fact, political scientists were coming to think that the strongest economic pressures in Congress came from the individual interests of its members who were, in general, part-time businessmen or business lawyers. Ownership in television stations, for example, was a particularly attractive business activity for politicians.

Foreign aid was another government support for business. Nations that could not otherwise have bought in the American market were enabled, and often compelled, to enter large contracts with American firms. Some old businesses, with established foreign outlets, were not enthusiastic about such government encouragement to newcomers. Advocates of expanding world trade, such as the *Wall Street Journal* and *Fortune*, argued against restricting the placement of orders based on foreign aid to suppliers in the United States.[17]

By the late 1950s American export firms were taking advantage of lower wages in Europe to invest in foreign enterprises, that is, exporting capital rather than goods. Since most of this money went to the highly developed nations, in the early 1960s the federal government sought to alter the flow by offering guarantees for certain types of investment in less developed areas. But by 1971 most of the $60 billion in direct investments abroad was in the leading industrial nations and most of the remainder in oil properties.

By no means were all the new interrelations with government welcomed by large companies. In 1937, with Thurman W. Arnold in charge of the antitrust division of the Department of Justice, emphasis on competition had been revived. His philosophy, endorsed by the administration, was to prosecute collusive agreements, rather than to try to break up big companies. By introducing more competition into semimonopolistic markets, Arnold hoped to lower prices and increase production. In 1940, prosecutions had reached eighty-seven a year, more than were brought during the entire "trust-busting" administration of Theodore Roosevelt. From 1940 to 1948, the Sherman Act was invoked by the Department of Justice more times than in the preceding fifty years.[18] In 1950, the Cellar-Kefauver Act extended the Clayton Act of 1914 to cover mergers that might simply be "against the public interest."

Extension of the provisions of the law, however, did not clarify its enforcement. A basic problem for business was that action might be initiated either by the Federal Trade Commission or the antitrust division of the Department of Justice, and their policies did not necessarily coincide. In general, the FTC spent its time investigating dishonest advertising and price-fixing, while the Justice Department proceeded against proposed mergers, but these distinctions were not always adhered to, nor were the orders of one authority binding on the other.

In September 1969 *Fortune* attacked the antitrust policy of the business-oriented Nixon administration, saying, "Unhappily, he is missing a rare opportunity to reform a sadly decayed field," and called for a bolder antitrust division that would "intervene in state and federal regulations — which often act less to protect consumers than to preserve business fiefdoms."[19]

Regardless of presidential attitudes and the energy of some government prosecutors, the results from 1950 to 1971 were not striking. The laws had been warped and twisted by generations of judicial decisions until their legal applications were far from clear. The chief effects of the many court actions, and particularly of a successful criminal prosecution of price-fixing by electrical company executives in 1960, were to make companies more careful in the creation of records that would indicate collusion in pricing and less anxious to drive out the medium-sized competitors who constituted proof that competition still existed.

In the export market the Webb-Pomerene Act of 1918 had allowed American firms to join international cartels without risking antitrust prosecution. International trade in raw materials, such as rubber, coffee, nitrates, potash, copper, and tin, fell under the control of cartels in which American companies participated. Use of patents and erection of branch plants in foreign nations also led to cartel arrangements. For the firms on the inside, the agreements spelled security and price maintenance; for those on the outside, they appeared to be barriers to progress. At the end of World War II, President J. Howard Pew of Sun Oil Company denounced cartels as "the primary reason for the backwardness of European industry. . . . Their effect has been to destroy initiative; close the door of opportunity for new individual entrepreneurs and small business units; encourage inefficiency; raise prices and thus lower the standard of living."[20] In spite of their unpopularity with many American businessmen, international cartels continued to thrive in later decades.

Business and Labor

For companies in the unionized industries that employed about a quarter of the labor force, one of the most important aspects of the new environment was nationwide collective bargaining. Although unions were restrained from sympathetic picketing and closed-shop contracts unless specifically voted upon, and made responsible for damages due to breach of contract by the Taft-Hartley Act of 1947, the law had little effect on the "cost push" inflation that was the rule from 1945 on.

Experience quickly demonstrated that it was better for companies in manufacturing industries with little or no price competition to compromise on higher wages and compensate through higher prices than to endure long strikes. On the other hand, small employers, (as in building construction) were at a great disadvantage in dealing with national unions. By pace-setting strikes organized labor was continually able to raise wages faster than either gains in productivity per worker or increases in the general price level. Many companies resisted organization by meeting union wages and benefits, so that union gains ultimately affected all of industry and real wages advanced in all but a few years of the period. While in manufacturing some of the increase in wages was compensated for by increases in productivity, in trade and service this was harder to accomplish, and the overall increase in American productivity was never sufficiently rapid.

A historian of business notes that around the end of the fifties "a pathological fear of inflation had taken the place of a pathological fear of government."[21] Yet the cure involved a contradiction so fundamental that political leaders hesitated to take effective action — to wit, the control of wages and prices by law in the interest of preserving free enterprise. By 1971, unions were negotiating annual wage increases of 10 to 15 percent, while the government was intermittently using monetary policy to try to keep inflation below 6 percent. The domestic result was depressed business because of high interest rates and uncertainty regarding the future value of money. Externally, exports were checked and the "balance of payments" deficit increased. By early August of 1971 both inflation and the trade deficit were advancing so rapidly that the President, acting under a recent Emergency Powers Act, declared a ninety-day wage-price freeze. At the end of this period wage and price boards were appointed to prevent unduly large increases, particularly by big business. In late 1971 and early 1972 these agencies had had some success in checking inflation, and economists were predicting a rate of 3 or 4 percent for the coming year.

There were, in addition, some long-run trends favorable to greater wage-price stability. Plant and construction workers who benefited the most from wage increases were collectively a declining segment of the labor force. In 1950 these and other "blue-collar" workers had outnumbered the "white" by a narrow margin, while by 1971 they were less than three-quarters as numerous. Or looked at another way, in a rapidly growing population their number increased only a little. Taking the national scene as a whole in 1971, there were nearly three-quarters as many managerial, proprietary, professional, and technical workers as blue collar. What the computer would do to these relations and to wage bargaining power in the succeeding decade was hard to guess.

In admission policies, many unions discriminated against blacks or in favor of other minority groups, but the changing environment of the larger cities and government action brought management more serious problems regarding job discrimination. As black migration from country to city took the place of the old European immigration, company hiring policies, particularly in the more desirable firms, failed to readjust to the new composition of the urban population. With the rise of the civil rights movement in the 1950s, the industrial states passed equal opportunity legislation and set up human rights commissions to enforce it. By the sixties civil rights groups and black militants were adding to the legal pressure on hiring policies.

Many big companies found themselves poorly equipped to meet the situation. While not as bad as pictured by Robert Townsend of Avis, who advocated the firing of every personnel department and replacement by a "one-girl people department," procedures were unquestionably biased and out of date. Educational credentials and job specifications were used as convenient devices for screening applicants, although they might have no demonstrable correlation with success on the job.[22] In fact, the hiring policies even of large companies might, as applied to any given applicant, be quite irrational or based on "nonability" criteria. An executive of a large New York bank said: "You can usually tell when a man was hired in this place by his last name. Thirty years ago we had a bias in favor of Germans and Swiss, even for the lowest level job. Then during the war we began to let the Irish in. By Korea we were employing Italians and Jews. Now we employ blacks and Puerto Ricans."[23]

Of 247 companies queried by Professor Jules Cohn, in the late 1960s 110 had set up special training programs for blacks, and most of the rest were doing something to alter their recruitment policies.[24] Manufacturing plants emphasized the young, while banks, public utilities, and other firms with tedious white-collar jobs were willing to train older blacks. Similar attention was not paid to other urban minority groups at the lower levels, and very little to any ethnic groups at the managerial level. Regarding the latter, the candidate was expected to fit the atmosphere of the company group, to belong to the same social clubs, perhaps even to live in a particular area; blacks, in particular, presented insoluble problems, although women too were essentially outsiders.

Only one of Professor Cohn's companies reported a special training program for women, but in any case an increase in their employment seemed almost certain. In spite of a large upswing in female employment during World War II, by 1950 the percentage of women in the labor force was again under 30 percent. Two decades later the figure was nearly 37 percent, with the decline of blue collar and the increase of government work both favoring continued growth. The different types of female employment had remarkably close totals. Listed in numerical order, retail trade, government, manufacturing, and service each employed from 4.9 to 6.0 million women.

Business and the Public

During the depression the old exhortatory forms of public relations were labeled as propaganda and became relatively ineffective or in some cases likely to produce the opposite results from those intended. There ensued seven or eight years of relative bankruptcy in both

financial support and new ideas. With business performance poor,
public-relations offices learned that it was action rather than fine talk
that counted. As A. H. Batten, president of an advertising agency, said
in 1937, "Any public relations worthy of the name must start with the
business itself. Unless . . . it can meet at every point the test of good
citizenship and usefulness to the community, no amount of public
relations will avail."[25]

The "new" public relations, from 1941 on, arose during a period of
continued prosperity in which performance by business exceeded most
citizens' expectations. Although statements by top executives may
often have done their company harm by making it appear that the
economic and social ideas of businessmen had not changed, the old
forms of public relations – speeches, news stories, advertisements –
were not abandoned. Public relations, however, came to be seen as a
"two-way street" which company officials as well as the public had to
explore. It was increasingly recognized by advisers that unless the
company lived up to the image they were trying to create, their effort
would fail. As a result the more advanced multiplant companies began
to conduct a realistic type of public relations among their workers and
in the local communities.

In the Du Pont Company, for example, the new public relations was
called the precinct system. Each of nearly one hundred separate plants
was charged with creating a friendly attitude toward the company
among its employees and in its area. The means to this end were wages
as high but no higher than those paid by the best employers in the area;
"fringe benefits" in excess of those generally incorporated in union
contracts, although few plants had outside unions; a strong emphasis
on safety and health; contributions to community activities and active
participation in them by the local executives. A General Electric
Employee Relations News Letter of January 7, 1953 urged: "First,
let our employees' families and their neighbors know what we are
trying to do (and are doing) to be good employers, good buyers of
local products and services; good tax payers, good contributors to
charity and other worthwhile projects, and good corporate and individual citizens." "When we put a manager in a town," said President

McHugh of the New York Telephone Company, "we say to him in effect, 'This is your town . . . you are going to be loyal to this community.' "[26] Some men who were rising rapidly in big companies moved on to other areas, but many middle-level executives spent their lives in one plant and became an integral part of the community.

Another public-relations development was the increase in foundations or institutes by which companies invested tax-free money in furthering public understanding through research or free services. From 1935 on, the Internal Revenue Service allowed companies to contribute 5 percent of their income to tax-exempt welfare or educational institutions. Gradually, by taking a broader view of the welfare of the company, the courts acquiesced in this diversion of stockholders' money. Passing contributions through the hands of a tax-exempt foundation created by the company had the advantage that money could be paid in only in years of high profits, but could be distributed to the beneficiaries of the foundation in uniform annual amounts.[27] Also, a foundation could practice more systematic philanthropy than busy top executives, who were inclined to follow their personal sentiments. Of Professor Cohn's companies thirty-six gave through foundations, but the total of all corporate giving in 1966 was only 6 percent of national philanthropy, and the rate was not increasing.[28]

In assessing these new corporate attitudes based on good relations from positive performance, two factors should be noted. First, the liberal policies of pay and contributions and the new assumption of social responsibility had grown up during a period of general prosperity. Second, these policies perhaps had continuing strength because of their suitability to the managerial role. As noted in Chapter 5, the managers of most big companies were not large owners of company securities and to many of them, at least, good employee and customer relations gave more personal satisfaction than their relations with the stockholders.

Consumer democracy was more emphasized as the ethical basis for the arbitrary powers of management than it had been in the earlier part of the century. The consumer by his choices was held to decide which products would continue on the market, and which companies would succeed. Like municipal democracy, this is true in a broad sense. If lack of enterprise by existing producers limits choices for too long a period, some outside company will probably enter that market with a more desirable product, just as a long period of corrupt machine control usually leads to a municipal reform movement; but the adjustment is far from automatic.

Two contrary trends may be noted in providing the goods the consumer wanted most at the lowest possible price. On the one hand, the cost of starting complicated mass-production processes increased greatly in the years after 1941. In the 1950s $100 million was probably too little with which to establish a successful automobile company. On the other hand, the great corporations increasingly became all-purpose companies with large capital resources that could be invested in anything promising a good continuing profit. Their specialists were constantly surveying the industrial field for soft spots in the production of other companies where competition would pay, or for new products that could find a market. The search on the part of both manufacturers and distributors to find new uses for old products was also part of the response to "consumer sovereignty."

Effects of New Mass Media

Radio and television gave a new effectiveness to both public-relations messages and advertising. The three national networks were big businesses themselves and all but a few of the local stations were run as profit-making operations. By 1971 there were over 5,000 radio broadcasting stations and nearly 700 producing television. More than in the case of newspapers, magazines, or moving pictures, the content of radio and television production was closely geared to the desires of advertisers. The latter wanted broadcasts with a general content favorable to the business of the sponsor, that would attract maximum audiences of the proper type. By World War II, audience size could be checked by a number of methods.[29]

The actual business arrangements were between advertising agencies and the managers of stations; unlike print media, where the agency designed the advertisement but not the rest of the periodical, broadcasting sponsors kept a close watch on the content of the shows on which their commercials appeared.

In addition to exerting a greater substantive control of media, the electronic advertiser reached a much larger percentage of those looking at the medium. An ad in a magazine or newspaper could easily be skipped and therefore reached only a small minority of the potential readers, whereas on radio or television it took the positive action of turning off the program to prevent absorbing some of the message. Thus, although total advertising expenditures remained a smaller percentage of the gross national product than in the decades before 1929, they probably had a greater effectiveness.

While advertisers seldom attempted direct propaganda in the content of sponsored shows, television emphasized high consumption and business-like values. Subconsciously viewers became attuned to certain standards and practices desired by sellers. Yet, in a business-oriented society this seemed nearly inevitable. Increased control by government, as was the case in most western European nations, appeared to make no striking change in this respect, while opening the way for equally subtle political influences.

Whether because of better public relations, higher levels of prosperity, or greater distrust of government, more Americans seemed to be accepting the existing business system as the least of the potential evils. The practices of communism had badly damaged the ideal of democratic socialism. Radical parties were negligible in strength, and the protests of the young were ill defined both economically and politically. Aside from foreign affairs, neither major party sponsored marked change in government policies generally designed in the interests of business. In 1955, a poll by *Look* magazine indicated 80 percent approval of business, although three-quarters of the respondents also thought existing types of regulation "necessary and proper." By 1971, the subject of general approval of business was no longer regarded as important enough to be included in the various polls.[30]

10 American Businessmen

The postwar environment and a subsequent generation of growth continued to produce rapid proliferation of small firms.[1] Big corporations might steal the newspaper headlines and magazine articles and to most foreigners typify the American business system, but the average businessman was in reality still a proprietor who owned a large share in a small enterprise. This remained true even if the term "businessman" was broadly interpreted to include administrators well below the top levels. Although no reliable figures are available, it appears certain that the total of all men occupying executive positions in the 35,000 medium-sized and big businesses in 1950 was less than the 3.5 million active proprietors and partners of unincorporated business alone. In 1971 these relations were much the same, and American business was still a realm of small operators.

The Realm of Small Business

More business establishments and more self-employment came with increasing affluence and developing technology. From 1930 to 1971 the population of the United States grew by two-thirds while the number of business firms increased from three to eight million. The fastest growing sector, a third of all businesses in 1971, was "service," comprising such diverse activities as beauty parlors and barbershops, professional sports and motels. A quarter of all enterprises were in retail trade, more than a sixth in banking, brokerage, insurance, real estate, and other financial operations, and only a twentieth in manufacturing.[2] In each of the trade and service categories, firms with as many as a hundred employees were few in number. The "business world" as one experienced it in daily American life was largely composed of brokers, independent experts on this or that, distributors, retailers, small manufacturers, and contractors. These men, with a keen eye to personal profit, gave a competitive, enterprising character to the economy in spite of the giant corporations in manufacturing, finance, and public utilities.

The ability of a man with little or no capital to start a retail or service business was aided by a number of factors. Supply companies that rented costly equipment to retailers were in a position similar to landlords who wanted to keep their commercial properties occupied. Pumps, display cases, refrigerator rooms, or restaurant fixtures made no money while idle or stored away. It was better to take a chance on a new operator. Thus it was ease of entry rather than prospective profit that governed the influx of entrepreneurs to any given line, and asset-debt-liquidity considerations were usually the major worries of the small businessman.[3]

Although 90 percent of the retailers remained small independent owners, they increasingly employed cooperative devices to assist in competition with chain stores. A so-called "voluntary chain" of independently owned stores, supplied by a central wholesale agency, might be cooperatively owned by its outlets. Some large supply agencies, such as Rexall Drugs, undertook the retail promotion of their products and gave advice as to management. By 1950 half of the food sales by independent stores originated in cooperative or voluntary chain arrangements.

Some economists maintain that retailers supplied by one large wholesaling firm are not really independent entrepreneurs. Often they cannot set their own prices, work out their own advertising and display systems, or freely choose what they will buy. Therefore, they should be regarded more as managers working on a commission basis. Against this it can be argued that the proprietor owns or rents his place of business, hires and fires his employees, governs his own time, makes many small but perhaps crucial choices, and carries on all relations with his customers. If one insists that a "free enterpriser" be completely uncontrolled in his business decisions, then, what with intercompany agreements and government regulation, there is little free enterprise left in the economy.

While chain stores in all fields of retailing grew rapidly in the twenties, and their spread after World War II seemed obvious to any observer, the effect on overall sales and numbers of establishments in the twenty years after 1945 was surprisingly small. Total chain outlets rose from 163,000 to 220,000, but the percentage of all retail sales by large chains (101 or more stores) rose only from just under 42 percent to slightly over 43 (in 1963). Meanwhile, the number of stores with no payroll declined from 650,000 to 570,000, although the total number of retail shops rose slightly (1967). From these figures the picture that emerges is one of multiplication of new specialty shops for an affluent society concealed by relative stability in the overall numbers of stores.

The chain had some advantages in buying, and generally more capital to work with, but technologically there was nothing that the chain could do in an individual outlet which an independently owned one could not duplicate. For example, the owner of an independent department store in Houston, Texas, said in 1950 that he did not find competition with the chain stores difficult. He worked harder than a chain-store manager and had less overhead, better customer relations, and more flexibility.[4]

In manufacturing there were also many opportunities for small enterprise. Garment-making of several varieties continued to need little investment and had sales outlets adjusted to the small shop. The same was true for manufacture of most knit goods and some other textiles. A farm family could operate a machine for full-fashioned hosiery in off hours and peddle their products to selling agents at prices that undercut the "big" mills with two or three hundred employees on union wages. Carpentry and other branches of building construction were largely handicraft trades. A builder could subcontract those parts of his job requiring gasoline shovels or bulldozers and operate with nothing more than working capital, mostly supplied by a local bank on the basis of the contract. Job printing was another example of small business from which thousands of little entrepreneurs made a living.

Professor Soltow's study of eighty small metal fabricating companies, started mainly in Massachusetts between 1890 and 1957, found a number of reasons for the success of these enterprises.[5]. To begin with, they entered markets where their entrepreneurs saw — on the basis of either knowledge or experience — a "niche" for a new supplier. Presumably as technology becomes more complex the number of such niches increases; at least the rate of entry for the last seventeen years of Soltow's period was above the long-term average. Considering the requirements of metal working, it is significant that a quarter of the firms in this latter period started with under $5,000 in capital.[6]

To give any comprehensive idea of the range of manufactures, from bread and rolls to pillows and mattresses, would take many pages. Basically they thrived because of the network of business relationships. When a small manufacturer wanted to expand he usually had to look for an additional "niche," and he could learn about such opportunities from helpful equipment salesmen, friends in big companies, local bankers who had confidence in him, or manufacturers of the needed productive equipment whom he might see at trade association meetings. Each of these men had some interest in seeing the manufacturer fill the need, in one of the many thousand markets that were too small for a big company to bother with.

In all the small ventures — trade, service, or manufacturing — an investment of as much as $5,000 by the manager himself appears to have been rare.[7] Often $4,000 or $5,000 were collected by mortgaging a house or taking friends or relatives in as active or silent partners. With no outside help, three or four employees in a particular line of business could pool their savings and strike out for themselves. All of these considerations made personal factors and trade connections dominant forces in locating the firm.

Certainly the life expectancy of the young enterprise, whether in trade, service, or manufacturing, depended to a large degree on the adequacy of the capital for the type of business. Sampling studies show that infant mortality was usually the result of too little money. But there were other important causes of failure. Many men who knew the practical end of the business lacked the ability to keep accounts and do the necessary paper work. Others might lack training in all aspects of the venture that had attracted them. Inadequate general education played a conspicuous part in a good many bankruptcies.[8]

As with human beings, life expectancy increased once infancy was past. Studies indicated high mortality through the second year, when, presumably, initial capital ran out.[9] A study of manufacturing enterprises in an eastern urban area of about 50,000 population showed a further variation resulting from general business conditions. A quarter of the firms starting between 1929 and 1938 fell by the wayside within an average of three years, and more than a third survived over ten years. For those starting during the more favorable period 1939 to 1944, only a fifth succumbed at an average life of three years and almost half lasted more than ten.[10] Often the retirement or death of the proprietor of an old, well-established firm led to merger or sale.

The great depression was harder on small business than on big. The little man's profit margin was usually smaller than that of big business in good years, and when profits turned into losses he lacked reserves to draw upon for additional working capital. Banks and even the Reconstruction Finance Corporation looked skeptically at loan applications from firms that had no profits, no cash, and little net worth. From 1932 to 1939 the RFC advanced only about $33 million in loans of under $50,000 each.[11] That small companies survived and by 1939 were 10 percent more numerous than at the height of the previous boom is testimony to the great desire of Americans to work for themselves and to refuse to admit defeat. The decade of prosperity from 1940 to 1950 increased the number of enterprises by 20 percent and added greatly to their financial strength.

In 1953, Congress established a Small Business Administration which took over the advisory functions of the Small Defense Plants Administration created for the Korean War, and the lending functions of the former Reconstruction Finance Corporation. Loans limited to $150,000 could be extended directly or by guaranteeing up to 90 percent of advances made by local banks. As noted earlier, the new agency defined small business as firms with from less than 100 to less than 1,000 employees depending upon the type of activity. Thus the vast majority of American businesses could qualify for aid.

From time to time Congress legislated additional aids to "small" business, in which many Congressmen had a personal share. An act of 1958 gave small business corporations tax advantages estimated at over $250 million a year, such as exempting those with less than ten shareholders from corporation taxes, allowing losses (as in partnerships) to be deducted from personal incomes, raising the surtax levels, and allowing accelerated depreciation on equipment worth less than $10,000. To deduct stock losses up to $25,000 from personal income, the stock issue could not exceed $500,000 or the total assets of the corporation $1 million.

Companies set up for the purpose of investing in small business were also given tax advantages. In 1961, when 360 such corporations had a capital of over $300 million, they were allowed to borrow up to half their paid-in capital from the SBA and invest up to $500,000 in any one "small" company. As time went on, amounts were increased in an effort to give the small or medium-sized firm some compensation for the advantages the giant firm might gain by financing from internal reserves. Both the SBA and many small business investment firms favored minority ethnic groups, but progress in this direction was slow. In 1968, even in central-city areas classed as "ghetto" only 18 percent of the business establishments were owned by Negroes, and for the total of metropolitan areas the figure was 2.3 percent. In fact, one analyst held that neither tax advantages nor SBA loans helped really small business.[12]

Medium-Sized Business

While by government definition there was only large business and small business, in actuality (as discussed in Chapter 5) there was a

middle group that shared some of the problems of both and in many
ways set the tone of American business. While in order to be their
own bosses and to rise to higher social levels, men moved from blue-
or white-collar jobs to small business proprietorships, with inadequate
regard for most of the considerations necessary for profit, the medium-
sized entrepreneur usually had business experience and was perhaps
the businessman nearest to the classic "profit-maximizer."[13] The
proprietors of these companies had substantial capital investment in
their business, were usually well educated, regularly sought expert
advice, and seldom shifted back and forth between ownership and
employment by others.

Taking firms with between 100 and 500 employees as largely
representative of this middle group (although SBA loans were available
to some enterprises with as many as 1,500 workers, and 500 is used
because of census classifications), it numbered 63,000 firms in 1968,
which employed about a quarter of the labor force. Many of the
firms, judged by number of employees, were big for their type of
activity. Brokerage, law, accounting, or engineering offices with 400
or 500 employees would ordinarily have many partners, swelling the
number of owner-enterprisers in relation to the figures for firms. In
contrast to the "managerial" attitudes of the administrators of great
business bureaucracies, these entrepreneurs were old-style capitalists,
and collectively they exercised great influence over business ideas and
policies.

Medium-sized companies, often with college-trained management,
operated successfully in almost every line of activity. A Los Angeles
paint maker, for example, thus described the basis for the success of
his medium-sized firm: "Our distribution is based on local service
which larger companies are unable to provide. Great assistance is given
to dealers who sell on exclusive agreements. We give advice on store
management, supply imprinted mailings for customers, business cards
for professional painters, local advertising, and tie-ups with other
merchandise. The personal attitude is stressed in dealer relations."
Similarly, a steel fabricator in the East explained that his shop would
make a boiler, casting, or other metal part of any size and type,
whereas a big company would make only its standard models.

This last illustration points to the rigidity of large-scale mass production. For a company that was geared to a series of assembly lines to make something new was, because of high overhead costs, usually more expensive than for a small firm; in addition, the big company might have no labor and supervision available for such a job.

While the large company with a research staff had become the chief business source of innovation or invention in fields of applied science, the smaller firm, where things were still tinkered with by hand or considered in relation to special needs, seemed likely to be responsible for a large number of simple improvements. The innovating businesses could hope that the inertia of their biggest competitors would allow the little innovator to get a bit more of the market by pushing new styles, patterns, and designs.

Their more precarious competitive position and the fewer people involved put a greater strain on the individual managers for both alertness and teamwork than in bigger organizations. For example, a candy manufacturer with gross revenues of several million dollars a year, finding sales and profits falling off and no managerial agreement as to causes or cures, ended the troubles by getting rid of three of the five senior officers and replacing them where necessary by routine administrators at much lower salaries. The two remaining top executives, working in harmony, quickly reversed the financial trend.[14]

Judged by a few studies, the more highly capitalized medium-sized companies had long lives. Gertrude G. Schroeder, for example, found that of 179 steel-ingot producers incorporated at some date between 1901 and 1948, only 51 had failed; and of the 62 that led a continuous individual company life, all but 8 had been created before World War I.[15]

Types of Business: Old and New

The world of business continued to increase in intricacy and specialization. Old functions such as marketing remained basically the same, but many specific processes changed. While the giant national companies tended to absorb wholesale distribution through their own regional outlets, particularly for their major products, the multiplication of machines, household equipment, hardware, and software, much of it made by small producers, expanded wholesaling. In addition, the new machines of all types needed more specialized service, and even the biggest companies were inclined to arrange for such work with local firms.

Real estate brokerage, in essence the oldest business in America, continued to flourish. Inflation made real property more attractive than stocks or bonds to many investors, particularly to the rich who could arrange through mortgages to make large capital gains without much taxable income. Even in 1971, the estimate that in the history of the United States more money had been made from land than from manufacturing or transportation might still be true. While real estate trading and management were often combined with insurance brokerage to create a substantial medium-sized company, a single man with a secretary could still operate on his own.

In the two decades of postwar prosperity bankers recovered much of the short-term commercial credit business that had fallen away due to stock and internal financing in the twenties and lack of business needs in the thirties. Furthermore, a new business in small consumer loans, initiated by nonbanking finance companies in the 1920s, was entered into by nearly all commercial banks. With careful credit scrutiny, losses on unsecured personal loans ran as low as 1 percent and high interest charges brought profits larger than on business paper.

The rigidities of American banking laws, including the national banking system's treatment of accounts in default, the need for liquidity, and consequent conservatism regarding new types of risk, kept bankers out of sales financing for dealers and consumers long enough for outside companies to develop and become strong. While some of these enterprises went back to the early years of the century, they multiplied rapidly with the rise of automobile financing in the 1920s. Surviving the prohibitions on installment finance during World War II by going into other activities, the stronger companies flourished in the postwar boom and new ones appeared, until by 1950 there were three giant companies and hundreds of smaller ones.[16]

Savings and loan associations of several types competed successfully with banks for long-term financing. Less restricted as to liquidity, they were allowed to pay certificate holders a higher interest rate than savings banks paid to passbook holders and by 1971 the associations held the largest amount in mortgages.

During the period following the war the total number of banks declined slightly from over 14,000 to about 13,500. With less than a hundred suspensions, the drop came chiefly from mergers. Meanwhile, the number of workers in finance, almost entirely administrative and white collar, nearly doubled to 3.7 million in 1971, a rate of increase exceeded only by that of service in general and government.

The Attack on Competitive Price

In many industries and in some other types of business where a few firms were dominant, prices were set by various forms of tacit agreement, so that wholesalers, retailers, and franchised dealers bought at uniform, administered prices. But they had to sell at whatever the market would bear, hence even large retailing chains engaged in keen price competition with one another. The small retailer generally sought to hold his customers by charge accounts, deliveries, and other special services. These cost money, and he could not set his prices as low as large-scale cash-and-carry stores. His salvation, therefore, appeared to lie in some means of enforcing uniform retail prices.

In 1937, the National Association of Retail Druggists and other small-business trade associations persuaded Congress to pass the Miller-Tydings Act, permitting states to fix the prices of branded articles at retail regardless of the Sherman Antitrust Law.[17] By 1941, the representatives of small retailers had persuaded forty-five states to pass fair-trade laws fixing prices of branded commodities. If the laws could have been enforced, they might have given the retailer price protection that would have increased his profits. But enforcement proved impossible. Discount houses that sold for cash in defiance of the law quickly appeared.

In 1951, the United States Supreme Court ruled that no one who had not signed an agreement to sell at the established price could be bound to do so by law. The next year, Congress — still influenced by the pressure of small-dealer associations — passed the McGuire Act to force all retailers to conform. Still, such laws remained hard to enforce. Secret discounting was hard to prove, and the producers were often in favor of such practices.

Finding that discounts worked automatically to reduce price when markets were overstocked, large manufacturers tended to maintain an advertised retail price, and let the dealer suffer the loss if he had to sell for less. Whether the entire system of legal price control worked for the benefit of small business or not was a moot question.

The Auxiliaries of Business

To a considerable degree medium-sized business was kept alive and healthy because specialized service firms duplicated, sometimes more expertly, the staff functions of the giant corporations. In the major metropolitan centers expert advice on almost any business problem could be bought from a specialist. Lawyers, credit agencies, and accountants were the oldest historic types of auxiliaries, and as the government moved into business from 1932 on, the services became indispensable. By the 1960s installment selling had spawned over 2,000 bureaus dealing in evaluation of consumer credit, some with careless and arbitrary policies that made government regulation seem likely.[18] Meanwhile, substantial, often nationwide, advisory firms developed for engineering, management, personnel, advertising, public relations, and computer services.

Hence the smaller firm, by hiring such service only when needed, might have relatively less overhead than the big company that retained such staff experts on regular salary. The smaller company also had the benefit of choosing between competing experts and minimizing the inevitable frictions between line and staff in its own office. On occasion even the biggest companies called in outside specialists in order to get views unbiased by company policies and politics (Chapter 11).

Less specific in their contribution to better business were outside organizations such as trade and professional associations. Both held meetings and published papers and journals containing useful information but, as in earlier decades, were restrained from collective action on prices or production by the antitrust laws. In the 1960s there were tens of thousands of such associations and their literature even in a special field was too voluminous for anyone but a specialist to read. To take radio advertising in the 1950s as an example, the American Association of Advertising Agencies, the American Communications Association, the American Marketing Association, the Association of National Advertisers, the Advertising Research Foundation, the Association of Radio News Analysts, the Research Society of America, the American Society of Composers, Authors and Publishers, the Institute of Radio Engineers, the National Association of Broadcast Engineers and Technicians, the Radio Directors Guild, the Radio Executives Club, and the Radio Research Council all had an interest.

Really small businessmen, the millions of proprietors with less than four employees, were relatively inactive in this complex associational life. Of 300,000 retail grocers in 1946, for example, only 91,000 belonged to a trade association.[19] To become active, a firm needed a manager who could be spared for meetings and reading, while most small proprietors lacked time, inclination, and money for the dues and travel. Much of the advice they received came from the commercial credit companies that lent them money, at very high rates, or the suppliers of the goods they sold.

Regional Differences

In recent decades businessmen everywhere in the United States have talked the same idiom, worn the same clothes, driven the same cars, used the same forms, and looked to the same corporations as models of achievement, yet this national business culture that makes it hard to tell whether one is in a bank in New York or Dallas covers many basic differences in business attitudes and situations. The United States during the middle twentieth century represented in one place or another the whole range of economic circumstances. There were marginal farmers barely able to subsist, living close to the most modern factories; there were "imperialist" investing regions and "colonial" areas needing development. Metropolitan capital markets like Chicago were related to backcountry agricultural regions in much the same way that London had been to South Africa or prewar Paris to Rumania.

In efforts made by underdeveloped areas of the United States to attract capital, the town or an organization of its business leaders was generally the active force, trying by gifts of money or land or remission of local taxes to bring industry and trade to their community. In 1964 more than 11,000 public and private organizations were trying to attract industries to particular areas. Local tax exemptions of up to ten years and a guarantee of adequate financing were frequently offered, as well as "industrial parks" and research and educational facilities. As soon as one county in a state started issuing tax-exempt bonds to raise money for industrial development, neighboring counties were likely to feel forced to follow.[20]

The big banks of larger cities sent their top officers around the country looking for new businesses or branch plants. With the rise of federal bureaucracy, government agencies and military installations became objects of solicitation. An air base, for example, might be the largest employer and spender in a city of 100,000 people. Even a school or college could be looked upon as a labor-employing and spending unit that enhanced the reputation of the community and thereby attracted other enterprises.

Between such extremes as New York State, which in 1967 had over $25 billion of value added to products by manufacturing, and Wyoming, which had $89 million, lay a host of intermediate states that illustrated at any given moment most of the historic stages in the substitution of industry and service for agriculture. Texas, for example, changed within a generation from a region largely agricultural to one that from the fifties on ranked among the first ten states in value added by manufacture. And, aside from the additions from oil and gas, most of the progress came after 1940.

Texas' rapid business growth came in spite of many social customs generally regarded in other underdeveloped areas as impediments to industrialization. The Texans of the early twentieth century, largely ranchers or cotton growers, had the leisurely ways associated with both agricultural life and the South. J. V. Farwell, one of the principal owners of the mammoth XIT Ranch, wrote in 1905 that the development of west Texas was "delayed *only* by the *slow* brain and muscle of native Texas people."[21] Such deeply ingrained patterns of culture change but slowly. Industrialization, even in the main manufacturing areas like Houston, Fort Worth, and Dallas, did not eliminate the older habits. As a college-trained Fort Worth manufacturer observed in 1950: "High pressure and fast tempo are not accepted."[22] Ranchers still owned much mid-city property in central and west Texas cities and often neither sold nor improved it.

Business development came about both by the movement of national firms into the area, and through the financing of local enterprises. The big banks of Houston in particular were continually on the lookout for national manufacturing companies that might build branch plants in Texas. Top executives of the banks traveled to big centers like Detroit or Chicago and personally argued the advantages they had to offer in raw materials, labor, and water transportation. The fact that they were operating within one closely united nation undoubtedly gave these salesmen of the less developed regions an advantage over similar efforts by Africans in London, and still more over those of Brazilians in New York.

If locally initiated enterprises were not big and secure enough, (like public utilities or large oil companies) to sell stock or bonds through Chicago or New York investment houses, they sought money from local capitalists and banks. In the early days, before World War II, banks geared to oil and cattle were disinclined to make industrial loans. Gradually one bank in a medium-sized city would begin to bid for this business. The more conservative banks could also bring in new capital by selling mortgages to large insurance or mortgage companies in the older regions.

Because of the national banking-act restriction that no bank could make a single loan equal to more than 10 percent of its capital, large loans in Texas had to be shared with either Dallas or Houston banks, and for loans of millions of dollars these banks in turn associated themselves with those of the nation's major financial centers.

While a number of successful local industrialists complained in the 1950s that "Texans are only venturesome in oil," slowness to underwrite new kinds of business was to a large extent reasonable caution. Industry and trade offered a myriad of different risks, and local entrepreneurs lacked experience. Absence of reliable administrative personnel is one of the major handicaps in all new areas. The first question that a capitalist who saw a new opportunity had to ask himself was, are there men around here who can do this? A Fort Worth banker explained, in 1950, that his "people were willing to venture only if management comes with industry."

Within Texas the national differences in development were mirrored on a lesser scale. Central and west Texas were "new" regions industrially, compared with the eastern Gulf Coast. In a city of the high plains such as Amarillo, the oil and cattle west continued to show the effect of the initial contacts with general industry. In 1950 almost every Amarillo business had been founded by its existing operator. Most of these pioneers lived their work and took little time for play. To visitors from the older industrial areas the pace seemed leisurely, but to the men of the old agricultural order the present seemed to mean "rushing all the time."

An intense pride in Amarillo and a desire to keep ahead of rival Lubbock, seventy-five miles to the south, led to continual efforts to attract business. The chamber of commerce established an Industrial Foundation with some hundred members to put up money for selected new enterprises. Such aid, however, was carefully allotted. A major aim was to encourage industries, such as food processing and farm implements, that were allied to Amarillo's position as an agricultural trade center.

In spite of the spread of general industry, the continuing strength of Texas economy and the chief source of individual wealth was oil. By granting in 1926 a 27.5-percent tax-free annual allowance for depletion of wells, Congress gave oil, and therefore Texas, a favored position in the national economy. Established to encourage wildcatting (the drilling of wells in unproven fields) the allowance tended to keep oil money employed in the further quest for oil. But oil operations require machinery, buildings, and all of the usual consumer supplies, so that the oil boom aided other forms of business as well.

Texas was the outstanding example of mid-twentieth-century development of a region with great natural resources. In contrast Southern California represented equally rapid growth in a new area which up to 1950 had no important resource save climate. Here population came first and business followed. The result was a young economy in light industry, luxury goods, and assembly work strikingly different from that in most other areas of the United States.

Many of the small manufacturers, wholesalers, and retailers that supplied the growing population were themselves migrants seeking to supplement an income on which they had planned to retire. Other entrepreneurs were men from similar lines of business elsewhere in the country who had wanted to move to California. Since these migrants could generally supply their own capital, there was a tendency to start too many enterprises and create severe local competition. Through the high transmountain freight rates and the difficulties of firms in quickly and properly supplying a distant market, infant industry in California received considerable protection from eastern producers.

The varied character of California enterprise, particularly following World War II, was reflected in the lending policies of the banks. Being larger institutions than the banks in Texas, they could afford to bring in expert personnel from the older financial centers to evaluate diverse risks: personnel which came, as did the population as a whole, mainly from the Middle West. But, in spite of the desire of these former mid-westerners to share large loans either on the coast or in Chicago, New York remained the chief source of funds for big participations. Wall Street indeed stretched across the continent.

The barrier of mountains and distance worked both for and against California. On the one hand, it gave local industry an advantage in the home market, and on the other, made it hard for the local man to expand into the national market because of high transportation costs.

High California wage rates, boosted by the war industries, were another hindrance to sales beyond the mountains. Consequently, successful West Coast firms tended to establish branch plants in the Middle West, the East, or in foreign nations.

The moving-picture industry, located in California originally because of the climate, was an exception to these difficulties, but as a home enterprise, looked at from either employment or capital investment, it was relatively small and declining. Its contribution to the growth of Los Angeles was more the creation of a glamorous rich, a smart and dashing elite that gave the city publicity but rather annoyed the chamber of commerce.

Anxious as the Southern Californians were to build industry, assembly of parts made elsewhere and distribution of goods to the local market remained the chief nonagricultural activities. Tourists or permanent visitors from other regions were regarded by many as the most valuable import. A leading banker suggested that Angelenos still lived by the old Arkansas adage that "one Yankee tourist is worth twice as much as a bale of cotton and is twice as easy to pick."

Bordering such precocious and naturally favored areas as Texas and California were other parts of the West where, granting the existing stage of technology, growth appeared to have leveled off in the period after World War II. This phenomenon was generally true of the continental area from the High Sierras to the wheat and corn belts of the prairie states. Exceptions occurred where coal, iron, uranium, or other mineral deposits prompted new operations such as the Geneva plant of United States Steel in Utah. But centers like Denver, Colorado, for example, in spite of sparse surrounding population could be regarded as the capitals of mature areas.

By the end of World War II the leading business institutions of Denver were in the hands of the second or third generation of family ownership, in contrast to Amarillo, 400 miles to the southeast, where practically no business save oil or cattle was in the hands of even the second generation. In 1950 no new hotels or office buildings marked Denver's streets. A vast Denver trade area, moreover, was being gradually eaten into by other metropolitan centers on its edges. Los

Angeles, San Francisco, Missoula, Kansas City had all encroached upon Denver's intermountain trade empire. "If opportunities exist here," said an editor, "they are undeveloped and require hard work to develop them." Yet in less than a decade after these gloomy words Denver was thriving from government agencies and military supply, gaining 21 percent in real value added by manufacture in the 1960s as against a metropolitan-area average of 11 percent.

Texas, Southern California, and Colorado illustrated a range of differing situations in United States business and economic growth. They also suggested the impermanence of any given phase. Colorado, the boom area of the late nineteenth century, was by 1950 relatively static, while Texas forged ahead. By 1955 Colorado and the other mountain states were starting to benefit from new oil, uranium, and government agencies. Time would no doubt bring plateaus of maturity to all rapidly developing areas, and subsequent changes in technology, new discoveries of natural resources, or an evolution in government policy might revive growth. Similarly, because of mid-century transportation costs and problems of water supply, some Los Angeles executives feared that the area was overdeveloped. Yet new methods of processing seawater, cheaper means of transportation, and the continued development of oil and natural gas might make such fears laughable to a future generation.

Everywhere in mid-century urban America the policies of the big national corporations could be seen and felt, but in none of the cities mentioned in the foregoing examples of Western growth did such influence appear to be dominant. In all three areas there were large branch plants of the leading corporations, each office ordinarily commanded by a vice-president. While these officers were accorded high respect and prestige, they appeared to take less part in community decisions and to do less to set the tone and tempo of business than the important local men. For example, in the 1950s if one great airplane company were to close its Fort Worth plant, 20 percent of the city's workers would have been out of jobs. Yet at business-club meetings and in the discussions of informal business groups regarding local policy, one could not detect any special influence from the presence of this company, except for the pressure of its union contracts upon the open-shop traditions of the community.

An inescapable conclusion from any effort to assess the relative importance and influence of small, medium, and big business, or of local, regional, or national branches, is that the subject had barely been approached in any systematic way by the 1970s. This lag in social analysis is partly explicable by the subtlety and ambiguity of many of the questions involved. To maintain that large companies have great power is akin to saying that sovereignty rests in government. In either case the practical question is how and in what channels is the power exerted. Furthermore, questions of the influence of big business lead at once to questions of the nature of influence in a community, and in turn to how people acquire the opinions that move them to action. In any event, the businessmen in the small- and medium-sized cities that contain the largest segment of American population thought they were still free enterprisers managing their own affairs. Reflecting deeply ingrained patterns of thinking, they worried more about being dominated by government than by big business.

11 Managerial Enterprise

Although some firms that by American standards are medium sized may be run by professional managers, in general one may equate managerial enterprise with bigness. While relatively more of such companies distinguish or differentiate American business from that of other nations, managerial enterprise is not typical of any Western capitalist economy. No census records the exact number of executives responsible for policy in large corporations, and therefore the extent of managerial enterprise has to be implied from other statistics measuring size.

The Continuing Character of Bigness

The data permit several definitions of what constitutes "big" or managerial business. For example, if one takes mass production as the essential measure, in 1971 some figure such as $100 million in annual sales might be selected; if capital invested is the important criterion, then the same figure in assets could be used; or if the emphasis is on hierarchically complex management, one or two thousand employees might seem a reasonable dividing line. However, none of these measures apply uniformly: a big bank has many administrators and few common workers, a manufacturing company in heavy industry the reverse. Ironically, the measure frequently used historically, because

204

it is easy to apply — that of assets or resources — has little relevance to any of the problems or advantages of bigness.

No matter what measure is selected, big companies have grown enormously since the 1920s. In 1928 F. W. Taussig and C. S. Jocelyn studied, by means of questionnaires, the backgrounds and careers of some seven thousand top-level business leaders whose names were taken from *Poor's Register of Directors.* In 1952 W. L. Warner and J. C. Abegglen sought, as nearly as possible, to duplicate the study in order to make comparisons. In the earlier study 13 percent of the executives were in firms with over $50 million in annual sales; in 1952 the same percentage were in firms with over $500 million in sales. Other groups reflect about the same tenfold rate of increase. Even with figures deflated to allow for the 50 to 60 percent increase in the general price level, big business had grown faster than national income or wealth.

In 1970, the lowest levels among *Fortune's* 500 largest industrial companies were $166 million in sales, $62 million in assets, and 1,273 employees, while for the largest (General Motors) the figures were $19 billion, $14 billion, and 696,000 respectively. In addition to the industrials *Fortune* had roughly comparable figures for fifty each of banks, insurance, retail, transportation, and utility companies. Together the 750 companies employed 20 million workers, or a little over a quarter of the labor force. The smallest number of employees in a single company was 850. Manufacturing companies were the largest employers, the 500 accounting for three-fourths of the total. If the next 500 biggest manufacturing companies are added, the list includes almost all of the industrials that share the major problems and benefits of bigness, while another 1.7 million workers are included. In noting that the 500 largest manufacturers bring over 40 percent of gross national product to the market, it should be remembered that this final payoff includes the contributions of thousands of small suppliers, transporters and service firms. Size falls off rapidly between the first and second 500 industrials; the latter produce only about 11 percent as much in value of finished product as the former and some companies have fewer than 500 employees.[1]

Although the giant corporations became steadily larger, for both business and legal reasons the degree of monopoly in specific markets did not notably increase.[2] Big companies usually found it more profitable to deploy surplus resources in new markets or new products rather than in fighting the price wars necessary to kill off major competitors, and the antitrust laws influenced policy strongly in the same direction. Thus, although several big companies grew three- or fourfold in real net assets or gross sales, because of diversification they did not greatly increase their share of their original markets.

That, in spite of adding only a minority part of the value of all goods and services, the big companies seemed to many people both typical and dominant was largely because their relatively few officers, their managerial enterprisers, provided the intellectual leadership of the world of business. The big companies had the expert staff to write learned speeches for their executives whether on science, technology, management, or public relations; they owned foreign companies and supplied the chief contacts with businessmen in other nations; and they had the trained manpower to represent their interests in meetings, conferences, legislatures, or government administrations. Yet all of this staff and these many functions made the managerial, social, and ethical problems of the big company increasingly complicated and difficult to solve.

The Evolution of Managerial Structure

Chairman Winthrop Aldrich's statement at the 1950 annual meeting of Chase Manhattan Bank that "the management of this institution is in the hands of the . . . directors. . . . The stockholders have no right to intervene," symbolizes the final death of the concept of stockholder democracy.[3] Stock could of course be bought by large outside financial interests and the proxies of small holders solicited, as in the formation of conglomerates by overhead tenders (Chapter 9), but this was still managerial manipulation. In fact, the rising concept of top managers (not the board of directors) as trustees for an equitable division of returns between stockholders, employees, customers, and the public at large reduced "ownership" to merely one of many claims on the operation of a company.[4]

The primary problem of management, however, was not so much the division of returns as the deployment of assets in such a way as to strengthen the company's position in its markets, which generally meant to maintain profits and sales volumes at least equal to those of major competitors. Such external effectiveness depended largely on internal management. From the 1940s on the chief elements in effective management were conceived to be a clear and efficient power structure with good communication between key members, and provisions for decision-making at the proper levels for the problems involved.

Simple as this formula may appear, its detailed application often presented enigmas that baffled the high command. One trouble was that there was no single type of big "organization." The period in which a corporation initially became large and the existing types of managerial ideas and technology placed their marks on the organization, so that management in each company reflected the accidents of its particular history. Furthermore, strong executives impressed their personal ideas on their corporate structures. When General Electric, for example, shifted presidents in the mid-1960s it went through a radical reorganization in its structure and methods of management.[5]

Another inescapable dilemma faced by management is that bureaucracies are both administrative agencies with productive functions to perform and personal power structures. The individual inevitably, or "humanly," prizes most his own success in the power structure. At critical junctures in competition within this bureaucratic power market a man may hope that the functioning of the corporation will "remain equal" (*ceteris paribus*) until his personal "enterprise" has won him the coveted job. If because of a secure market position this usually happens, the successful men of power in a company may ultimately find themselves poorly informed about the detailed workings of the organization, and what is worse, not very much interested.

Thus there was surprisingly little transfer of new ideas generated in business schools or specialized agencies to presidents and board chairmen who were confident of their correct intuitive reactions to business situations. Many times these dominant individuals were right, the "new" was an intellectual fad that would pass (such as worker intelligence testing in the 1920s), but there were limits in very complex situations to the substitution of tacit reactions for knowledge and good organization.

Standard Oil Company (New Jersey), for example, found in 1943 after the resignation or death of three strongmen who had dominated company affairs for more than twenty years, that it was well behind the current conceptions of advanced management. Congressional hearings on patent cartels revealed lack of adequate knowledge among top executives, and the parent company had neither personnel nor public-relations departments. An outside expert told the subsequently created head of the latter department, "your first job may involve lifting the company's management out of traditional conceptions."[6]

By 1960 the structure of most big industrial companies had come to be somewhat similar to the system introduced by Alfred Sloan, with the backing of the du Ponts, at General Motors in the 1920s (Chapter 5). The plan depended on removing the burden of specific administrative functions from top management, the creation of semi-autonomous divisions for different products or services, and coordinating the whole through both staff and line committees. In General Motors the largest divisions were directly represented in top management by vice-presidents, while smaller divisions had vice-presidential representation by groups. The president and a vice-president were responsible for all the line (production) divisions, and the chairman and vice-chairman of the board for the staff (information and coordination) divisions. In all, about 500 major executives were required to manage this largest manufacturing company.[7]

As combating the effects of depression speeded diversification in big companies, more adopted a multidivisional system. High postwar profits and limitations on further expansion in old markets worked in the same direction. Change was not rapid because presidents who readily visualized the value of plant reorganization could not foresee profits arising from the same flexible approach to systems of management. Since such practical men recognized the need for meeting pressing problems, however, the diversification of products gradually forced the adoption of multidivisional management.[8]

While industrial sociologists hold that there is "a general tendency for successful and continuing organizations to accumulate functions," special circumstances, such as product diversification and relations with government, encouraged the growth of new departments.[9] The rise of outside managerial and technological consulting services and the development of specialized study in business schools also led big companies to seek to internalize some of the new learning through expansion or creation of staff organizations and even in relatively small companies involved with rapidly changing military technology, government grants created research and development departments.

The particular departmental system of a company had major effects on business policy. "In decision-making," writes Arthur M. Johnson, "the external world emerges through the intervening mind of administrative man . . . contingent upon perceptions that are influenced by the firm's organizational structure."[10] In the decentralized corporation, for example, the "thrust of decision" comes from "divisional and departmental managers," who are less governed by external events and more concentrated on internal company problems than are top management.[11] The routing of decisions and data is also important: those that pass through sales emerge at the top or bottom in different form than those going through engineering.

This is one of the reasons that companies develop an atmosphere or climate; in one company the aspiring executive talks the language of systematic management, in another improvement of production, and in another of advertising or sales.[12] In the 1960s organizational climate became a subject for research in business schools. Renato Tagiuri says that organizational climate "(a) distinguishes the organization from other organizations, (b) is relatively enduring over time, and (c) influences the behavior of people in the organization."[13] It is an intangible total environment that gradually affects the personality of the person exposed to it.[14] In any case it is an element that all thoughtful and sensitive executives recognized and tried either to alter or reinforce.

While human relations were of primary importance in business, they were inextricably bound up with financial results. High corporation taxes, carryovers for losses, accelerated depreciation, and excess-profits levies during World War II and the Korean War made methods of accounting an increasing influence on business policy. Although control of operations through accounting went back to the nineteenth century, the methods now became far more sophisticated, particularly with the advent of the computer in the 1950s, and controllers became more important in top management. "What other executives are apt not to notice," said *Fortune* in 1962, "is that financial managers are extending their influence far beyond the familiar functions of controllers and treasurers." In 1949, not a single member of the Controllers' Institute was a vice-president; by 1961, its membership included 235 such officers.[15]

The increasing prestige of controllers was paralled by new and difficult professional problems in accounting. Hard-headed executive Robert Townsend complained in 1970 that "No accounting system is very good, and all of them are infinitely variable."[16] In the 1950s and the 1960s older issues were aggravated by inflation, adjustment to computers, and the continuing executive resistance to strict financial surveillance. The latter may have been somewhat responsible for the fact that a leading economist could claim in 1971 "that all the 'profit' increases between 1966 and 1969 were due to loose accounting, not to any improvement in real earnings."[17] Like engineering, accounting faced the problem of providing information in forms useful for nonprofessionals, and failure to communicate accurately could have serious results.

The Managers

Undoubtedly in the middle decades of the century the whole managerial group, including everyone from assistant managers or superintendents on up, was the most rapidly growing segment of the population. Since the Bureau of Labor Statistics did not differentiate these employees from proprietors of small business and changed its basis for classifications between 1940 and 1971, it is impossible to give any exact picture of the growth. During periods of general prosperity medium-sized businesses joined with big in adding many thousands of managers to their simple or intricate hierarchies.

By 1971 businessmen working in firms large enough to have such intermediate management had at their command the education, nationwide contacts, and company resources that allowed them to set manners, attitudes, and habits of living. Too immersed in company affairs to bother with political activities at the lower levels, they probably exerted less influence than the more numerous local business owners and lawyers, but in most other spheres they came to be regarded as the nation's top-level elite.

The group covered a wide range of income and social background, from presidents with incomes in the hundreds of thousands to the $15,000-a-year junior executives, from men with doctor's degrees to those with less than high-school education, from men of inherited wealth and position to those whose fathers had been laborers. Futher more, the chances for men from diverse middle- or lower-class origins to achieve top executive status appeared to be increasing. In the Taussig and Jocelyn study of 1928, for example, only 11 percent of the business leaders had fathers who were laborers; in the Warner and Abegglen comparative study of 1952, there were 15 percent from these ranks. A similar increase occurred in the group from white-collar homes. On the other hand, in the earlier analysis 37 percent had fathers who were major executives or owners of large business; by 1952 only 32 percent had such favorable origins.[18] In 1964 a study made by the *Scientific American* of 1,000 executives in the 600 largest corporations showed 23 percent with fathers classed as "poor" and only 12 percent with those classed as "wealthy." Less open to dispute regarding definitions was the finding that all but 24 percent of these 1,000 executives had college or graduate degrees.[19]

Regardless of origin all executives of big companies had certain things in common: they held their jobs because of personal managerial ability, they occupied a defined position in a graded hierarchy, they looked to increasing salary, perhaps with bonuses, as the chief form of financial remuneration for their work, and they were part of an organization that functioned best through cooperation and good personal relations. These common attributes led to popular discussion of executives as a single group.

As knowledge became more important, recruitment for special types of managerial posts, rather than mere hiring of young men for the company as a whole, increasingly became the rule. Interviewers from the big companies visited university campuses and selected the men, and occasionally women, that management thought they might need. Since the big companies had a good deal of leeway in the use of their funds, managerial candidates could be "stockpiled" against possible shortages. In the meantime they could be kept occupied with company training programs.[20]

As illustrated in the recession of 1969-1970, this practice coupled with high degrees of educational specialization introduced a new insecurity into lower and middle management. In the depression of the thirties large companies had tried to retain their managerial personnel at lower pay. Although in the Warner-Abegglen study of 1952 only 27 percent of the top executives had worked for only one company, they presumably had shifted in the course of upward mobility. By 1970 mobility because of unemployment became the lot of a number of specialized middle-managers, and changes in both managerial and plant technology threatened to accentuate rather than arrest the trend.

The same types of continuous change prevented the development of general formulas for promotion. If "systems men" worked out specifications for a certain job, it often appeared that the men who had in fact performed the job reasonably well before it was classified lacked the required qualifications.[21] Continuous attention was, of course, given to this crucial problem of avoiding errors in promotion. Performance in training programs, psychological testing, wife-screening, and elaborate annual assessment by superiors were all resorted to in the 1950s, but no single system won general acceptance.[22] Since companies continued to differ widely in needs and "personality" or "climate," a man who failed to progress in one company might do well in another. In most situations optimism, self-confidence, and good judgment regarding other people were necessary attributes, but undefined traits of personality joined with push and pull to keep actual promotions largely independent of the theories of specialists in management.

By the 1960s analysts both inside and outside the big companies were thoroughly aware of the manifold problems inherent in the successful operation of business bureaucracy.[23] Some dilemmas, such as the conflict between the desire to destroy competitors for promotion prompted by personal ambition, and the cooperation with them demanded for the welfare of the company, were basically insoluble. It could be hoped, however, that by company stress on the importance of "managerial teams" intelligent human beings would be led to strike a constructive balance. Other problems such as complacency or inbred custom could be met by frequently moving young executives from one plant to another. Not only did they meet new co-workers with different backgrounds, but the company came to form their most important community. "Refresher" courses of various kinds were offered to middle-level executives. Both carrot and stick tactics were pursued by different types of top executives. In the 1950s, for example, it was considered best at General Electric to turn an accounting record of poor results over to the manager himself and thereby challenge him to solve his own problems. "There can be little doubt that the feeling of confidence and trust in the company that even casual contact with General Electric managers reveals, is directly traceable to this practice of using information for self-control rather than control from above."[24] Experimentation in measures for control and morale were still going on in 1971.[25]

A Knowledge Revolution?

In any power structure the opening of new avenues to the top menaces those located midway along the old routes. In the case of the new staff men of the period 1945 to 1970 the threat to the old-line managers was basic because the staff represented a potential triumph of knowledge over experience — an incipient revolution in the type of men in control of American business. The staff experts were men with college and graduate degrees whose duty was to tell older, experienced men — many of whom had not finished college — how to improve their operations. Since the staff employees were younger, and had a much higher rate of job mobility than the line, they were less likely to be attuned to company attitudes and traditions. Tensions inevitably mounted and workers, foremen, and plant managers often joined in tacit combinations to invalidate the recommendations of the young upstarts.[26]

Hence the "knowledge revolution" proceeded more at the pace of a Thirty Years War than a sudden take-over. Since specialized consultants were readily indentified as goads used by top management to stir up complacent line operators, it was necessary for staff men to proceed with tact and caution. Where opposition was great and radical change was needed, it might seem better for morale to have outside consultants make the recommendations. Instances were reported of staff members secretly sharing large research and development budgets with line departments in order to win their cooperation. While this involved no personal stealing, it gave the controller's office a false impression of how resources were being used.[27] A general incentive for staff officers to try to win the support of line in the internal power struggle was that in most companies there were more highly paid line than staff positions and the advancing young man welcomed a chance to shift over at some point in his career.

As with most revolutionary movements the proponents were divided among themselves. In the sixties one group expected the computer to be a powerful support for the assault on tacit experience, one that would quickly flatten multistep line hierarchies by doing much of the work of middle management. But for a decade at least, experience held its ground. Even in the middle ranks, business problems remained stubbornly humanistic and demanded tacit thinking by men as well as statistical reports by machines. Ingenious staff plans were often found to concentrate too much on experimental designs and not enough on the real dimensions of the problem. After acquiring some 60,000 computers in fifteen years, only half of 2,500 large companies were able to affirm without qualification that they had received their money's worth.[28]

The less mathematically inclined part of the forces of knowledge gained support for new ideas in both big companies and among management consultants from the study of foreign subsidiaries. Here the exponents of American ideas of systematic management ran up against not only the usual bastions of traditional experience, but also areas trapped with strange customs and values. The results were highly educational for both home-office and field representatives, and not conducive to more faith in either predesigned systems or computer analysis. To academicians, consultants, and staff advisers in corporations the foreign experiences emphasized the study of cultural values, which involved nonquantified social theory, and gave a new turn to the knowledge revolution. Previous assumptions were seen to be "culture bound" to a degree unrealized by either scholars or practical men. For example, it had been an axiom of American management study that reward was the best, perhaps the only, reliable incentive for both good morale and innovation and that security was the enemy of initiative. Studies soon revealed that in Japan security with low rewards had produced a will to work and innovate that seemed equal or superior to that in the United States. By the 1960s these new ideas were widely spread, but as with the new thought of the 1920s, tangible effects on management came slowly.

Top Management

In the upper as well as the middle reaches of management, incentive through financial reward remained a general feature of the American system. Options to buy stock at rates that it was hoped would be less than the future market price, annual gifts of nontransferable stock, cash bonuses, and generous pensions were all used to attract and hold able executives.[29] But it is doubtful that most of these men performed because of financial rewards. More likely they worked hard for self-fulfillment and prestige among their peers and regarded income chiefly as a sign of success.

The need for mutual respect if a team of top executives was to function smoothly was an additional force tending to produce a degree of
like-mindedness or a company atmosphere. After World War II,
particularly in the 1950s, decision by group or committee action
became popular; few steps were taken without unanimous approval,
an apparent harmony that was often the reflection of the personality
of a dominant leader.[30]

The half-dozen men at the top in most giant companies were im-
pelled to think cautiously and in long-run terms. Caution was essential
not only because of the large commitments involved, but also the
threat of the many legal penalties for error in the form of stockholder
suits or government prosecutions. Long-time horizons were necessary
because major actions by enormous companies took many years to
plan and complete. Although immediate expenditures might be altered
from month to month or year to year, such long-range planning was
probably a stabilizing force in the business cycle.[31] That a director or
stockholder who had not been a party to the discussions involved in
planning for the future could not be allowed to influence policy, was
an inevitable result of the characteristics of management.

Specifically, top decision-makers were faced with the problem of
utilizing the maximum amount of available information in such a way
as to make the fewest errors and, with good luck, achieve some outstanding successes. The framework for decision might include governmental or public considerations, but the focus was, strictly and properly, on business risks and problems. A leading investment banker said,
"I survive by virtue of my competitors' mistakes — if they did not
make about as many as I do I would be an ex-businessman."[32]
Townsend held, "My batting average on decisions at Avis was no
better than .333".[33] "Unaided," wrote George A. Boehm, "the human
mind cannot possibly weigh the manifold complexities involved in . . .
the operation of an enterprise producing hundreds of products for
millions of customers."[34]

The best aids would have been comprehensive theories that could
justify uniform rules and procedures, but in the relatively young
world of multiproduct, multidivisional management reliable theories
were sadly lacking. As late as World War II, most of the writing on

management dealt with the problems of single units rather than those of large enterprise.[35] Aside from personal experience, the substitute for theory was vast masses of empirical data which, after 1955, came to be more or less organized by computer programs. So-called "decision theory" in the 1960s was made up of some relatively simple formulas for handling such material, but almost inevitably by "yes or no" choices rather than "maybe" or "wait and see."

Just to reduce the mass of day-to-day and month-to-month results to a form suitable for overall policy decisions involved formidable dilemmas. For example, unless subordinates screened the data in some systematic way the chief executives would be overloaded, but screening introduced elements of very human judgment regarding exclusion that reduced the information available at the top.[36] Again, the data generally brought with them no reliable rules for evaluation or classification, and in the end the executive was forced to rely on intuitive or tacit judgment. Furthermore, at the level of the final distillation or screening, it was often hard to tell from the computerized material what had really taken place.

The usual efforts at resolving these difficulties involved seeking to increase flexibility in securing additional specific information, not only at the top, but wherever it could be useful — in business language, "reaching far into departments"; having as many decisions as possible made at low levels where the real facts were known; and securing much upper-level staff interpretation of what was going on. But as of 1971 Herbert A. Simon, one of the nation's chief administrative theorists, saw no easy solution to information problems. "Today's computers are moronic robots," he said, "and they will continue to be so as long as programming remains in its present primitive state. . . . Computers must be taught to behave at a higher level of intelligence. This will take a large, vigorous research and development effort."[37]

The Value of Bigness

As counterweights to the managerial difficulties and increasingly high overhead expenses involved in operating giant firms,[38] there were, of course, compensating advantages. High long-run costs for research and development were more readily borne, advertising budgets were generally lower in relation to sales, and dealers could be more numerous, which in turn made market positions more secure. Yet in the very largest companies each division might be big enough to achieve all the efficiencies due to size without help from a top holding corporation devoted to management. While large-scale operations could cut costs, in practice pricing policies allowed independent small companies to remain in competition. This relatively secure command of the market and the large percentage of income that would in any case be absorbed by taxes was thought by some critics to lead to easy-going policies that David Riesman called "conspicuous production," manifested in such things as overly elaborate executive procedures and more employees than necessary.

Since historical reality does not often include laboratory-like tests of competing systems, it has been impossible to determine whether or not great business empires promoted efficiency and growth at a more rapid rate than smaller specialized firms. Many businessmen suspected the efficacy of what they regarded as overly large organizations, while the managers of the latter and their scholarly supporters held that size and efficiency increased side by side. Europeans, resenting the spread of American enterprise in their nations, held that it was not efficiency, but rather power, that went along with size.

12 Business and Social Change

Without regard to the internal efficiency or inefficiency of the multi-plant, multiproduct giants that eventually developed in certain types of business, the initial pressures of technology and the market in all nations undergoing industrialization led to a steady increase in the size of firms. By 1971 large corporations in every advanced economy dominated the production of such industrial necessities as steel, motors, rail or air transport, and electric light and power. For this reason, most of the plans for stimulating further industrialization centered around the creation of great facilities, such as the Fiat plant in Russia, for making the essential basic products. Furthermore, in managing this type of production there were international similarities that created common problems.

Often concealed by differences in government and custom, there also came to be a wide range of similarities in the structure of the highly industrial "mass societies," whether one looked at Czechoslovakia, Great Britain, or the United States. Everywhere varying amounts of small business had survived and promised to be regenerated, perhaps in spite of socialist governments, as the automation incorporated in more advanced technology eliminated the need for men in basic production. The internal stability of the national economies all depended on increasing mass consumption, on high levels of education by those with talent, and on economic administration by at least tolerably efficient bureaucracies. Ideas governing such organizations differed somewhat, just as the national cultures and political traditions of all countries differed, but managers whether in government or private enterprise faced the common problems of effective human relations and the provision of tolerably satisfactory careers under conditions largely established by similar means of production and resulting types of consumption.

A Changing World of Business

An important factor differentiating nation from nation was the per-capita level of production of consumer goods. At the highest levels (such as in the United States) new interests, attitudes, and demands were generated that would presumably appear everywhere, in the course of time, as other nations — "socialist" or "capitalist" — reached a similar educational and economic stage. In these stages of affluence or high consumption, history suggested a new spread of small enterprise.

In the decades from 1900 on, the assembling and marketing of the basic utilities, such as automobiles or prepared foods, became routinized in the hands of large corporations. The continuously new opportunities for meeting or creating demand were in making better components to sell to the final assemblers, new luxury or novelty items for consumers which might be marketed directly, and better services for either business firms or household customers. In the sixties and early seventies service, used in a broad sense to include facilitating home life and travel, seemed the most promising area of American business expansion. Services for consumers covered a multitude of diverse operations from education to providing campsites for tourists, while in business firms they stretched from essentially middleman services in bringing highly specialized producers and customers together, as in types of printed electric circuits, to editing and publishing thousands of different small periodicals. As seen in Chapter 9, providing computer time and advice on programming was rapidly becoming a major type of service.

These hundreds of thousands of entrepreneurs generally operated on a small scale and even in the United States few became large capitalists. Really big disposable capital came to be "institutionalized," to reside mainly in the liquid assets of various types of funds, insurance companies, banks, or giant corporations. While in the capitalist world a few hundred big, well-known operators could draw upon these pools of credit for buying companies and forming business empires, lending or investment firms themselves were, in all nations, run by professional managers primarily thinking in terms of security in relation to rates of return on the disposable capital of the financial corporation.

Unquestionably, in perennially optimistic America, both the would-be empire builders and the financial institutions made costly mistakes and were often, as claimed by Thorstein Veblen, an upsetting element in capitalism, but the total effect of financial manipulation on both production and the nation's output was undoubtedly small. The welfare of the economy and the world depended far more on increasing understanding of technology and management, and on alertness to new opportunities in both production and service.

In fact, the twentieth century may be looked upon in retrospect as the period of the rise of management, characterized by more managers per worker in both small business and large, more study and writing about how to manage the multifarious activities of advanced industrial society, and intensive consideration of the problems of moderate to big corporate hierarchies — a subject useful to both business and government.

Challenges to Management

Throughout the century the thousands of students and practitioners of management were concerned with four major problems: adjusting to rapid technological change; learning how to control large spread-out organizations; maintaining the morale of workers in big plants; and the need for dealing ever more closely with government.

Increasingly complex technology had first required the hiring of more college-trained experts for managing plants, for new staff departments such as engineering, or for occasional help and advice such as in public accounting or advertising. The advent of electronic devices, particularly the computer in the third quarter of the century, made much routine clerical and administrative work by human beings unnecessary, along with some of the management functions involved, and this change threatened to proceed much further in the same direction. It also seemed likely to overwhelm the remaining executives with an unmanageable amount of partially processed information. The immediate administrative problem, therefore, in all big organizations was how to decentralize decision-making in the most effective way. In the long run, further technological advance might ease the situation by leading to less employment and fewer business problems in the highly automated giant firms. They could then become more routine providers of basic utilities, which would add to the increasing number of the next generation of workers and managers serving in smaller, more easily controlled units in trade and service.

Up to 1971, however, the problem of decision-making in big corporations grew rather steadily in both scope and difficulty. While the proportion of workers in manufacturing remained fairly constant at about a quarter of the labor force, the absolute number of industrial firms grew more slowly and the biggest became very much larger. Except for some eccentrics like Henry Ford, chief executives soon realized the greater efficiency of moderate-sized plants employing no more than a few thousand workers; consequently, larger corporations did not necessarily lead to larger plants. The result of this trend and technological advance was more efficient production but probably increased strain on top management in running plants located in distant areas.[1]

Periods of crisis, usually initiated by unusual forces such as war or depression, gradually forced executives to give more thought to all the problems of management, or business per se, and less to those of technologically efficient production. As good production became a second-level engineering problem, head-office management and marketing — both hinging on human relations — became the major concerns. The spread of foreign subsidiaries and branches, particularly from the 1950s on, demonstrated that the intricacy and strangeness of the problems might exceed the imagination and abilities of a particular management. For example, in 1950 when a strong-minded president took over control of one of the half-dozen largest manufacturing companies with world-wide branches, he found "it was dedicated principally to 'security, complacency and mediocrity.' "[2] How widespread such weaknesses may have become is, of course, impossible to estimate, but the general history of large bureaucracies emphasized the problems faced by all of big business.

In the early 1970s there was still no real science of management on which to rely, but rather a number of theories and rules developed from experience and some unrelated systems for handling measurable or routine sistuations. Marked successes were still scored by men like Robert Townsend, who favored abolition of business schools that educated men for top management.[3]

Lack of theory as to what was most important led to a deluge of miscellaneous information and overworked executives. According to *Fortune,* a "typical" manager's complaint was, "It's all I can do to move the papers on my desk. . . .I've got to read all the stuff that comes in. I've got to know these things. . . .Any other kind of reading? When am I supposed to have time for it?"[4] Yet a nearly contemporary critic noted an opposite, and equally understandable, reaction to too much unrelated information — rejection, and resort to easy or conventional solutions. The president of the biggest advertising agency of the late 1950s said that this was "the high tide of mediocrity, the great era of the goof-off. The land has been enjoying a stampede away from responsibility. It is populated with. . . executives whose minds are on the golf-course."[5]

The problem of determining policy was further complicated by a major internal division present even in moderately small firms, one that distinguished business from government bureaucracy: the difference between the influences of administration and enterprise. An engineer running a plant, an accountant keeping the books, or most of the army of specialists in larger companies were oriented toward professional efficiency in their own task, with ultimate market considerations far removed from their daily activities. Other things being equal, the larger the bureaucracy the higher the ratio of such administrators to market, or profit-oriented, enterprisers.

While top executives were inclined to think of these specialists as nonbusinessmen, the difference was probably caused by position in the business hierarchy rather than by personal character. An attitude test in a large chemical firm showed that the values placed on theoretical, economic, aesthetic, social, political, and religious considerations did not vary substantially between research scientists, research managers, and executives, suggesting that the apparent differences in interest came from the immediate requirements of their job rather than from basic differences in personality.[6] This finding was reassuring from the standpoint of the operation of the career ladder, but offered no cure for the interim conflicts arising from status within the company.

The continuing tension in management-labor relations was also largely a matter of difference in situation rather than internalized goals or values. Both sides wanted personal recognition and better incomes for themselves, to be spent on much the same amenities of life, but management felt more responsible for preserving the market position of the company while labor felt free to demand the largest share of total sales revenue that could be won from management. Furthermore, executives were a small group and other employees a large mass, so that wage concessions to the latter cost more. On the whole, national unions won inflationary wage settlements which, in spite of the fact that three-quarters of the total labor force was nonunion, tended directly or indirectly to raise all wages. Directly, employers wishing to preserve nonunion shops met union conditions; indirectly, the "wage-push" inflation in manufactured goods forced some cost-of-living adjustment in all types of wages.

This desire to avoid unionization emphasized another aspect of labor-management relations involving a principle operative from top to bottom of business organizations: the maintenance of hierarchical lines of power. Unions, through shop stewards, had always violated this principle by talking back to foremen and preventing the most flexible use of the work force. By the 1960s a new generation of both blacks and whites, educated in a period stressing the national tradition of equality, resisted arbitrary authority, even without the aid of unions. Locally organized strikes, slowdowns, and absenteeism were the main weapons of resistance by labor. The resulting confusion and low productivity made it appear that men of the affluent Western world, particularly in America and Britain, were losing the will to work; in truth, the problem might be one of a need for better methods, communication, and understanding.

While sharing the same basic American values, the difference in position between men in business and men in government was great enough to produce distrust and hostility. As the mayor of Minneapolis said in the early 1960s: "We have not yet evolved in America an understandable and acceptable role or status for the politician."[7] Yet as industrialism advanced, the interrelationships of businessmen and "politicians" continually increased in number and some firms depending on government contracts were practically joint enterprises. Furthermore, since "the norms of society . . . are usually integrated by the dominant institution," it was to be expected that much if not most political reform and regulation, particularly in local and state government, would have been inspired by businessmen, with most of the opposition financed by other businessmen.[8] As the problems of industrial society led to more regulatory commissions on all levels of government, businessmen and their lawyers did more arguing before such tribunals or with influential legislators and made relatively fewer appearances in the courts, which had always been slow and expensive and now became recourses of last resort. Since most commissions tended to become guardians of the existing status of the interests they regulated, businessmen as a whole probably favored the trend from courts of law to administrative tribunals.

Each individual businessman was inevitably in conflict with government over rates of taxation, and starting with World War I, taxes and methods of accounting for tax purposes became major considerations from the standpoint of profit. High and complicated taxes undoubtedly encouraged mergers and unscrupulous manipulations, both of which were traditionally unwanted by the public, but no other nation

found substantially better ways of raising the enormous sums needed
for military-welfare states.

A Continuing Business Society

At mid-century four social scientists studied "The American Business Creed," both the "classic" ideas of the individual enterpriser and
those of the managerial group. They saw the creed as an ideology
justifying those aspects of conventional business action that raised
doubts in the mind of either the businessman or the public.[9] They also
found that the business creed differed only in emphasis from other
American attitudes such as those of farmers, politicians, professional
men, or laborers. Among all these groups there appeared to be no
manifest disputes as to basic values.[10] Most Americans were held to
believe in individualism, involving freedom and moral responsibility;
materialism and productivity; practical realism; purposeful activity;
the goal of progress; adventurous optimism; competition; and
democracy.[11] But the differences in emphasis between the self-
justifications of the manager and those of the proprietor were
important.

The American manager's assumption of social responsibilities and
the role of mediator or judge between the demands of organized labor,
administrative employees, producers, distributors, consumers, and
stockholders emphasized the professional, judicial, objective approach
to both company and social problems. The managerial role also put a
premium on careerism and the manipulation of people, on opportun-
istic adjustment to changing situations rather than adherence to
immutable principles. It was frequently said that the old entrepreneurial values such as hard-headed ruthless competition, supported
according to a railroad president by an "economics to harden men's
hearts," that had built industrial enterprise in the nineteenth century
were no longer needed or appropriate. The newer attitudes, however,
seemed to apply more to the few businessmen employed by big corporations than to the vast majority of owner-managers.

The many magazine articles which discussed the managerial group tended to overemphasize extreme cases. One overall generalization, however, seemed sound: the styles and fashions set by the managerial elite were closer to those of the mass of the people than had been the case in an earlier day. Partly this reflected the fact that the customs of the society as a whole had been standardized by a technology that gave it the automobile, motion picture, and television, but it also depended somewhat on the requirements of a democratically oriented careerism needed for the efficient operation of large organizations. Eccentrics were not readily accepted in managerial circles; the cult of the average man, always implicit in American culture, had gained further strength.

Growing standardization of manners also came from frequent moves to new areas. In a big company the rising executive was likely to be moved three or more times from one branch to another before he reached his final office. This led to a growth of suburban developments for middle-income families, which many of the families expected to leave within a few years and in which the habits and customs of the big company office were reflected in gregariousness, cooperation, and conformity.

Further blurring the distinctions between small businessmen and professional managers were common habits of life and material aims. One often had to look closely to see the small gradations in taste and manners between the college-educated vice-president and the high-school-educated shopkeeper. A well-standardized business culture reinforced by mass media had softened local color and class distinctions. Despite broad differences in economic activity, businessmen and other Americans were becoming more alike.

In these world-wide changes resulting from mass production and consumption, the United States was in a leading position. As products and services grew ever more varied, so did the careers open to young Americans. Scholarship aid for specialized education was increasingly available, and the range of specialties continually growing. A small business could be started as easily as in previous decades, and the proprietor, using the help available from the Small Business Administration and other government agencies, appeared to have a better chance for success than his predecessors. Successful careers in big business were more open to talent than in the days of smaller organization and continuing family influence. Partly from the evolution of the business system itself the United States was gaining in economic and social democracy.

The critical, skeptical climate of the sixties and seventies, however, emphasized conflicts within business and those between the old business or American values and emerging, contrary ones, still too nebulous to take clear political or social form. Rebelliousness by youth, shown in business not only at the plant level but also by young administrators, obvious in the universities in the form of demands for more democracy and social consciousness, and erupting in the slums as destructive protests against racism and poverty, became of urgent importance, yet lay outside the traditional interests of business. A full-page advertisement of the Olin corporation at the end of 1967 read in inch-high letters: UNFORTUNATELY COLLEGE KIDS DON'T EVEN DISLIKE AMERICAN BUSINESS, in half-inch letters below: THEY JUST IGNORE IT. The text of the ad explained: "That's our biggest problem. Because dislike, at least, would give us a chance for dialogue. But indifference just closes the door in our face. So each June, business goes right along losing more bright young people to teaching, public service, government, and other non-business fields for the wrong reason."[12]

Still, the smoke may readily have exceeded the severity of the fire. Youth is mercurial, whereas the forces of tradition are steady and enduring. By the 1970s the degree of protest seemed lower, and in any case the advance of a more rounded American civilization or a higher level of industrialism was bound to react against the old dominance of recruitment for business. In 1970 a resurvey of "Middletown," made famous as an urban laboratory by the Lynds in the 1920s and 1930s, indicated little change in basic American values. "From businessmen . . . to newspaper editors, to factory workers, to clergymen its residents agree that the city is still largely motivated by middle-class, materialistic, individualist attitudes. The business class still runs

Muncie (the real name), as it did when the Lynds were here, and sets its achievement values."

It could be argued that Muncie, Indiana is small-city, "mid-America," not the East or West Coast, and that the old values may be deteriorating first on the more cosmopolitan fringes, but it still seems probable that inflation, unemployment, and the adjustment of management to technology are more immediate menaces to business than loss of interest by the coming generation. Whether with the end of the phase of industrialism oriented to factory production and the coming of greater abundance more widely distributed, men will lose interest in the making and distribution of goods still seems a problem of the rather distant future.

Notes

Chapter 1. Business as an American Institution

1. William Miller, "American Lawyers in Business and Politics," *Yale Law Journal* (January 1951), p. 68n.

2. Henry C. Potter, *The Citizen in His Relation to the Industrial Situation* (New Haven: Yale University Press, 1902), p. 162.

3. André Siegfried, *America Comes of Age* (New York: Harcourt Brace, 1927), p. 165.

4. Francis X. Sutton, Seymour E. Harris, Carl Kaysen, and James Tobin, *The American Business Creed* (Cambridge: Harvard University Press, 1956), p. 23.

5. Ralph Henry Gabriel, *The Course of American Democratic Thought* (New York: Ronald Press, 1940), p. 155.

6. Lewis Atherton, *Main Street on the Middle Border* (Bloomington: University of Indiana Press, 1954), p. 28.

7. Carl Snyder, "American Captains of Industry," *American Monthly Review of Reviews* 25 (April 1902), 418 and 432. In 1902, of a sample of children asked to choose whom they would most like to resemble, only 1.6 percent said "businessmen, industrialists, or financiers." See Fred I. Greenstein, "New Light on Changing American Values: A Forgotten Body of Survey Data," *Social Forces* 42 (May 1964), 445.

8. Theodore Roosevelt, "Solitude and Longitude Among Reformers," *Century Magazine* 60 (June 1900), 216.

9. Quoted in Allan Nevins and Frank E. Hill, *Ford: The Times, the Man, the Company* (New York: Scribners, 1954), p. 579.

10. Atherton, *Main Street on the Middle Border,* p. 3.

11. *The Autobiography of William Allen White*, pp. 4, 131, and 429. See also pp. 51, 62, 98, 101, 114, 179, 187, 219, 244, and 325. References as published in the *New Yorker*, 20 April 1946, p. 90.

12. William Miller, "American Historians and the Business Elite," *Journal of Economic History* 9 (November 1945), 204.

13. Atherton, *Main Street on the Middle Border*, p. 23.

14. William Jennings Bryan, Cross of Gold Speech, 8 July 1896, quoted in Henry Steele Commager, ed., *Documents of American History* (New York: Crofts, 1934), p. 175.

15. Quoted in Matthew Josephson, *The President Makers* (New York: Harcourt, Brace, 1940), p. 74.

16. *Ibid.*, p. 86.

17. *Ibid.*, p. 75.

18. Claude G Bowers, *Beveridge and the Progressive Era* (Boston: Houghton Mifflin, 1932), p. 68.

19. Charles E. Perkins (president, Chicago, Burlington & Quincy Railroad) to Thomas Potter, 18 November 1884, quoted in Thomas C. Cochran, *Railroad Leaders, 1845-1890: The Business Mind in Action* (Cambridge: Harvard University Press, 1953), p. 437.

Chapter 2. The Technological and Economic Base

1. See Thomas C. Cochran, *Social Change in Industrial Society* (London: George Allen and Unwin, 1972), chap. 1.

2. Lewis Mumford, *Technics and Civilization* (New York: Harcourt, Brace, 1934), pp. 151-210.

3. Allan Nevins and Frank E. Hill, *Ford: The Times, the Man, the Company* (New York: Scribners, 1954), p. 348.

4. Geroge V. Thompson, "Intercompany Technical Standardization in the Early Automobile Industry," *Journal of Economic History* 14 (winter 1954), 6.

5. Thomas C. Cochran, *The Pabst Brewing Company: The History of an American Business* (New York: New York University Press, 1948), p. 211.

6. In 1914 the total value of electrical supplies was under $350 million. Except where otherwise noted, statistics prior to 1960 are from the U. S. Bureau of the Census, *Historical Statistics of the United States, Colonial Times to 1957* (Washington: Government Printing Office, 1960).

7. See James J. Flink, *America Adopts the Automobile, 1895-1910* (Cambridge: MIT Press, 1970).

8. But some of the associates had already advanced well over $10,000 in materials and equipment. Nevins and Hill, *Ford,* p. 238.

9. W. C. Durant persuaded the du Pont family to buy the Chevrolet Company, and the Chevrolet Company in turn bought control of General Motors.

10. Melvin T. Copeland, "Marketing," in *Recent Economic Changes* (New York: McGraw-Hill, 1929), vol. 1, p. 323.

11. *Ibid.,* p. 391.

12. *Detroit News,* 24 November 1922, quoted in Keith Sward, *The Legend of Henry Ford* (New York: Rinehart, 1948), p. 198.

13. E. I. du Pont de Nemours & Company, *Du Pont: The Autobiography of an American Enterprise* (New York: Scribners, 1951), p. 92.

14. See William J. Cunningham, "Transportation: Part I, Railways," in Copeland, *Recent Economic Changes,* vol. 1.

15. Gertrude G Schroeder, *The Growth of Major Steel Companies, 1900-1950* (Baltimore: Johns Hopkins Press, 1952), p. 197. Of sixty-two steel-ingot producers listed in 1948, all but sixteen had been incorporated before 1906, and only one after 1941 (*ibid.,* p. 201).

16. Evelyn H. Knowlton, *Pepperell's Progress* (Cambridge: Harvard University Press, 1949), p. 333.

17. Daniel Creamer, *Capital and Output Trends in Manufacturing Industries, 1880-1948,* Occasional Paper No. 41 (New York: National Bureau of Economic Research, 1954), p. 31.

18. *Ibid.,* p. 5.

Chapter 3. Big Business and Finance

1. Norman Beasley, *Knudsen: A Biography* (New York: McGraw-Hill, 1947), p. 71.

2. Temporary National Economic Committee, Monograph 13, Senate Committee Report, 76th Congress, 3rd session (Washington: Government Printing Office, 1941), p. 19.

3. Quoted in Frederick Lewis Allen, *Lords of Creation* (New York: Harpers, 1935), p. 280.

4. Frederick Lewis Allen, *The Great Pierpont Morgan* (New York: Harpers, 1949), p. 251; and Thomas Lamont, *Henry P. Davison* (New York: Harpers, 1933), p. 76.

5. Report of the Committee Appointed to Investigate the Concentration of Control of Money and Credit, House Report 1593, 62nd Congress, 3rd session, 1913, p. 89.

6. Quoted in Allen, *Lords of Creation*, pp. 187-188.

7. House Report 1593, pp. 105-106.

8. Quoted in Alpheus Thomas Mason, *Brandeis — A Free Man's Life* (New York: Viking, 1946), p. 211.

9. O. W. Underwood, *Drifting Sands of Party Politics* (New York: Century, 1928), p. 289.

10. Benjamin Strong in Edwin W Kemmerer, *The ABC of the Federal Reserve System* (Princeton: Princeton University Press, 1918), p. ix.

Chapter 4. The Structure of Business

1. Adolph A. Berle, Jr. and Gardiner C. Means, *The Modern Corporation and Private Property* (New York: Macmillan, 1932), p. 33. The Snyder-Tucker general price index advanced 84 percent. See U. S. Bureau of Census, *Historical Statistics of the United States, 1789-1945* (Washington: Government Printing Office, 1949), p. 231.

2. See Adolph A. Berle, Jr., *The 20th Century Capitalist Revolution* (New York: Harcourt, Brace, 1954).

3. Joseph D. Phillips, *Little Business in the American Economy* (Urbana: University of Illinois Press, 1958), pp. 57-58.

4. See Temporary National Economic Committee, Investigation of Concentration of Economic Power, Monograph 17, *Problems of Small Business* (Washington: Government Printing Office, 1941).

5. Phillips, *Little Business,* p. 64.

6. See James H. Soltow, *Origins of Small Business Metal Fabricators and Machinery Makers in New England, 1890-1957* (Philadelphia: American Philosophical Society, 1965).

7. Edward A. Duddy and David A. Revzan, *Marketing: An Institutional Approach* (New York: McGraw-Hill, 1947), pp. 252 and 257.

8. *Ibid.,* pp. 155 and 199.

9. Boris Emmet and John E Jeuck, *Catalogues and Counters: A History of Sears, Roebuck and Company* (Chicago: University of Chicago Press, 1950), p. 295.

10. *Ibid.,* p. 266.

11. Alvin J. Silk and Louis W. Sears, "The Changing Nature of Innovation in Marketing: A Case Study of Selected Business Leaders, 1852-1958," *Business History Review* 37, (autumn 1963), 191-194.

12. Alfred D. Chandler, Jr., *Giant Enterprise: Ford, General Motors and the Automobile Industry* (New York: Harcourt, Brace, World, 1964), p. 161.

13. See "How to Sell Automobiles," *Fortune,* February 1939, pp. 71-78 and 105-109.

14. Alfred M. Lee, *The Daily Newspaper in America* (New York: Macmillan, 1930), p. 527.

15. Frank Presbry, *The History and Development of Advertising* (Garden City, N.Y.: Doubleday, Doran, 1929), p. 435.

16. *Ibid.,* pp. 525-527.

17. *Ibid.,* p. 550.

18. See Merle E. Curti, "The Changing Concept of Human Nature, in the Literature of American Advertising," *Business History Review* 41 (winter 1967), 335-357.

19. Otis Pease, *The Responsibilities of American Advertising* (New Haven: Yale University Press, 1958), p. 35.

20. Alan R. Raucher, *Public Relations and Business, 1900-1929* (Baltimore: Johns Hopkins Press, 1968), pp. 116-130.

21. Pease, *American Advertising,* p. 171n.

22. *Ibid.,* p. 13. Estimates are by *Printers Ink,* the chief trade journal.

23. *Ibid.,* p. 24.

24. Quoted from Edward L. Bernays, *Public Relations* (Norman: University of Oklahoma Press, 1952), p. 57.

25. Kenneth M. Myers, "ABC and SRDS: The Evolution of Two Special Advertising Services," *Business History Review* 24 (autumn 1960), 308-309.

26. See for example Edwin L. Shuey, *Factory People and Their Employers* (New York: Lentilhon, 1900).

27. See Milton J. Nadworny, "Frederick Taylor and Frank Gilbreath: Competition in Scientific Management," *Business History Review* 31 (September 1957), 23-33.

28. The Pabst Brewing Company expanded in this manner in 1904. See Thomas C. Cochran, *The Pabst Brewing Company: The History of an American Business* (New York: New York University Press, 1948).

29. For this and other aspects of the two laws see Sidney Ratner, *Taxation and Democracy in America* (New York: Wiley, 1967), pp. 292-297 and 333-338.

30. Much of the following information comes from James Don Edwards, "Accounting in the United States from 1913 to 1928," *Business History Review* 32 (spring 1958), 74-101.

31. Marian V. Sears, "The American Businessman at the Turn of the Century," *Business History Review* 30 (December 1956), 397-402.

32. Arthur J. Eddy, *The New Competition* (New York: Appleton, 1912), p. 100.

33. *Iron Age,* 6 February 1908, quoted in Arthur R. Burns, *The Decline of Competition* (New York: McGraw-Hill, 1936), p. 79.

34. Burns, *Decline of Competition,* pp. 52-55 and 73.

35. Maple Flooring Manufacturers Association v. U.S., 268 U.S. 563.

36. Louis Galambos, *Competition and Cooperation: The Emergence of a National Trade Association* (Baltimore: Johns Hopkins Press, 1966), p. 137.

37. *Ibid.,* p. 139.

38. Alfred D. Chandler, Jr., "Structure of American Industry in the Twentieth Century," *Business History Review* 43 (autumn 1969). p. 257.

39. Simon Kuznets, *National Income: A Summary of Findings* (New York: National Bureau of Economic Research, 1946), p. 53.

Chapter 5. Inside the Firm

1. An intensive effort to recover such records in 1951 in a city of 40,000 population yielded no substantial returns. Information had to be secured through interviews. See Sidney Goldstein, *The Norristown Study* (Philadelphia: University of Pennsylvania Press, 1961).

2. See Temporary National Economic Committee, Investigation of Concentration of Economic Power, Monograph 17, *Problems of Small Business* (Washington: Government Printing Office, 1941); Joseph D. Phillips, *Little Business in the American Economy* (Urbana: University of Illinois Press, 1958); and Kurt B. Mayer and Sidney Goldstein, *The First Two Years: Problems of Small Firm Growth and Survival* (Washington: Small Business Administration, 1961).

3. See Goldstein, *The Norristown Study,* pp. 151-165; and James H. Soltow, *Origins of Small Business Metal Fabricators and Machinery Makers in New England, 1890-1957* (Philadelphia: American Philosophical Society, 1965).

4. Frederick W. Taylor, *Scientific Management* (New York: Harpers, 1911), pp. 6-7.

5. *Ibid.*, pp. 25-26; and Joseph A. Litterer, "Systematic Management: The Search for Order and Integration," *Business History Review* 35 (winter 1961), 463-464.

6. Selig Perlman in a paper prepared for a meeting of the American Jewish Historical Society, Poughkeepsie, New York, 1954.

7. Henry Ford, in collaboration with Samuel Crowther, *My Life and Work* (Garden City, N. Y.: Doubleday, Page, 1922), p. 125.

8. See Milton J. Nadworny, *Scientific Management and the Unions, 1900-1932* (Cambridge: Harvard University Press, 1955).

9. Henry Eilbert, "The Development of Personnel Management in the United States," *Business History Review* 33 (autumn 1959), 346-355.

10. Norman J. Wood, "Industrial Relations Policies of American Management," *Business History Review* 34 (winter 1960), 412.

11. National Industrial Conference Board, *Employee Magazines in the United States* (New York: NICB, 1925), pp. 2-4. The largest number were monthlies (*ibid.*, p. 29).

12. National Industrial Conference Board, *Industrial Relations Programs in Small Plants* (New York: NICB, 1929), p. 7.

13. Loren Baritz, *Servants of Power: A History of the Use of Social Science in American Industry* (Middletown, Conn.: Wesleyan University Press, 1960), pp. 65 ff.

14. Reinhard Bendix, *Work and Authority in Industry: Ideologies of Management in the Course of Industrialization* (New York: Wiley, 1956), p. 291.

15. Ernest Dale, "Hamilton McFarland Barksdale and the Du Pont Contributions to Systematic Management," *Business History Review* 36 (summer 1962), 145.

16. Bendix, *Work and Authority*, p. 294.

17. NICB, *Industrial Relations in Small Plants*, p. 13.

18. Most of the plans were in "open-shop" companies (*ibid.*, p. 22).

19. Ford, *My Life and Work*, pp. 18 and 92.

20. Quoted in William Z. Ripley, *Main Street and Wall Street* (Boston: Little, Brown, 1927), p. 121.

21. See James Burnham, *The Managerial Revolution* (New York: John Day, 1941); and Oswald Knauth, *Managerial Enterprise* (New York: Norton, 1948).

22. Paul H. Giddens, *Standard Oil Company (Indiana): Oil Pioneer of the Middle West* (New York: Appleton-Century-Crofts, 1955), pp. 403 ff.

23. Testimony of Myron W. Watkins in Temporary National Economic Committee, Monograph 13, p. 99.

24. See Alfred D. Chandler, Jr., *Strategy and Structure: Chapters in the History of American Industrial Enterprise* (Garden City, N.Y.: Doubleday, Anchor Books, 1966).

25. "The Growth of the Firm: A Case Study: The Hercules Powder Company," *Business History Review* 34 (spring 1960), 2.

26. Joseph A. Litterer, "Alexander Hamilton Church and the Development of Modern Management," *Business History Review* 35 (summer 1961), 214.

27. *Strategy and Structure*, p. 4. I am indebted to Professor Chandler for many ideas in this section.

28. *Railroads: Their Origins and Problems* (New York: J. & J. Harper eds., Harper & Row, 1969), p. xxiv.

29. For names and dates see Bendix, *Work and Authority*, p. 287n.

30. Don D. Lescohier, "Working Conditions," in John R. Commons, *History of Labor in the United States, 1896-1932*, vol. 3 (New York: Macmillan, 1935), p. 328n.

31. Chandler, *Strategy and Structure*, pp. 299 ff.

32. See Mira Wilkins, *The Emergence of Multinational Enterprise: American Business Abroad from the Colonial Era to 1914* (Cambridge: Harvard University Press, 1970).

33. Robert B. Davis, "An American Enterprise Abroad: American Radiator Company in Europe, 1895-1914," *Business History Review* 43 (autumn 1969), 333.

34. Bendix, *Work and Authority*, p. 214.

35. Andrew Carnegie, *The Empire of Business* (Garden City, N.Y.: Doubleday, Page, 1902), pp. 192, 200, 201-202, and 13.

36. C. H. Buford, "How to Become a Railroad President," *What's New*, November 1949, pp. 12-13.

37. Thomas C. Cochran, *Railroad Leaders, 1845-1890: The Business Mind in Action* (Cambridge: Harvard University Press, 1953), pp. 127 – 128.

38. Francis X. Sutton, Seymour E. Harris, Carl Kaysen, and James Tobin, *The American Business Creed* (Cambridge: Harvard University Press, 1956), p. 55.

39. Everett E. Hagen, "The Internal Functioning of Capitalist Organizations," *Journal of Economic History* 30 (March 1970), 223.

40. William H. Henry, "The Business Executive: The Psychodynamics of a Social Role," *American Journal of Sociology* 54 (January 1949), 287.

41. Herrymon Maurer, *Great Enterprise: Growth and Behavior of the Big Corporation* (New York: Macmillan, 1955), p. 90.

42. *Ibid.*, pp. 90 ff.

43. John L. McCaffrey, "What Corporation Presidents Think about at Night," *Fortune*, September 1953, p. 128.

44. Willaim B. Whyte, Jr., "How Hard Do Executives Work?" *Fortune,* January 1954, p. 109.

45. McCaffrey, "Corporation Presidents," pp. 128-140.

46. See National Industrial Conference Board, *Employee Magazines in the United States* (New York: NICB, 1925).

47. Carl D. Thompson, *Confessions of the Power Trust* (New York: Dutton, 1932), p. 14.

48. Knauth, *Managerial Enterprise,* p. 28.

49. See N. R. Danielian, *AT & T* (New York: Vanguard, 1939), pp. 102-103; and Arthur A. Bright, Jr., *The Electric-Lamp Industry* (New York: Macmillan, 1949), pp. 384-391. Paul G. Clark, in *Structure of the American Economy,* Wassily Leontief, ed. (New York: Oxford University Press, ed. 2, 1951) pictures the investment policy of AT&T as a kind of automatic adjustment to new demand on a basis worked out by engineers. Entrepreneurial decisions do not appear explicitly.

50. Knauth, *Managerial Enterprise,* pp. 45-46.

51. Sutton et. al., *Business Creed,* p. 360.

52. Edward L. Bernays, *Public Relations* (Norman: University of Oklahoma Press, 1952), pp. 87 and 91; see also Alan R. Raucher, *Public Relations and Business, 1900-1929* (Baltimore: Johns Hopkins Press, 1968).

53. Bernays, *Public Relations,* pp. 87-88.

54. Danielian, *AT&T* p. 302.

55. *Ibid.,* p. 304.

56. See Eric F. Goldman, *Two-Way Street: The Emergence of the Public Relations Counsel* (Boston: Bellman, 1948).

57. Morrell Heald, "Managerial Responsibility to Society: The Growth of an Idea," *Business History Review* 31 (winter 1957), 378.

58. David F. Hawkins, "The Development of Modern Financial Reporting Practices among American Manufacturing Corporations," *Business History Review* 37 (autumn 1963), 137-160.

59. Danielian, *AT&T,* pp. 183 and 192.

Chapter 6. Business and the Nation

1. "Disarming the Trusts," *Atlantic Monthly* 85 (January 1900), 50.

2. People of the State of New York v. North River Sugar Refining Co., 24 NE 834 (1890).

3. State, *ex rel.* v. Standard Oil Co., 49 Ohio 137 (1892); 30 NE 279 (1892).

4. Mark Sullivan, *Our Times* (New York: Scribners, 1927), Vol. 2, p. 314.

5. United States v. E. C. Knight Company, 156 U.S. 1 (1895).

6. Theodore Roosevelt, *Autobiography* (New York: Scribners, 1912), p. 427.

7. Addystone Pipe and Steel Co. *et al.* v. United States, 175 U.S. 211 (1899).

8. See Robert H. Wiebe, *Businessmen and Reform: A Study of the Progressive Movement* (Cambridge: Harvard University Press, 1962); Gabriel Kolko, *The Triumph of Conservatism: A Reinterpretation of American History, 1900-1916* (New York: Free Press of Glencoe, 1963); and Kolko's *Railroads and Regulation, 1877-1916* (Princeton: Princeton University Press, 1965).

9. Lawrence M. Friedman and Jack Ladinsky, "Social Change and the Law of Industrial Accidents," *Columbia Law Review* 67 (January 1967), 65-66; Albert K. Steigerwalt, *The National Association of Manufacturers, 1895-1914: A Study in Business Leadership* (Grand Rapids: Bureau of Business Research, Graduate School of Business Administration, University of Michigan, 1964), pp. 160-163; and Robert Asher, "Business and Workers Welfare in the Progressive Era: Workmen's Compensation Reform in Massachusetts, 1880-1911," *Business History Review* 43 (winter 1969), 453.

10. Quoted in William Z. Ripley, ed., *Trusts, Pools and Corporations* (New York: Ginn, 1905), p. 470.

11. Roosevelt, *Autobiography*, pp. 429-430.

12. Quoted in Henry R. Seager and Charles A. Gulick, Jr., *Trust and Corporation Problems* (New York: Harpers, 1929), p. 400.

13. *Ibid.*, p. 422.

14. H. G. S. Noble, "The New York Stock Exchange in the Crisis of 1914," quoted in Humphrey B. Neill, *The Inside Story of the Stock Exchange* (New York: B. C. Frobes, 1950), p. 191.

15. Paul A. C. Koistinen, "The Industrial-Military Complex in Historical Perspective," *Business History Review* 40 (winter 1967), 380-381.

16. Robert D. Cuff, "Bernard Baruch: Symbol and Myth in Industrial Mobilization," *Business History Review* 43 (summer 1969), 117.

17. Grosvenor B. Clarkson, *Industrial America in the World War* (Boston: Houghton Mifflin, 1923), p. 233.

18. *Ibid.*, p. 235.

19. Robert D. Cuff, "A Dollar-a-Year Man in Government: George N. Peak and the War Industries Board," *Business History Review* 40 (winter 1967) p. 414.

20. J. N. Froomken, "Automation," *International Encyclopedia of the Social Sciences* (New York: Macmillan and Free Press, 1968), vol. 1, p. 482.

21. Raymond Goldsmith, *A Study of Saving* (New York: National Bureau of Economic Research, 1954), vol. 1, pp. 48 and 59.

22. Simon Kuznets, *National Income: A Summary of Findings* (New York: National Bureau of Economic Research, 1946), p. 53.

23. Michael E. Parish, *Securities Regulation and the New Deal* (New Haven: Yale University Press, 1970), p. 147.

24. Quoted in Broadus Mitchell, *Depression Decade: From New Era through New Deal, 1929-1941* (New York: Rinehart, 1947), p. 163.

25. Paul M. Mazur, *American Prosperity* (New York: Viking, 1928), p. 250.

26. Quoted in Frederick Lewis Allen, *Lords of Creation* (New York: Harpers, 1935), p. 335.

27. Arthur F. Burns, *New Facts on Business Cycles* (New York: National Bureau of Economic Research, 1950), pp. 7-17.

28. John Kenneth Galbraith, *The Great Crash, 1929* (Boston: Houghton Mifflin, 1961), p. 116.

29. Senate Banking and Currency Committee, *Hearings on the Banking Act of 1935* (Washington: Government Printing Office, 1936), p. 406.

30. John M. Keynes, *A Treatise on Money,* vol. 1, *The Pure Theory of Money* (London: Macmillan, 1930), p. 349.

31. Arthur F. Burns, *Business Cycle Research and the Needs of Our Times* (New York: National Bureau of Economic Research, 1953), p. 4.

32. James D. Richardson, ed., *A Compilation of the Messages and Papers of the Presidents* (Washington: Government Printing Office, 1898), vol. 9, p. 390.

33. National Industrial Conference Board, *Studies in Enterprise and Social Progress* (New York: NICB, 1939), p. 125.

34. "Everybody Ought to be Rich", *Ladies' Home Journal* 44 (August 1929), 299, quoted in John A. Penrod, "The Literature of the Great Depression" (Ph.D. thesis, University of Pennsylvania, 1954), p. 58.

Chapter 7. The Great Depression

1. Leonard P. Ayres, chart published by Cleveland (Ohio) Trust Company, 1942 (later editions available).

2. Herbert Hoover, *Memoirs of Herbert Hoover: The Great Depression, 1929-1941* (New York: Macmillan, 1952), p. 2.

3. Samuel L. Clemens, *Mark Twain in Eruption,* ed. Bernard De Voto (New York: Harpers, 1940), p. 17.

4. Paul W. Litchfield, *Industrial Voyage* (New York: Doubleday, 1954).

5. Quoted in Richard Hofstader, *The American Political Tradition* (New York: Knopf, 1948), p. 325.

6. *Ibid.,* p. 326.

7. Report of the Committee on Recent Economic Changes, Herbert Hoover, chairman, *Recent Economic Changes in the United States* (New York: McGraw-Hill, for the National Bureau of Economic Research, 1929) vol. 1, p. 139.

8. The argument as stated here is condensed with minor changes from Arthur F. Burns, *The Instability of Consumer Spending,* 32nd annual report, National Bureau of Economic Research (New York, 1952).

9. John M. Keynes, *The General Theory of Employment, Interest and Money* (New York: Harcourt, Brace, 1936), p. 320.

10. *Ibid.,* p. 96.

11. Simon Kuznets, *National Income: A Summary of Findings* (New York: National Bureau of Economic Research, 1948), p. 99.

12. Simon Kuznets, "Economic Growth and Income Inequality," *American Economic Review* 45 (March 1955), 7.

13. Harold G. Moulton, *Formation of Capital* (Washington: Brookings Institution, 1935), pp. 158-159.

14. Milton Friedman and Anna J. Schwartz, *The Great Contraction, 1929-1933* (Princeton: Princeton University Press, 1965), pp. 46 ff.; see also Giulio Pontecorvo, "Investment Banking and Security Speculation in the Late 1920's," *Business History Review* 32 (summer 1958), 183-185; and for a general discussion of the character of the depression, Thomas Wilson, *Fluctuations in Income and Employment* (New York: Pitman, 1942).

15. Wilson, *Fluctuations,* pp. 156-162.

16. Friedman and Schwartz, *The Great Contraction,* pp. 46 ff.

17. For two contrasting industries see Sidney Fine, *The Automobile under the Blue Eagle: Labor, Management, and the Automobile Manufacturing Code* (Ann Arbor: University of Michigan Press, 1963); and Louis Galambos, *Competition and Cooperation — The Emergence of a National Trade Association* (Baltimore: Johns Hopkins Press, 1966).

18. Franklin D. Roosevelt, "Message to World Economic Conference," London, 1933.

19. Grace Beckett, "Effect of the Reciprocal Foreign Trade Agreements on the Foreign Trade of the United States," *Quarterly Journal of Economics* 54 (November 1940), 93.

20. Michael E. Parish, *Securities Regulation and the New Deal* (New Haven: Yale University Press, 1970), p. 217.

21. David F. Hawkins, "The Development of Modern Financial Reporting Practices among American Manufacturing Corporations," *Business History Review* 37 (autumn 1963), 160.

22. Parish, *Securities Regulation*, p. 220.

23. Victor Carosso, "Washington and Wall Street: The New Deal and Investment Bankers, 1933-1940," *Business History Review* 44 (winter 1970), 427-441.

24. Sidney Fine, *Sit-down: The General Motors Strike of 1936-1937* (Ann Arbor: University of Michigan Press, 1969), pp. 194-195, 235 ff., and 274-297.

25. Hoover, *The Great Depression*, pp. 433-434.

26. Eric F. Goldman, *Rendezvous with Destiny* (New York: Knopf, 1952), p. 365.

27. For the rather involved history of this tax, which was reduced the following year and repealed in 1939, see Sidney Ratner, *Democracy and Taxation in America* (New York: Wiley, 1967), pp. 472 ff.

28. *American Yearbook 1940*, p. 382.

Chapter 8. Business and War

1. For a general discussion see Paul A. C. Koistinen, "The Industrial-Military Complex in Historical Perspective: The Interwar Years," *Journal of American History* 56 (March 1970), 830-839.

2. "Forum of Executive Opinion," *Fortune*, October 1940, pp. 75 and 165.

3. *Historical Statistics of the United States*, p. 65.

4. Norman Beasley, *Knudsen: A Biography* (New York: McGraw-Hill, 1947), p. 270.

5. See Bureau of the Budget, *The United States at War: Development and Administration of the War Program by the Federal Government* (Washington: Government Printing Office, 1946), p. 105.

6. P. W. Litchfield, *Industrial Voyage: My Life as an Industrial Lieutenant* (Garden City, N.Y.: Doubleday, 1954), p. 290.

7. Civilian Production Administration, Bureau of Demobilization, *Industrial Mobilization for War: History of the War Production Board and Predecessor Agencies, 1940-1945* (Washington: Government Printing Office, 1947), vol. 1, pp. 63 and 147.

8. *Ibid.*, pp. 149-150.

9. Donald Nelson, *Arsenal of Democracy: The Story of American War Production* (New York: Harcourt, Brace, 1946), p. 176.

10. Bureau of the Budget, *The U. S. at War*, pp. 105 ff.

11. *Arsenal of Democracy*, p. 224.

12. *Ibid.*, p. 212.

13. Bureau of the Budget, *The U. S. at War*, p. 113.

14. *Ibid.*, p. 114.

15. CPA, *Industrial Mobilization*, vol. 1, pp. 216-222.

16. *Ibid.*, pp. 631-632.

17. *Ibid.*, p. 312.

18. *Arsenal of Democracy*, p. 284.

19. In what I have tried to make a balanced discussion, there are no major factual differences between the studies by the Bureau of the Budget, the Civilian Production Administration, and Donald Nelson. Consequently a footnote will only be used where one study differs from the other two.

20. *Arsenal of Democracy*, p. 409.

21. CPA, *Industrial Mobilization*, vol. 1, pp. 852-853.

22. Bureau of the Budget, *The U. S. at War*, p. 477.

23. CPA, *Industrial Mobilization*, vol. 1, p. 861.

24. Frederic C. Lane, *Ships for Victory: A History of Shipbuilding under the U.S. Maritime Commission in World War II* (Baltimore: Johns Hopkins Press, 1951), pp. 208-210.

25. Henrietta Larson and associates, *New Horizons, 1927-1950. History of Standard Oil Company (New Jersey)* (New York: Harper & Row, 1971), pp. 440-470.

26. Courtney R. Hall, *History of American Industrial Science* (New York: Science Library, 1954), p. 414.

Chapter 9. A New Environment for Business

1. See Alfred D. Chandler, Jr., "The Structure of American Industry in the Twentieth Century: A Historical Overview," *Business History Review* 43 (autumn 1969), 255-298.

2. Herman E. Kroos, *Executive Opinion: What Business Leaders Said and Thought, 1920-1960*, (Garden City, N.Y.: Doubleday, 1970), p. 8.

3. *Time*, 9 July 1956, p. 74.

4. All recent statistics, unless otherwise noted, come from appropriate volumes of the *Statistical Abstract of the United States*. For this reference, for example, see 1970, p. 519.

5. *Fortune*, January 1971. Of corporate spending of $3 billion, only 18 percent was classified as "basic" (pp. 106-117).

6. *Business Week,* 5 June 1971, devoted an issue to computers. See pp. 61-63.

7. *Ibid.,* p. 90.

8. J. N. Froomkin, "Automation," *New International Encyclopedia of the Social Sciences,* vol. 1, pp. 482 ff., and *Fortune,* August 1971, p. 144.

9. Committee on Government Operations, United States Senate, *The Rural to Urban Population Shift a National Problem,* 90th Congress, 2nd session, (Washington: Committee Print, 1968), pp. 36-43.

10. *Time,* 15 March 1954, p. 100.

11. Sidney Fine, *Laissez-Faire and the General Welfare State* (Ann Arbor: University of Michigan Press, 1956), p. 399.

12. Lawrence M. Friedman, "Legal Rules and the Process of Social Change," *Stanford Law Review* 19 (April 1967), 836.

13. E. Pendleton Herring, *Public Administration and Public Interest* (New York: McGraw Hill, 1936), p. 173; and Friedman, "Legal Rules."

14. A. D. H. Kaplan, *Big Enterprise in a Competitive System* (Washington: Brookings Institution, 1954), p. 31.

15. *Time,* 10 December 1951, p. 91.

16. Philip Sharecoff, "S.B.A. Under Fire," *New York Times,* 12 May 1971, sec. 3, p. 3.

17. Thomas V. Di Bacco, "American Business and Foreign Aid: The Eisenhower Years," *Business History Review* 41 (spring 1967), 25.

18. Joe S. Bain, "Industrial Concentration and Anti-Trust Policy," in Harold F. Williamson, ed., *Growth of American Economy* (New York: Prentice-Hall, 1951), p. 879.

19. *Fortune,* September 1969, p. 103.

20. Quoted in Charles R. Whittlesey, *National Interest and International Cartels* (New York: Macmillan, 1946), p. 6.

21. Kroos, *Executive Opinion,* p. 278.

22. Robert Townsend, *Up the Organization: How to Stop the Corporation from Stifling People and Strangling Profits* (New York: Knopf, 1970), p. 144. Charles E. Silberman said in *Fortune,* September 1963, p. 99, that "in the aggregate corporate voluntary action has fallen desperately short of what needs to be done."

23. Jules Cohn, *The Conscience of the Corporation: Business and Urban Affairs, 1967-1970* (Baltimore: Johns Hopkins Press, 1971), p. 31.

24. *Ibid.,* pp. 24-25.

25. Quoted in Edward L. Bernays, *Public Relations* (Norman: University of Oklahoma Press, 1952).

26. Quoted in Eugene Staley, ed., *Creating an Industrial Civilization: A Report of the Corning Conference* (New York: Harpers, 1952), p. 143.

27. See Morrell Heald, *The Social Responsibilities of Business: Company and Community, 1900-1960* (Cleveland: Case Western Reserve University, 1970), pp. 247-251.

28. Cohn, *Conscience of the Corporation*, pp. 10-12.

29. See Matthew N. Chappell and C. E. Hooper, *Radio Audience Measurement* (New York: Stephen Dye, 1944).

30. See *Public Opinion Quarterly*, 1964 on, for absence of such discussion.

Chapter 10. American Businessmen

1. Alfred D. Chandler, Jr., "The Structure of American Industry in the Twentieth Century: A Historical Overview," *Business History Review* 43 (autumn 1969), 274. See also Committee on the Judiciary of the United States Senate, Subcommittee on Antitrust and Monopoly, *Hearings* (Washington: Government Printing Office, 1964), testimony of M. A. Adelman, p. 240; and George Soule, *Planning U.S.A.* (New York: Bantam, 1967), p. 152.

2. The rounded figures from the *Statistical Abstract 1970* are for the year 1967, but the rate of change is very gradual.

3. Joseph D. Phillips, *Little Business in the American Economy* (Urbana: University of Illinois Press, 1958), p. 19.

4. This and other Southwestern interview material is the result of a trip taken for this purpose in 1950, made possible by grants from the American Philosophical Society and the University of Pennsylvania.

5. *Origins of Small Business Metal Fabricators and Machinery Makers in New England, 1890-1957* (Philadelphia: American Philosophical Society, 1965).

6. *Ibid.*, p. 21.

7. In a sample of 81 businesses started in Providence, Rhode Island, in 1958 and 1959 less than a third had over $5,000 in capital. See Kurt B. Mayer and Sidney Goldstein, *The First Two Years: Problems of Small Firm Growth and Survival* (Washington: Small Business Administration, 1961), p. 52.

8. *Ibid.*, pp. 81-86.

9. *Ibid.*, pp. 5-6.

10. Sidney Goldstein and Kurt B. Mayer, "Patterns of Business

Growth and Survival in a Medium-Sized Community," *Journal of Economic History* 17 (June 1957), 193-206.

11. Temporary National Economic Committee, Investigation of Concentration of Economic Power, Monograph 17, Problems of Small Business (Washington: Government Printing Office, 1941), p. 230.

12. Mabel Newcomer, "The Little Businessman," *Business History Review* 35 (winter 1961), 512.

13. Kurt B. Mayer and Sidney Goldstein, "Manual Workers as Small Businessmen," in Arthur B. Shostak and William Gomberg, eds., *Blue Collar World: Studies of the American Worker* (Englewood Cliffs, N.J.: Prentice-Hall, 1964), pp. 537-541.

14. Renato Tagiuri, Paul R. Lawrence, Rosalind C. Barnett, and Dexter Dempley, *Behavioral Science Concepts in Case Analysis: The Relationship of Ideas to Management Action* (Boston: Harvard Graduate School of Business Administration, 1968), pp. 65-67.

15. Gertrude G. Schroeder, *The Growth of Major Steel Companies, 1900-1950* (Baltimore: Johns Hopkins Press, 1952), pp. 201-202.

16. Clyde William Phelps, *Financing the Installment Purchases of the American Family: The Major Function of the Sales Finance Corporation* (Baltimore: Commercial Credit Company, 1954), pp. 38-39.

17. An Act of 1936 forbade price discrimination in selling to middlemen.

18. "Credit Bureaus Near a Day of Judgement," *Business Week,*17 August 1968, pp. 44 and 46.

19. Phillips, *Little Business,* p. 118.

20. Eugene Lichtenstein, "Higher and Higher Go the Bids for Industry," *Fortune,* April 1964, p. 118.

21. XIT Ranch Papers, Panhandle-Plains Historical Museum, Canyon, Texas.

22. This and following opinions are from personal interviews conducted by the author in 1950 and again in the early 1960s.

Chapter 11. Managerial Enterprise

1. *Fortune,* May 1971, pp. 172 ff., and June 1971, pp. 100 ff.

2. *Fortune,* November 1969, p. 2.

3. *Time,* 13 February 1950, p. 82.

4. Frank Abrams of Standard Oil in *Fortune,* August 1960, p. 108.

5. *Fortune,* October 1970, p. 92.

6. Henrietta M. Larson, Evelyn H. Knowlton, and Charles S. Popple, *New Horizons, 1927-1950. History of the Standard Oil Company (New Jersey)* (New York: Harper & Row, 1971), p. 444; see also pp. 442-454.

7. Peter F. Drucker, *Concept of the Corporation* (New York: John Day, 1946), pp. 42-44.

8. Alfred D. Chandler, Jr., *Strategy and Structure: Chapters in the History of American Industrial Enterprise* (Garden City, N.Y.: Doubleday, Anchor Books, 1966), pp. 376-396.

9. Wilbert E. Moore, *The Conduct of the Corporation: A Spirited Invasion of the Privacy of Big Enterprise* (New York: Vintage, 1962).

10. Arthur M. Johnson, "Agenda for the 1970's: The Firm and the Industry," *Journal of Economic History* 31 (March 1971), 113.

11. Walter Guzzardi, Jr., "The Young Executives, III" *Fortune,* September 1964, p. 161.

12. *Fortune,* October 1953, p. 268.

13. "The Concept of Organizational Climate," in Renato Tagiuri and George H. Litwin, eds., *Organizational Climate: Explorations of a Concept* (Boston: Harvard Graduate School of Business Administration, 1968), p. 27.

14. George H. Litwin, "Climate and Behavior Theory," in Tagiuri and Litwin, *Organizational Climate,* p. 58.

15. *Fortune,* January 1962, pp. 81-85.

16. Robert Townsend, *Up the Organization: How to Stop the Corporation from Stifling People and Strangling Profits* (New York: Knopf, 1970), p. 41. Townsend built up the Avis car rental corporation in the 1960s.

17. Dr. Otto Eckstein, head of Data Research Company, *Time,* 2 August 1971, p. 59.

18. W. Lloyd Warner and James C. Abegglen, *Occupational Mobility in American Business and Industry, 1928-1952* (Minneapolis: University of Minnesota Press, 1955), p. 45.

19. *New York Times,* Sunday, 30 May 1965, "Business," p. 1.

20. *Fortune,* August 1953, pp. 150-152 for General Electric program.

21. See Roy Lewis and Rosemary Stewart *The Managers: A New Examination of the English, German and American Executive* (New York: Mentor, 1961), pp. 82 ff.

22. *Time,* 12 November 1951, p. 105; and William H. Whyte, *Is Anybody Listening* (New York: Simon & Schuster, 1952), p. 180.

23. For a more detailed discussion see Thomas C. Cochran, *Social Change in Industrial Society: The United States* (London: George Allen and Unwin, 1972), chap. 7.

24. Peter F. Drucker, *The Practice of Management* (New York: Harpers, 1954), p. 132.

25. Everett E. Hagan, "The Internal Functioning of Capitalist Organizations," *Journal of Economic History*, 30 (March 1970), 228-229.

26 See H. L. Wilensky, "Work Careers and Social Integration," in Tom Burns, ed., *Industrial Man: Selected Readings* (Baltimore: Penguin, 1969), pp. 132-133.

27. M. Dalton, "Conflicts between Staff and Line Managers," in Burns, *Industrial Man*, p. 262.

28. *Fortune*, October 1969, p. 3. See also Harry Levinson, *The Exceptional Executive: A Psychological Conception* (Boston: Harvard Graduate School of Business Administration, 1969) and C. West Churchman, *Challenge to Reason* (New York: McGraw-Hill, 1969).

29. Because of Securities Exchange Commission rulings these payments to the top officers were reported annually to the stockholders.

30. Herrymon Maurer, *Great Enterprise: Growth and Behavior of the Big Corporation* (New York: Macmillan, 1955), pp. 147 and 210-217. Mr. Maurer's book is based on a detailed analysis of fifty of the largest companies.

31. *Ibid.*, pp. 128-131.

32. Albert J. Hettinger, Jr., in Milton Friedman and Anna J. Schwartz, *The Great Contraction, 1929-1933* (Princeton: Princeton University Press, 1965), pp. 125-126.

33. Townsend, *Up the Organization*, p. 115.

34. *Fortune*, April 1962, p. 128.

35. Chandler, *Strategy and Structure*, p. 351.

36. See Anthony G. Gettinger, "Complications in the National Decision-Making Process," in Martin Greenberger, ed., *Computers, Communications and the Public Interest* (Baltimore: Johns Hopkins Press, 1971), pp. 73-84.

37. "Designing Organizations for an Information Rich World," in Greenberger, *Computers*, p. 46.

38. In 1939, for example, administration of the "parent," non-producing Standard Oil (New Jersey) cost 6 percent of net income; from 1945 to 1949 it ran from 10.7 to 10.8 percent (Larson *et al.*, *New Horizons*, p. 605).

Chapter 12. Business and Social Change

1. Robert Townsend, *Up the Organization: How to Stop the Corporation from Stifling People and Strangling Profits* (New York: Knopf, 1970), p. 65.

2. Ralph Cordiner, quoted in *Fortune*, March 1961, p. 135.

3. Townsend, *Up the Organization*, p. 71.

4. *Fortune*, May 1954, p. 117.

5. Charles Hendrickson Brower in *Time*, 2 June 1958, p. 81.

6. Renato Tagiuri, Paul R. Lawrence, Rosalind C. Barnett, and Dexter C. Dunphy, *Behavioral Science Concepts in Case Analysis:The Relationship of Ideas to Management Action* (Boston: Harvard Graduate School of Business Administration, 1968), p. 96.

7. Edward C. Banfield and James Q. Wilson, *City Politics* (Cambridge: MIT Press, 1964), p. 246.

8. William H. Form and Delbert C. Miller, *Industry, Labor and Community* (New York: Harper & Row, 1960), p. 5.

9. Francis X. Sutton, Seymour E. Harris, Carl Kaysen, and James Tobin, *The American Business Creed* (Cambridge: Harvard University Press, 1956), pp. 3 ff.

10. *Ibid.*, p. 285.

11. *Ibid.*, pp. 251-262.

12. *International Herald Tribune*, 14 December 1970, p. 7.

Index

Abegglen, J. C., 205, 211, 212
Abrams, Frank, 155
Accountants of America, Institute of, 68
Accounting, 68, 210
Adams, Brooks, 11, 12
Adams, Charles Francis, Jr., 83
Adams, Franklin P., 80
Adams, Henry, 11, 106
Administration, *see* Management
Advertising, 22, 63–66. *See also* Public relations
Aerospace industry, 160, 174
Agriculture, shift from, 197. *See also* Farmers
Airplanes, 16, 31–32, 142
Alcott, Bronson, 12
Aldrich, Winthrop D., 111, 206
American Association of Advertising Agencies, 66
American Federation of Labor, 132, 135
American Management Association, 84
American Public Accountants, Association of, 67
American Radiator Co., 85
American Society of Public Accountants, 68
American Telephone & Telegraph Co., 21, 22, 44, 92; use of films, 93; increase in stockholders, 94
American Tobacco Co., 81

Antitrust legislation, 96. *See also* Cellar–Kefauver Act; Clayton Act; Sherman Act
Appersons, the, 24
Army and Navy Munitions Board, 144, 146, 149
Arnold, Thurman W., 176
Assembly line, 20; in Ford plant, 26
Associated Advertising Clubs of the World, 66
Associated Press, 64
Atherton, Lewis, 7, 9
Atomic energy, 161
Audit Bureau of Circulation, 64
Austria, 126
Autocar, 29
Automation, 18–20, 26; after World War II, 161
Automobiles, 16; insurance, 28; effects, 163–165; prestige from, 168–169. *See also* Motor vehicles
Automotive industry, World War II, 140–141, 148
Avery, C. W., 27
Avis Co., 216

Baker, George F., 46, 47, 48, 172; and Pujo committee, 49–50
Balchen, Bernt, 32
Bankers, *see* Banks; Investment bankers
Bankers Trust Co., 47, 49

This book, Thomas C. Cochran writes, is "neither a hostile critique nor an apology for the actions involved in modern business, but rather an effort to record well-authenticated parts of the history that should be of importance to both businessmen and scholars." He emphasizes that while the purpose of business is to produce and distribute goods and services for profit, business has great importance too as a social institution.

Readers familiar with the outstanding contributions of Mr. Cochran will welcome this complete revision and expansion of his pioneer study, *The American Business System* (HUP 1957). The *New York Times* lauded this earlier volume as "a palatable way to imbibe some worthy ideas of top economists, political leaders and businessmen." Since the study was written at a time when there was a lack of secondary literature devoted to the history of business, it was primarily directed toward the economics of business development in this country. In the present volume the author approaches his subject from a new direction by synthesizing the